COURTIER and COMMONER
in ANCIENT CHINA

SELECTIONS FROM THE *History of*
The Former Han BY PAN KU

Translated by BURTON WATSON

COLUMBIA UNIVERSITY PRESS

New York and London

*Portions of this work were prepared under a contract
with the U.S. Office of Education for the production
of texts to be used in undergraduate education. The
texts so produced have been used in the Columbia College Oriental Humanities program and have subsequently been revised and expanded for publication in
the present form. Copyright is claimed only in those
portions of the work not submitted in fulfillment of
the contract with the U.S. Office of Education. The
U.S. Office of Education is not the author, owner, pub-
lisher, or proprietor of this publication, and is not to
be understood as approving by virtue of its support
any of the statements made or views expressed therein.*

LIBRARY OF CONGRESS CATALOGING IN PUBLICATION DATA
Pan, Ku, 32–92.
  Courtier and commoner in ancient China.
  "Translations from the Oriental classics."
  Translation of selections from Han shu.
  Includes bibliographical references.
    1. China—History—Han dynasty, 202 B.C.-220 A.D.
    I. Title.
DS748.P3   1974   931   73-18003
ISBN 0-231-03765-1 (cloth)
ISBN 0-231-08354-8 (pbk.)

Printed in the United States of America

To Hans Bielenstein

CONTENTS

INTRODUCTION 1

TRANSLATOR'S NOTE 10

Han Shu 54: THE BIOGRAPHIES OF LI KUANG AND SU CHIEN 12

Han Shu 63: THE BIOGRAPHIES OF THE FIVE SONS OF EMPEROR WU 46

Han Shu 65: THE BIOGRAPHY OF TUNG-FANG SHUO 79

Han Shu 67: THE BIOGRAPHIES OF YANG WANG-SUN, HU CHIEN, CHU YÜN, MEI FU, AND YÜN CH'ANG 107

Han Shu 68: THE BIOGRAPHIES OF HO KUANG AND CHIN MI-TI 121

Han Shu 71: THE BIOGRAPHIES OF CH'ÜAN PU-I, SHU KUANG, YÜ TING-KUO, HSÜEH KUANG-TE, P'ING TANG, AND P'ENG HSÜAN 158

Han Shu 74: THE BIOGRAPHIES OF WEI HSIANG AND PING CHI 174

Han Shu 78: THE BIOGRAPHY OF HSIAO WANG-CHIH 198

Han Shu 92: THE BIOGRAPHIES OF THE WANDERING KNIGHTS 222

Han Shu 97 A-B: ACCOUNTS OF THE FAMILIES RELATED TO THE EMPERORS BY MARRIAGE (EXCERPTS) 247

INDEX 279

COURTIER and COMMONER
in ANCIENT CHINA

INTRODUCTION

THE HAN SHU OR HISTORY OF THE FORMER HAN by Pan Ku (A.D. 32–92), which deals with the period from 206 B.C. to A.D. 23, is one of the most renowned and influential of all Chinese historical works. Admired for the rich detail of its narrative and the purity and economy of its style, it served as a model for the official histories that were compiled in later centuries to cover all the dynasties of Chinese imperial history. From the time of its appearance in the first century A.D. until the present, no one in China or the countries within the sphere of Chinese cultural influence could consider himself truly educated who was not thoroughly familiar with its pages.

The Chinese have since ancient times been avid readers and writers of history, and historical texts figure among the earliest works in the language. Most important of these is the *Ch'un ch'iu* or *Spring and Autumn Annals,* a chronicle of the state of Lu for the period 770–450 B.C. which was traditionally supposed to have been compiled by Confucius, and the commentaries upon this text, particularly the *Tso chuan* or *Tso Commentary,* which explain the historical background of the events recorded in the *Annals* and expound its didactic significance.

These and other early historical texts, however, were probably put together by many hands over a period of years and for the most part lack any unifying form or outlook. The earliest integral work of history by a known author is the *Shih chi* or *Records of the Historian* by Ssu-ma Ch'ien (145?–90? B.C.), a text in 130 chapters written around 100 B.C. It is a history of the entire past, from the time of the sage rulers of high antiquity down to the period of the writer, and also includes accounts of foreign lands and peoples as they were known to the Chinese. Thus it is far broader in scope and richer in content than any of the works preceding it.

In form as well, Ssu-ma Ch'ien's work differs radically from earlier historical texts. It is divided into five sections: *chi* or annals, devoted to the ruling dynasties of antiquity or, in the case of the Han, to the lives of individual rulers; *piao* or chronological tables; *shu* or treatises, historical essays on subjects of special importance such as religion, economics, ritual, etc.; *shih-chia* or "hereditary houses," accounts of important feudal states or families; and *lieh-chuan*, biographies of eminent statesmen, generals, philosophers, literary figures, or men who for some other reason seemed to the historian to merit a place in the history of the period. The work ends with an account of the historian himself and his aims, and a table of contents containing brief summaries of each chapter.

This, the so-called *chi-chuan* or "annal and biography" form, was adopted by Pan Ku in his *Han shu*, though he eliminated the *shih-chia* or "hereditary house" division and made other minor changes in terminology. But whereas the *Shih chi* deals with events occurring over a span of two thousand years or more, Pan Ku's work is confined to the period of the Former Han, which lasted from 206 B.C. to A.D. 8, and the brief reign of the usurper Wang Mang, A.D. 9 to 23, a span of 230 years. His work is thus the first to limit itself to the history of a single dynasty, a practice that became common in later Chinese historiography.

Ssu-ma Ch'ien, a scholar-official at the court of Emperor Wu (r. 140–87 B.C.), had not finished the writing of his great history when he aroused the emperor's ire by speaking out in defense of his friend Li Ling, a Han general who surrendered to the Hsiung-nu tribes in 99 B.C. (see p. 29). Accused of lese majesty for his impertinence, he was handed over to the law officials and subjected to the process of intimidation and torture that constituted Han legal procedure, until in desperation he acknowledged his guilt. He was sentenced to death but was permitted to undergo the punishment of castration instead. He chose to suffer this humiliation rather than commit suicide so that he might finish the writing of the *Shih chi*.

Pan Ku, though considerably more fortunate, sufferred a somewhat similar experience. His father Pan Piao (A.D. 3–54), a scholar and possessor of a superb private library, began work on a continuation of the *Shih chi*, which ends its narrative around 100 B.C., though how far he had progressed by the time of his death we do not know. Pan Ku took up his father's labors but decided that, rather than produce a mere continuation of the *Shih chi*, he would undertake a history of the entire Former Han period. He had not devoted himself to this task for long, however, when someone submitted a letter to the ruler, Emperor Ming (r. A.D. 58–77), accusing him of attempting as a private citizen to write a history of the Former Han, which had been ruled by members of the same Liu family to which Emperor Ming belonged. Pan Ku was taken to prison in the capital for questioning and his writings were confiscated.

In the eyes of the Chinese, the writing of history was an undertaking of extreme gravity. Confucius in compiling the *Spring and Autumn Annals* was believed to have passed moral judgment upon the men and events it recorded through the terminology which he employed, and this concept of the seriousness and didactic import of historical writing continued to be accepted in later ages, though historians modestly disclaimed any ability to imitate the judgments of the sage.

An incident close to the time of Pan Ku attests to the political importance that attached to works of history. In the reign of Emperor Ch'eng (r. 32–7 B.C.), one of the Han princes who had come to pay his respects at court asked the emperor if he might receive copies of certain philosophical works and "the Book of the Grand Historian," i.e., the *Shih chi* of Ssu-ma Ch'ien, a text that at the time was not widely circulated. The emperor consulted one of his high ministers but was advised to deny the request: the philosophical works, it was argued, often contradict the Confucian Classics and do not represent the teachings of the sages, while the *Shih chi* records "the wily and expedient schemes of the diplomats of the Warring States period, the unusual measures resorted to by the advisers at the time of the founding of the Han, and all the strange occurrences in the realm of the heavens, the strategic points in the layout of the land, information that should not be in the hands of the feudal lords." (*Han shu* 80, biography of Liu Yü, King Ssu of Tung-p'ing.) Thus, according to such a view, works of history could be of real danger to the ruling house if read by the wrong persons.

Emperor Ming, it would seem, was particularly suspicious of Pan Ku's efforts as a historian because, during the time of the usurper Wang Mang and the chaotic years that accompanied his overthrow and the establishment of the Later Han (A.D. 25–220), numerous works of propaganda had appeared prophesying the victory of one or another aspirant to the throne and claiming to give proofs of his divine election, and the emperor no doubt surmised that Pan Ku's work was of a similar dubious nature. When he examined Pan Ku's writings, however, he revised his opinion and not only released the historian but appointed him to a post in the imperial archives and encouraged him to continue his literary labors. Pan Ku was thus given access to government files and was allowed to complete the writing of his history under highly favorable circumstances. The *Han shu* was probably finished around A.D. 80 and is said to have won immediate acclaim among the scholars of the day.

Pan Ku's work is in 100 chapters, though many of these are of such length as to be divided into two or more *chüan* or sections, the actual number of *chüan* being 120. For the first hundred years of the Former Han, he relied heavily on the work of Ssu-ma Ch'ien, often taking over entire chapters from the *Shih chi* with only minor stylistic revisions. In dealing with the century that followed and the period of Wang Mang, he no doubt made use of the writings of his father and other scholars who had written continuations to the *Shih chi,* though the exact nature of his indebtedness is difficult to determine, since these earlier continuations no longer exist. Because, unlike the *Shih chi,* his work is confined to the history of a single dynasty, one that was the direct ancestor of that under which he himself wrote, it is more consciously the celebration of a particular ruling house. Also, his work is more orthodoxly Confucian in outlook than that of Ssu-ma Ch'ien, though it is difficult to say to what extent this may be due to the personalities of the two historians and to what extent it reflects a difference in the ages in which they lived. Finally, perhaps because he wrote about events somewhat removed in time rather than of his own day, as had Ssu-ma Ch'ien in the latter pages of the *Shih chi,* his work possesses an air of calmness and objectivity, in contrast to the passionate and highly personal approach of Ssu-ma Ch'ien. Even in the *tsan* or appraisal sections which conclude most of the chapters, in which the historian allows himself to speak in his own voice, Pan Ku, unlike Ssu-ma Ch'ien, seldom mentions his own experiences as they relate to the events of the narrative or gives any evidence of strong personal involvement. Rather he is the model of the cool and impartial purveyor of truth, keeping his own private feelings discreetly veiled from view.

The "annals" chapters of the *Han shu,* devoted to the reigns of individual emperors, consist almost entirely of a dry recital of official acts and pronouncements, with little clue to the personalities and private lives of the rulers. The chronological tables and treatises are rather specialized in nature and often of only limited interest to the ordinary reader. It is the 70 chapters of the *lieh-chuan* or biography section which form the heart of Pan Ku's work, the chapters which have been most attentively read and remembered in later ages, and it is accordingly from this section that I have drawn the ten chapters in my selection.

I have attempted first of all to select those chapters that are of the greatest literary interest and have had the most influence on Chinese literature and culture. At the same time I have tried to illustrate some of the ways in which Pan Ku adapted and revised the material he took from the *Shih chi,* the manner in which he grouped men of similar personality or pursuit in one chapter, the vivid, novelistic style that characterizes his narrative, and the rich ironies and psychological subtlety in which it abounds. It has often been remarked that in ancient China historical works such as the *Shih chi* and *Han shu* appealed to tastes that in other literary traditions were satisfied by works of fiction. Something of the literary skill and impact of Pan Ku's work will, I hope, be apparent in the chapters I have translated.

I have for the most part avoided passages that are merely copied from the *Shih chi;* in the first chapter of my selection, however, the reader will encounter one such passage. Pan Ku, evidently approving wholeheartedly of his predecessor's work, took over Ssu-ma Ch'ien's biography of the general Li Kuang almost verbatim from chapter 109 of the *Shih chi.*[1] To this he added the biographies of Li Ling and Su Wu, which constitute one of the most celebrated and moving passages in the entire *Han shu* and the source of inspiration to countless writers and painters of later ages. The third chapter in my selection, the biography of the court jester Tung-

---

[1] The reader who wishes to make a comparison will find Ssu-ma Ch'ien's version of the biography translated in my *Records of the Grand Historian of China* (Columbia University Press, 1961), vol. 2, pp. 141–54, and *Records of the Historian: Chapters from the Shih chi of Ssu-ma Ch'ien* (Columbia University Press 1969), pp. 260–73.

fang Shuo, likewise deals with a figure who became extremely popular in later fiction and folklore and contains passages of wit and banter which, however questionable as history, remain remarkably humorous even today. It also illustrates the practice so common among Chinese historians of copying into a man's biography lengthy excerpts from his writings, a practice that has aided immensely in the preservation of important early works of Chinese literature.

The fifth chapter, the account of the statesman Ho Kuang and his family, represents perhaps the highest achievement of Pan Ku's art as a biographer. Unfolding with all the somber inevitability of a Greek tragedy, the chapter traces Ho Kuang's rapid rise to power, to the point where he could actually depose an emperor who had been called to the throne, and then, with his death, settles down to the grim and intricate tale of how his descendants, through evil and abuse, brought about the eventual destruction of the family.

Here and in similar accounts of doom, one will note the historian's attention to omens and portents. The Chinese of the time believed that the human, natural, and supernatural worlds are intimately linked and that evil and misrule in human society, particularly by those in high position, could occasion dislocations in the realm of nature, bringing about the appearance of weird creatures, unusual meteorological phenomena, or other strange occurrences. Pan Ku is careful to record such unusual occurrences in his biographical chapters and to suggest the human crimes and errors that he believed generated them, and he even included a lengthy chapter, the "Treatise on the Five Elements," devoted entirely to lists of such portents and their historical significance.

The next to the last chapter in my selection, "The Biographies of the Wandering Knights," is an example of the so-called collective biographies, chapters devoted to men of a particular profession, temperament, or life style. Ssu-ma Ch'ien had included a number of such chapters in his work, and Pan Ku took over the format of the wandering knights chapter, as well as the first three biographies in it, from *Shih chi* 124 (translated in *Records of the Grand Historian of China*, vol. 2, pp. 452–61). The *yu-hsia* or wandering knights were adventurers or local bosses who often assisted persons in trouble or offered their services in the carrying out of private vendettas. In the preface to his chapter, Ssu-ma Ch'ien, while acknowledging the faults of the knights, had praised them for their willingness to aid the oppressed and to abide by their word. Pan Ku, however, disapproved of such a sympathetic attitude and when he took over Ssu-ma Ch'ien's material, he discarded the preface and wrote one of his own condemning the knights and taking a strong "law and order" position in regard to their activities. Here Pan Ku appears as a revisionist, correcting what he regarded as errors of judgment and opinion in the work of his illustrious predecessor.

I have in most cases attempted to present entire chapters so that the reader may see how Pan Ku grouped his biographies and shaped them formally, though I have made a few cuts here and there to avoid taking up space with material of markedly inferior interest. I have prefaced each chapter with a translation of the summary of it which appears in the table of contents in chapter 100B of the *Han shu*. The last chapter in my selection, on the ladies of the harem, however, represents only a fraction of the numerous biographies of empresses and imperial concubines contained in *Han shu* 97. (Ssu-ma Ch'ien had dealt with the empresses in chapter 49 of his history, but Pan Ku shifted them to the end of his work, which he no doubt felt was a more suitable position for material dealing with women.) I have begun with the biography of Madam Li, where Pan Ku's account begins to differ significantly from its prototype in the *Shih chi*, and have endeavored to include the passages of greatest literary and historical interest. Because of the poetry that adorns so many of them and the often pathetic and shocking nature of their contents, the reader, I believe, will find these biographies among the most vivid and engrossing of the entire selection.

The *Shih chi* of Ssu-ma Ch'ien, because of the vast scope and richness of its contents, possesses a variety and excitement that are unmatched in all of Chinese historiography. Pan Ku's work, dealing with the history of a single dynasty, tends to be less varied in tone and content, though at the same time it is more detailed. It moves at a slower pace, and much of its narrative is made up of lengthy quotations from edicts, memorials, letters, and records of criminal investigations, often sordid in the extreme. Lacking the verve and romantic appeal of the *Shih chi*, it has a grim realism and air of brooding grandeur all its own, and for this reason, and because of the incalculable influence it has had on later Chinese literature and historiography, it deserves to be as well known as its famous predecessor.

The chapters that follow are arranged more or less chronologically, but because they are made up of biographies, the reader will encounter a certain degree of overlap in the narrative and will find himself moving back and forth in the reigns of a succession of emperors. It may be helpful at this point, therefore, to give a brief outline of the political history of the period.

The Han, which dated the beginning of its rule from 206 B.C., was founded by Liu Pang, customarily referred to by his posthumous title Kao-tsu. After his death in 195 B.C., his consort Empress Lü assumed power and placed many of the male members of her clan in positions of authority; for a time it appeared as though the Liu family might be overthrown, a fact often referred to in later Han history when similar instances of the overweening power of an empress's clan arose.

In 140 B.C., after several decades of relative peace and prosperity, the youthful Emperor Wu came to the throne and set about busily extending the hegemony and might of the dynasty. He launched repeated campaigns against the Hsiung-nu, a nomadic people living north of China in the region of the Gobi Desert, as will be apparent from the first chapters of my selection. The other event of his reign that the reader will find most often referred to is the downfall of the heir apparent Prince Li, Emperor Wu's son by Empress Wei. Falsely accused of practicing black magic against his father, the prince finally despaired of gaining a fair hearing and in 91 B.C. led an abortive revolt that ended with his suicide. Because of the Chinese concept of corporate responsibility, all the members of his family were put to death except one infant grandson, the future Emperor Hsüan.

Emperor Wu was succeeded by Emperor Chao (r. 86–74 B.C.), a boy who did not live long enough to exercise actual rule; all power was in the hands of the statesman Ho Kuang, who had been charged by Emperor Wu with the care of the young ruler. After Emperor Chao's death, Ho Kuang summoned to the throne a grandson of Emperor Wu, the king of Ch'ang-i, but, displeased with his conduct, summarily dismissed him and set up Emperor Hsüan in his stead. Emperor Hsüan (r. 73–49 B.C.) proved a highly capable ruler and under him the Han reached a pinnacle of prosperity and wellbeing. He was succeeded by Emperor Yüan (r. 48–33 B.C.), an enthusiastic patron of Confucian learning, and Emperor Ch'eng (r. 32–7 B.C.), who is remembered chiefly for his infatuation with the dancing girl Chao Fei-yen and her younger sister.

Emperor Ch'eng's mother Empress Dowager Wang saw to it that members of her clan were assigned positions of eminence, and from this time on the government was dominated by the Wang family. They were temporarily eclipsed during the reign of Emperor Ai (r. 6–1 B.C.), but under his successor Emperor P'ing (r. A.D. 1–6), Empress Dowager Wang's nephew Wang Mang rose to greater and greater prominence until, in A.D. 9, he announced the expiration of Han rule and the founding of a new dynasty called the Hsin. After struggling vigorously to consolidate and maintain his power, he was overthrown by members of the Liu family in A.D. 23, who proclaimed the restoration of the Han.

The Han was the first of the great imperial ages, and the *Han shu* preserves a priceless record of its achievements and failures. It details the struggles for power that were to vex so many later dynasties, the threat posed by the emperor's maternal relatives, accorded high position by the ruler because of Confucian injunctions to honor one's parents and kin; the danger latent in a body of eunuchs overseeing the imperial harem and interposing themselves between the ruler, often a mere child, and his ministers. It is a dreary record, full of bureaucratic rivalries, plots, malcontent and bloody execution. Without romanticism or idealization it presents the reader with the facts, hopeful, as all works of history must be, that to some degree the sorrows of the past may be a lesson to the future.

TRANSLATOR'S NOTE

THE HAN SHU IS FAMOUS for the severe economy of its style, but it is an economy bought at times at the price of ambiguity and outright opaqueness. The commentaries by Yen Shih-ku, Wang Hsien-ch'ien, and others have elucidated many of the obscurities, but there remain passages which allow of varying interpretations and I am by no means confident that I have understood the text aright. I have based my translation on the *Han-shu pu-chu* of Wang Hsien-ch'ien (1900), and have consulted with gratitude the modern Japanese translations of selected chapters from the *lieh-chuan* section of the *Han shu* by Honda Wataru in *Kanjo, Go-kanjo, Sangokushi retsuden,* Chūgoku koten bungaku taikei #13 (Tokyo, Heibonsha, 1968), and Miki Katsumi in *Shiki, Kanjo,* Sekai bungaku zenshū #4 (Tokyo, Chikuma Shobō, 1970); and the two superbly annotated selections from the *Han shu* included in the *Liang-Han wen-hsüeh-shih ts'an-k'ao tzu-liao* (Peking, 1962).

A complete translation of the imperial annals and the biography of Wang Mang has appeared in the three volumes by Homer H. Dubs, *The History of the Former Han Dynasty* (London, Kegan Paul, 1938–55), and two of the treatises, those on economics and the penal code, have been translated in Nancy Lee Swann, *Food and Money in Ancient China* (Princeton, Princeton University Press, 1950), and A. F. P. Hulsewé, *Remnants of Han Law* (Leiden, E. J. Brill, 1955) respectively. Few English translations from the biography section, however, have so far been published, and to the best of my knowledge the chapters in my selection appear here for the first time in English. In preparing these I have followed the same principles and procedures as in the case of my earlier translations from the *Shih chi*. I am aware that some scholars find my annotation inadequate, but I would stress that, as in the case of the *Shih chi*, my translations are intended primarily for the reader who wishes to acquaint himself with the literary qualities of the *Han shu* and to observe the historian's general methods and approach, rather than for the specialist in Han history, who must in any event consult the original. Material enclosed in parentheses, such as Pan Ku's frequent cross-references to other sections of the history, is found in the original text. With the exception of dates, easily ascertainable from other sections of the history, all additions of mine are enclosed in brackets.

I wish here to extend my thanks to Professor Matsushita Tadashi and the librarians of Wakayama Daigaku for allowing me to use the university libraries in the preparation of this translation. The Columbia College Committee on Oriental Studies generously supplied the funds that made this translation possible.

LI KUANG, SIMPLE AND SINCERE, truly captured the hearts of his men. Stretching his bowstring, he pierced a stone; his might awed the northern neighbors. He fought his way through seventy battles, in the end to die in an army camp. Li Kan bore a grudge against Wei Ch'ing, but he was shot down by Ho Ch'ü-ping. Because Li Ling failed to take his own life, he brought disgrace to his time and extinction to his family. Su Wu, faithful to his mission, would not dishonor his lord's command. So I have transmitted the Biographies of Li Kuang and Su Chien.[1]

LI KUANG

Li Kuang was a native of Ch'eng-chi in Lung-hsi Province. Among his ancestors was Li Hsin, a general of the state of Ch'in, who pursued and captured Tan, the crown prince of Yen.[2] The art of archery had been handed down in the Li family for generations.

In the fourteenth year of Emperor Wen's reign (166 B.C.) the Hsiung-nu entered the Hsiao Pass in great numbers. Li Kuang, as the son of a distinguished family, was allowed to join the army in the attack on the barbarians. He proved himself a skillful archer, killing and capturing a number of the enemy, and was rewarded with the position of cavalry attendant in the inner palace. He fre-

[1] This and the summaries which head the other chapters of the translation are taken from Pan Ku's table of contents in *Han shu* 100B.

[2] Tan had sent a man to the Ch'in court in an unsuccessful attempt to assassinate the king, who later became the First Emperor of the Ch'in.

quently accompanied Emperor Wen on his hunting expeditions, striking down the most ferocious beasts. Emperor Wen remarked, "What a pity you were not born at a better time! Had you lived in the age of Emperor Kao-tsu, you would have had no trouble in winning a marquisate of at least ten thousand households."

When Emperor Ching came to the throne, Li Kuang was made general of palace horsemen. At the time of the revolt of Wu and Ch'u, he served as a cavalry commander under the grand commandant Chou Ya-fu, joining in the attack and distinguishing himself at the battle of Ch'ang-i. But because he had accepted the seals of a general from the king of Liang without authorization from the Han government, he was not rewarded for his achievements when he returned to the capital.

Following this he was transferred to the post of governor of Shang-ku Province, where he frequently engaged in skirmishes with the Hsiung-nu. The director of dependent states Kung-sun K'un-yeh went to the emperor and, with tears in his eyes, said, "There is no one in the empire to match Li Kuang for skill and spirit and yet, trusting to his own ability, he repeatedly engages the enemy in battle. I am afraid one day we will lose him!" The emperor thereupon transferred Li Kuang to the post of governor of Shang Province.

At this time the Hsiung-nu invaded Shang Province. Emperor Ching sent one of his trusted eunuchs to join Li Kuang, ordering him to train the troops and lead them in an attack on the Hsiung-nu. The eunuch, heading a group of twenty or thirty horsemen, was casually riding about the countryside one day when he caught sight of three Hsiung-nu riders and engaged them in a fight. The three Hsiung-nu, however, shot and wounded the eunuch and were near to killing all of his horsemen. The eunuch barely managed to flee back to the place where Li Kuang was. "They must be out hunting eagles!" said Li Kuang, and galloped off with a hundred horsemen in pursuit of the three Hsiung-nu. The Hsiung-nu, having lost their horses, fled on foot. After they had journeyed twenty or thirty li,[3] Li Kuang caught up with them and, ordering his horsemen to fan out to the left and right of them, began to shoot at them. He killed two with his arrows and took the third one alive. As he had guessed, they were eagle hunters.

Li Kuang had bound his prisoner when, climbing a hill, he spied

[3] One li is about one third of an English mile.

several thousand Hsiung-nu horsemen in the distance. The Hsiung-nu, catching sight of Li Kuang and his men, supposed that they were a decoy sent out from the main body of the Han forces to lure them into combat. They made for a nearby hill in alarm and drew up their ranks on its crest.

Li Kuang's horsemen were thoroughly terrified and begged him to flee back to camp as quickly as possible, but he replied, "We are twenty or thirty li away from the main army. With only a hundred of us, if we were to try to make a dash for it, the Hsiung-nu would be after us in no time and would shoot down every one of us. But if we stay where we are, they are bound to think we are a decoy from the main army and will not attack."

Instead of retreating, therefore, Li Kuang gave the order to his men to advance. When they had reached a point some two li from the Hsiung-nu ranks, he told his men, "Dismount and undo your saddles!"

"But there are so many of them, if we undo our saddles, what will we do if they attack?" his men asked.

"They expect us to run away," said Li Kuang. "But now if we undo our saddles and show them we have no intention of leaving, they will be more convinced than ever that there is something afoot."

One of the Hsiung-nu leaders came out on a white horse to reconnoiter. Li Kuang mounted again and, with ten or so of his horsemen, galloped after the barbarian leader and shot him down. Then he returned to his group, undid his saddle, turned his horse loose and lay down on the ground. By this time night was falling and the Hsiung-nu, thoroughly suspicious of what they had seen, still had not ventured to attack. They concluded that the Han leaders must have concealed soldiers in the area and be planning to fall upon them in the dark, and so during the night they withdrew. When dawn came Li Kuang finally managed to return with his group to the main army.

After this Li Kuang was assigned to the governorship of Lung-hsi, Pei-ti, Yen-men, and Yün-chung provinces in succession.

When Emperor Wu came to the throne (140 B.C.), his advisers informed him of Li Kuang's fame as a general, and he made Li Kuang the colonel of the guard of the Eternal Palace.

At this time Ch'eng Pu-chih was the colonel of the guard of the Palace of Lasting Joy. Ch'eng Pu-chih had been a governor in the border provinces and a garrison general at the same time as Li

Kuang. When Li Kuang went out on expeditions to attack the Hsiung-nu, he never bothered to form his men into battalions and companies. He would make camp wherever he found water and grass, leaving his men to set up their quarters in any way they thought convenient. He never had sentries circling the camp at night and beating on cooking pots, as was the custom, and in his headquarters he kept records and other clerical work down to a minimum. He always sent out scouts some distance around the camp, however, and he had never met with any particular mishap.

Ch'eng Pu-chih, on the other hand, always kept his men in strict battalion and company formation. The sentries banged on the cooking pots, his officers worked over their records and reports until dawn, and no one in his army got any rest. Ch'eng Pu-chih once expressed the opinion, "Although Li Kuang runs his army in a very simple fashion, if the enemy should ever swoop down on him suddenly he would have no way to hold them off. His men enjoy plenty of idleness and pleasure, and for that reason they are eager to fight to the death for him. Life in my army may be a good deal more irksome, but at least I know that the enemy will never catch me napping!"

Li Kuang and Ch'eng Pu-chih were both famous generals at this time, but the Hsiung-nu were more afraid of Li Kuang, while the Han soldiers for the most part preferred to serve under him and disliked being under Ch'eng Pu-chih's command. Ch'eng Pu-chih advanced to the position of palace counselor under Emperor Ching because of the outspoken advice he gave the emperor on several occasions. He was a man of great integrity and very conscientious in matters of form and law.

Sometime later, the Han leaders attempted to entice the *Shan-yü* into entering the city of Ma-i, concealing a large force of men in the valley around the city to ambush the Hsiung-nu.[4] At this time Li Kuang was appointed as cavalry general under the command of Han An-kuo, the leader of the supporting army. As it happened, however, the *Shan-yü* discovered the plot and escaped in time, so that neither Li Kuang nor any of the other generals connected with the plot achieved any merit.

Four years later (129 B.C.) Li Kuang, because of his services as colonel of the guard, was made a general and sent north from

---

[4] *Shan-yü*, a Hsiung-nu word, is the title held by the leader of the Hsiung-nu nation.

Yen-men to attack the Hsiung-nu. But the Hsiung-nu force he was pitted against turned out to be too numerous and succeeded in defeating Li Kuang's army and capturing him alive.

The *Shan-yü* had for a long time heard of Li Kuang's excellence as a fighter and had given orders, "If you get hold of Li Kuang, take him alive and bring him to me!" As it turned out, the barbarian horsemen did manage to capture Li Kuang and, since he was wounded, they strung a litter between two horses and, laying him on it, proceeded on their way about ten li. Li Kuang pretended to be dead but managed to peer around him and noticed that close by his side was a young Hsiung-nu boy mounted on a fine horse. Suddenly he leaped out of the litter and onto the boy's horse, seizing the boy and whipping up the horse. After galloping twenty or thirty li he succeeded in catching up with what was left of his army. Several hundred Hsiung-nu horsemen came in pursuit, but he snatched the bow from the boy and shot and killed his pursuers. In this way he was able to escape.

When he got back to the capital, he was turned over to the law officials, who recommended that he be executed for losing so many of his men and being captured alive. He was allowed to ransom his life and was reduced to the status of commoner.

For several years he lived in Lan-t'ien, among the Southern Mountains, adjoining the estate of Kuan Ch'iang, the grandson of Kuan Ying, the former marquis of Ying-yin.

One evening Li Kuang, having spent the afternoon drinking with some people out in the fields, was on his way back home, accompanied by a rider attendant, when he passed the watch station at Pa-ling. The watchman, who was drunk at the time, yelled at Li Kuang to halt.

"This is the former General Li," said Li Kuang's man.

"Even present generals are not allowed to go wandering around at night, much less former ones!" the watchman retorted, and made Li Kuang halt and spend the night in the watch station.

Shortly after this, the Hsiung-nu invaded Liao-hsi, murdered its governor, and defeated General Han An-kuo. Han An-kuo was transferred to Yu-pei-p'ing, where he died, and the emperor forthwith summoned Li Kuang to be the new governor of Yu-pei-p'ing. When he accepted the post, Li Kuang asked that the watchman of Pa-ling be ordered to accompany him, and as soon as the man reported for duty Li Kuang had him executed. Then he submitted a letter to the throne explaining what he had done and apologizing for his offense.

The emperor replied: "Generals are the claws and teeth of the nation. The *Rules of the Marshal* [5] says that when a general rides in his carriage, he does not bow in greeting from the carriage bar, and when a death occurs, he does not don mourning. He calls out his brigades and deploys his troops in order to bring the unsubmissive to their knees, to unite the hearts of all the soldiers of the three armies, and to pool the strength of his fighting men. Therefore, when his anger blazes forth, there is terror for a thousand miles, and when his power is made manifest, ten thousand creatures bow low. In this way his fame may become known even to the Yi and Mo barbarians, and his awe and majesty strike fear into neighboring lands. To requite anger and wipe out injury, to cast off, to destroy, to do away with, to kill—this is what I expect from my generals! If you come with doffed hat and bare feet, knocking your forehead on the ground and begging for punishment, you will be fulfilling no wish of mine! Now, general, you will be good enough to lead your troops and turn the shafts of your wagons to the east, slowing your pace at Po-t'an, so as to keep an eye on Yu-pei-p'ing while autumn is at its height." [6]

When Li Kuang was in the border provinces, the Hsiung-nu referred to him as "The Flying General." They stayed away from the region for several years and did not dare cross the frontier.

Li Kuang was out hunting one time when he spied a rock in the grass which he mistook for a tiger. He shot an arrow at the rock and hit it with such force that the tip of the arrow embedded itself in the rock. Later he discovered that it was a rock, but another day when he tried shooting at it again, he was unable to pierce it.

Whatever province Li Kuang had been in in the past, whenever he heard that there was a tiger in the vicinity he always went out to shoot it in person. When he got to Yu-pei-p'ing he likewise went out one time to hunt a tiger. The beast sprang at him and wounded him, but he finally managed to shoot it dead.

When Shih Chien died, the emperor summoned Li Kuang to take his place as chief of palace attendants.

In the sixth year of *yüan-so* (123 B.C.) Li Kuang was again made

---

[5] A work on military affairs attributed to late Chou times.

[6] The Hsiung-nu were most likely to attack in the autumn, when their horses were well fed and in top condition.

a general and sent with the general in chief Wei Ch'ing to proceed north from Ting-hsiang. Most of the other generals who took part in the expedition killed or captured a sufficient number of the enemy to be rewarded for their achievements by being made marquises, but Li Kuang's army won no distinction.

Three years later Li Kuang, as chief of palace attendants, was sent to lead a force of four thousand cavalry north from Yu-pei-p'ing. Chang Ch'ien, the Po-wang marquis, leading ten thousand cavalry, rode out with Li Kuang but took a somewhat different route. When Li Kuang had advanced several hundred li into enemy territory, the Hsiung-nu leader known as the Wise King of the Left appeared with forty thousand cavalry and surrounded Li Kuang's army. His men were all terrified, but Li Kuang ordered his son Li Kan to gallop out to meet the enemy. Li Kan, accompanied by only twenty or thirty riders, dashed straight through the Hsiung-nu horsemen, scattering them to left and right, and then returned to his father's side, saying, "These barbarians are easy enough to deal with!" After this Li Kuang's men felt somewhat reassured.

Li Kuang ordered his men to draw up in a circle with their ranks facing outward. The enemy charged furiously down on them and the arrows fell like rain. Over half the Han soldiers were killed, and their arrows were almost gone. Li Kuang then ordered the men to load their bows and hold them in readiness, but not to discharge them, while he himself, with his huge yellow crossbow, shot at the subcommander of the enemy force and killed several of the barbarians. After this the enemy began to fall back a little.

By this time night had begun to fall. Every one of Li Kuang's officers and men had turned white with fear, but Li Kuang, as calm and confident as though nothing had happened, worked to get his ranks into better formation. After this the men knew that they could never match his bravery.

The following day Li Kuang once more fought off the enemy, and in the meantime Chang Ch'ien at last arrived with his army. The Hsiung-nu forces withdrew and the Han armies likewise retreated, being in no condition to pursue them. By this time Li Kuang's army had been practically wiped out. When the two leaders returned to the capital, they were called to account before the law. Chang Ch'ien was condemned to death for failing to keep his rendezvous with Li Kuang at the appointed time, but on payment of a fine he was allowed to become a commoner. In the case of Li

Kuang it was decided that his achievements and his failures canceled each other out and he was given no reward.

Li Kuang and his cousin Li Ts'ai had begun their careers as attendants at the court of Emperor Wen. During the reign of Emperor Ching, Li Ts'ai managed to accumulate sufficient merit to advance to the position of a two thousand picul official. During the *yüan-so* era of Emperor Wu's reign, he was appointed a general of light carriage and accompanied the general in chief Wei Ch'ing in an attack on the Hsiung-nu Wise King of the Right. His achievements in this campaign placed him in the middle group of those who were to receive rewards and he was accordingly enfeoffed as marquis of Lo-an. In the second year of *yüan-shou* (121 B.C.) he replaced Kung-sun Hung as chancellor of the central court. In ability one would be obliged to rank Li Ts'ai very close to the bottom, and his reputation came nowhere near to equaling that of Li Kuang. And yet Li Kuang never managed to obtain a fief and never rose higher than one of the nine lower offices of government, that of colonel of the guard, while even some of Li Kuang's own officers and men succeeded in becoming marquises.

Li Kuang was once chatting with Wang So, a diviner who told men's fortunes by the configurations in the sky, and remarked on this fact. "Ever since the Han started attacking the Hsiung-nu, I have never failed to be in the fight. I've had men in my command who were mere company commanders or even lower and who didn't even have the ability of average men, and yet twenty or thirty of them have won marquisates. I have never been behind anyone else in doing my duty. Why is it I have never won an ounce of distinction so that I could be enfeoffed like the others? Is it that I just don't have the kind of face to become a marquis?"

"Think carefully, general," replied Wang So. "Isn't there something in the past that you regret having done?"

"Once, when I was governor of Lung-hsi, the Ch'iang tribes in the west started a revolt. I tried to talk them into surrendering, and in fact persuaded over eight hundred of them to give themselves up. But then I went back on my word and killed them all the very same day. I have never ceased to regret what I did. But that's the only thing I can think of."

"Nothing brings greater misfortune than killing those who have already surrendered to you," said Wang So. "This is the reason, general, that you have never gotten to be a marquis!"

Over a period of forty some years, Li Kuang served as governor of seven provinces. Whenever he received a reward of some kind, he at once divided it among those in his command, and he was content to eat and drink the same things as his men. His family enjoyed no unusual wealth—in fact, to the day of his death he never discussed matters of family fortune. He was a tall man with long, apelike arms. His skill at archery seems to have been an inborn talent, for none of his descendents or others who studied under him were ever able to equal his prowess. He was a very clumsy speaker and never had much to say. When he was with others he would draw diagrams on the ground to explain his military tactics or set up targets of various widths and shoot at them with his friends, the loser being forced to drink. In fact, archery was his chief source of amusement.

When he was leading his troops through a barren region and they came upon some water, he would not go near it until all his men had finished drinking. Similarly he would not eat until every one of his men had been fed. He was very lenient with his men and did nothing to vex them, so that they all loved him and were happy to serve under him. Even when the enemy was attacking, it was his custom never to discharge his arrows unless his opponent was within twenty or thirty paces and he believed he could score a hit. When he did discharge an arrow, however, the bowstring had no sooner sounded than his victim would fall to the ground. Because of this peculiar habit he often found himself in considerable difficulty when he was leading his troops against an enemy, and this is also the reason, it is said, that he was occasionally wounded when he went out hunting wild beasts.

In the fourth year of *yüan-shou* (119 B.C.) the general in chief Wei Ch'ing and the general of swift cavalry Ho Ch'ü-ping set off with a large force to attack the Hsiung-nu. Li Kuang several times asked to be allowed to join them, but the emperor considered that he was too old and would not permit him to go. After some time, however, the emperor changed his mind and gave his consent, appointing him as general of the vanguard.

Wei Ch'ing crossed the border, captured one of the enemy and learned the whereabouts of the *Shan-yü*. He therefore decided to take his own best troops and make a dash for the spot, ordering Li Kuang to join forces with the general of the right Chao I-chi and ride around by the eastern road. The eastern road was rather long and roundabout and, since there was little water or grass in the region, it presented a difficult route for a large army to pass over. Li

Kuang therefore asked Wei Ch'ing to change the order. "I have been appointed as general of the vanguard," he said, "and yet now you have shifted my position and ordered me to go around by the east. I have been fighting the Hsiung-nu ever since I was old enough to wear my hair bound up, and now I would like to have just one chance to get at the *Shan-yü*. I beg you to let me stay in the vanguard and advance and fight to the death with him!"

Wei Ch'ing had been warned in private by the emperor that Li Kuang had already had a lot of bad luck in the past. "Don't let him try to get at the *Shan-yü*, or he will probably make a mess of things!" the emperor had said. Also, at this time Kung-sun Ao, who had recently been deprived of his marquisate, was serving as a general under Wei Ch'ing, and Wei Ch'ing wanted to take him along with him in his attack on the *Shan-yü* so that Kung-sun Ao would have a chance to win some distinction. For these reasons he removed Li Kuang from his post as general of the vanguard.

Li Kuang was aware of all this and tried his best to get out of obeying the order, but Wei Ch'ing refused to listen to his arguments. Instead he sent one of his clerks with a sealed letter to Li Kuang's tent and orders to "proceed to your division at once in accordance with the instructions herein!" Li Kuang did not even bother to take leave of Wei Ch'ing but got up and went straight to his division, burning with obvious rage and indignation and, leading his troops to join those of the general of the right Chao I-chi, set out by the eastern road. They lost their way, however, and failed to meet up with Wei Ch'ing at the appointed time. Wei Ch'ing in the meantime engaged the *Shan-yü* in battle, but the latter fled and Wei Ch'ing, being unable to capture him, was forced to turn back south again. After crossing the desert, he joined up with the forces of Li Kuang and Chao I-chi.

When Li Kuang had finished making his report to Wei Ch'ing and returned to his own camp, Wei Ch'ing sent over his clerk with the customary gifts of dried rice and thick wine for Li Kuang. While the clerk was there, he began to inquire how it happened that Li Kuang and Chao I-chi had lost their way, since Wei Ch'ing had to make a detailed report to the emperor on what had happened to the armies. Li Kuang, however, refused to answer his questions.

Wei Ch'ing sent his clerk again to reprimand Li Kuang in the strongest terms and order him to report to general headquarters at once and answer a list of charges that had been drawn up against him. Li Kuang replied, "None of my commanders was at fault. I was the one who caused us to lose our way. I will send in a report myself."

Then he went in person to headquarters and, when he got there, said to his officers, "Since I was old enough to wear my hair bound up, I have fought over seventy engagements, large and small, with the Hsiung-nu. This time I was fortunate enough to join the general in chief in a campaign against the soldiers of the *Shan-yü* himself, but he shifted me to another division and sent me riding around by the long way. On top of that, I lost my way. Heaven must have planned it like this! Now I am over sixty—much too old to stand up to a bunch of petty clerks and their list of charges!" Then he drew his sword and cut his throat.

When word of this reached the common people, those who had known him and those who had not, old men and young boys alike, were all moved to tears by his fate. Chao I-chi was handed over to the law officials and sentenced to death, but on payment of a fine he was allowed to become a commoner.

Li Kuang had three sons, Tang-hu, Chiao, and Kan, all of whom were palace attendants. One day when Emperor Wu was amusing himself with his young favorite Han Yen, the boy behaved so impertinently that Li Tang-hu struck him and drove him from the room. The emperor was much impressed with Tang-hu's ability. Li Tang-hu died young. Li Chiao was made governor of Tai Province. Ho and Tang-hu both died before their father. Li Kan was serving in the army under the general of light cavalry Ho Ch'ü-ping when his father committed suicide.

The year after Li Kuang's death his cousin Li Ts'ai, who was serving as chancellor, was presented by the emperor with a gift of land alongside the funerary park of Emperor Ching at Yang-ling upon which to construct his grave. He was supposed to receive a plot of twenty *mou*, but he surreptitiously appropriated an additional three *ch'ing*, and then sold some of it for a price of over 400,000 cash.[7] He also appropriated one *mou* of land from the outer precincts of the sacred roadway leading to the mausoleum, using it as the site for his own burial place. He was scheduled to be handed over to the prison officials, but he committed suicide.

Li Kan served as a commander under Ho Ch'ü-ping, taking part

[7] One *ch'ing* was equal to about 57 English acres; there were 100 *mou* in a *ch'ing*.

in an attack on the Hsiung-nu Wise King of the Left. He fought bravely in the attack, seizing the pennants of the barbarian king and cutting off many heads. He was rewarded by being enfeoffed as a marquis in the area within the Pass, receiving the revenue from a town of two hundred households.[8] In addition he was appointed to replace his father Li Kuang as chief of palace attendants.

Sometime afterwards, deeply resentful at the general in chief Wei Ch'ing for having brought about his father's disgrace, he struck and wounded Wei Ch'ing. Wei Ch'ing, however, hushed up the incident and said nothing about it. Shortly afterwards, Li Kan accompanied the emperor on a trip to Yung. When the party reached the Palace of Sweet Springs, an imperial hunt was held. Ho Ch'ü-ping, angry that Li Kan had wounded Wei Ch'ing, took the opportunity to shoot and kill Li Kan. At this time Ho Ch'ü-ping enjoyed great favor with the emperor, and the emperor therefore covered up for him, giving out the story that Li Kan had been gored and killed by a stag. A year or so later, Ho Ch'ü-ping died.

Li Kan had a daughter who became a lady in waiting to the heir apparent and was much loved and favored by him. Li Kan's son Li Yü also enjoyed favor with the heir apparent, but he was somewhat fond of profit. He was also very brave. Once, drinking with a group of palace attendants and courtiers, he began to abuse and insult them. They did not dare to make any reply, but later complained about him to the emperor. The emperor summoned Li Yü and ordered him to fight and kill a tiger with his sword. He was lowered by rope into the tiger pen, but before his feet had touched the ground the emperor gave the command to have him hauled up again. Li Yü swung his sword and cut the rope that was tied to him, determined to kill the tiger. The emperor, impressed by such spirit, had him rescued from the tiger pen and dropped the matter.

Tang-hu had a son named Li Ling who was born after Tang-hu died. He led a force of troops in an attack on the Hsiung-nu but was defeated in arms and surrendered to the barbarians. Later someone reported that Li Yü was planning to run away and join his cousin Li Ling. He was handed over to the law officials and died.

[8] "Marquis within the Pass" was the lowest rank in the landed nobility; those with this title did not receive outright possession of a fief but resided in the capital and enjoyed the revenue from an estate assigned to them.

LI LING

Li Ling's polite name was Shao-ch'ing. As a young man he was made an attendant in the inner palace, at the same time being appointed supervisor of the Chien-chang Palace. He was good at horsemanship and archery and treated people well. Modest and deferential, he gave way to others and thereby gained wide fame. Emperor Wu, seeing in him qualities reminiscent of his grandfather Li Kuang, put him in charge of a force of eight hundred cavalry. Li Ling penetrated over two thousand li into Hsiung-nu territory, passing Chü-yen and observing the lay of the land, but he returned without having caught sight of the enemy. On his return he was appointed a chief commandant of cavalry and was put in command of a force of five thousand men chosen for their bravery and determination. He taught archery in the provinces of Chiu-ch'üan and Chang-i, preparing them to ward off attacks from the Hsiung-nu.

Several years later, when the Han dispatched the Sutrishna general Li Kuang-li to attack Ta-yüan, Li Ling was put in charge of five companies of soldiers and ordered to follow in the rear.[9] By the time he reached the border, however, the Sutrishna general had already started home. The emperor sent Li Ling a letter, and in accordance with the instructions contained in it, he left his clerks and officers at the border and, with five hundred light cavalrymen, set out from Tun-huang and proceeded as far as the Salt River, where he met the Sutrishna general and returned with him to the border. Once more Li Ling was ordered to remain in the area, this time to garrison Chang-i.

In the second year of t'ien-han (99 B.C.) the Sutrishna general led a force of thirty thousand cavalry out of Chiu-ch'üan to attack the Wise King of the Right at the Heavenly Mountains. Li Ling was summoned to court, the emperor intending to put him in charge of baggage and supplies for the Sutrishna general, but when he was received in audience at the Martial Terrace, he kowtowed and put forth this request: "The men in my command with whom I have been garrisoning the border are all brave soldiers of the Ching and Ch'u region, master swordsmen of unusual ability. They have the

---

[9] Li Kuang-li, brother of Emperor Wu's favorite, Madam Li, was given the title Sutrishna general because his assignment was to conquer the city of Erh-shih or Sutrishna in the Central Asian state of Ta-yüan or Ferghana, an assignment which he carried to completion.

strength to strangle tigers, the skill to hit whatever target they name. I request that I be put in charge of a battalion of them and allowed to proceed to the south of Mount Lan-kan, and thus split the *Shan-yü's* troops so that he will be unable to concentrate all his forces on a confrontation with the Sutrishna general."

"Where would I get the men?" said the emperor. "I've already put a number of armies into the field—I have no cavalry to give you!"

But Li Ling replied that it was not a matter of cavalry. "I propose to use a small force to attack a large one. With five thousand foot soldiers, I'll wade right into the *Shan-yü's* court!"

The emperor, impressed by such bravado, gave his permission and accordingly ordered the chief commandant of strong crossbowmen Lu Po-te to lead his men and follow after Li Ling until he met up with him along the way. Lu Po-te, who had earlier held the title of General Who Calms the Waves,[10] was humiliated at the thought of acting as rear guard for Li Ling and submitted a report stating that, since it was autumn and the Hsiung-nu horses were well fed, it was no time to engage them in battle. "I would like to detain Li Ling here, and when spring comes, we will march out together with the cavalry from Chiu-ch'üan and Chang-i, five hundred men for each of us, and launch a concerted attack on the east and west ranges of Mount Chün-chi—then we will be certain to capture the enemy!"

When the letter was presented to the emperor, he was furious and suspected that Li Ling, repenting of his plan and no longer wishing to go on the expedition, had instructed Lu Po-te to submit the letter. He then dispatched an order to Lu Po-te stating, "I tried to give Li Ling some cavalry but he said he wanted to use a small force to attack a large one. Now the enemy has invaded Hsi-ho. You will be good enough to lead your troops and proceed to Hsi-ho to block the Kou-ying road." He also ordered Li Ling to set out in the ninth month, crossing the border at the Outpost for Blocking the Enemy. When Li Ling had reached the Lung-le River that flows south of the eastern range of Mount Chün-chi, he was to scout about in search of the enemy. If he saw no sign of the Hsiung-nu, he should then follow the old road that had been made by Chao P'o-nu, the marquis of Cho-yeh, until he reached the City

---

[10] In 112 B.C. Lu Po-te took part in the campaign against the state of Southern Yüeh, sailing down the Hui River to attack P'an-yü, the capital of Southern Yüeh in the region of present-day Canton.

for Receiving Surrender, where he should rest his men. He was to take advantage of the dispatch riders there to send word to the emperor, reporting the conversations that had taken place between him and Lu Po-te and giving a full account of his activities.

In accordance with these instructions Li Ling took his five thousand foot soldiers and set out from Chü-yen, marching north for thirty days until he reached Mount Chün-chi, where he halted and made camp. He drew up maps of all the mountains, rivers, and land formations that he had passed and dispatched a horseman under his command named Ch'en Pu-lo to return and submit them to the emperor. When Ch'en Pu-lo was summoned to audience, he described how Li Ling was able to inspire his men to fight to the death for him. The emperor was exceedingly pleased and appointed Ch'en Pu-lo as a palace attendant.

When Li Ling reached Mount Chün-chi, he suddenly found himself face to face with the *Shan-yü*, who surrounded his army with some thirty thousand cavalry. The Han army, positioned in the area between two mountains, used its big wagons to make a fortification of sorts. Li Ling then led his soldiers outside the ring of wagons and drew them up in ranks, those in the front line bearing lances and shields, those in the rear, bows and crossbows. He issued orders saying, "When you hear the sound of the drum, advance. When you hear the sound of the gong, halt!"

The enemy, noting how small the Han army was, advanced directly toward the camp. Li Ling attacked, engaging them in hand to hand combat, and as the thousand crossbows fired all at once, a victim fell with each twanging of the bowstring. The Hsiung-nu turned and fled back to the hills, where the Han army pursued them, attacking and killing several thousand men. The *Shan-yü*, greatly alarmed, called up some eighty thousand or more cavalry from the forces in the regions to the left and right and attacked Li Ling. Li Ling alternately fought and retreated, marching south for several days until he reached a mountain valley, where he continued the battle. Of his officers and men who had been wounded by arrows, those who had suffered three wounds were loaded onto the small carts, those who had suffered two wounds pulled the carts, and those with only one wound carried arms and fought.

Li Ling said, "My men seem to be losing their spirit—why don't they get to their feet when the drum sounds? Could it be that there are women in the army?" When the army had first set out, many of the wives of bandits from east of the Pass who had been transported to the border had followed along with the army, giving themselves as wives to the soldiers, and they were hidden in the wagons in large numbers. Li Ling instituted a search and had all those who were found put to the sword. The next day when the battle was resumed, his men cut off over three thousand enemy heads.

Li Ling led his troops southeast along the old road from the city of Lung, and when they had marched for four or five days, they found themselves in the midst of the reeds and rushes of a huge swamp. The enemy, being upwind, set fire to the brush, but Li Ling ordered his men to start fires of their own and in this way saved them.

They pushed south until they came to the foot of a hill. The *Shan-yü*, who had taken up a position on top of the hill to the south, ordered his son to lead the cavalry and attack Li Ling, but Li Ling's army, being on foot, fought with them among the trees and once more killed several thousand men.[11] Then they fired their double-shot crossbows at the *Shan-yü*, who fled down the hill.

This day they captured one of the Hsiung-nu who gave this account: "The *Shan-yü* has said, 'These are crack troops of the Han and cannot be overcome by attack. Day and night they are drawing us farther south toward the border—surely they must have troops lying in wait to ambush us!' But the household administrators and other tribal leaders all said, 'If the *Shan-yü* in person leads thirty or forty thousand cavalry in an attack on a few thousand men of the Han and still can't wipe them out, then we will never again be able to make the tribes on our borders submit to us. We will only give the Han cause to be even more contemptuous of the Hsiung-nu people. We should start fighting again in the valley and put forth all our effort. Forty or fifty li more and we will be out in open ground. If at that point we still can't crush them, then that will be the time to withdraw!' "

At this time Li Ling's men found themselves harder and harder pressed. The Hsiung-nu cavalry were numerous and engaged them in twenty or thirty skirmishes a day. They in turn wounded or killed over two thousand of the enemy who, failing to gain the advantage, were about to quit the scene. Just then a scout of Li Ling's army, one Kuan Kan, having been humiliated by his com-

---

[11] The Hsiung-nu, being mounted, were at a disadvantage as long as the Chinese were in confined or wooded areas. Their hope was to catch the Chinese out in the open.

pany commander, slipped away and surrendered to the Hsiung-nu, telling them all he knew—that there were no relief troops coming to rescue Li Ling, that his arrows were almost gone, that he alone was leading the force, along with the marquis of Ch'eng-an, each with a company of eight hundred men, marching in the front rank with flags of yellow and white. He advised the Hsiung-nu to use their best cavalry to shoot at them, in which case they could be wiped out.

(The marquis of Ch'eng-an was a native of Ying-ch'uan. His father, Han Ch'ien-ch'iu, formerly prime minister to the king of Chi-nan, had volunteered to join in the attack on Southern Yüeh and had been killed in battle. Emperor Wu had enfeoffed his son Han Yen-nien as a marquis, and the latter was accompanying Li Ling as a company commander.)

The *Shan-yü* was overjoyed to get hold of Kuan Kan and his information, and dispatched the cavalry to make an all out attack on the Han army, shouting at the top of their voices, "Li Ling! Han Yen-nien! Hurry up and surrender!" Then they blocked the trail and pressed their attack with even greater fury. Li Ling was in a valley, the enemy on the hillsides, and from four sides the volleys of arrows fell on him like rain. The Han army pushed south, but while they were still one day's march from Mount Ti-han, they used up the last of their five hundred thousand arrows, and accordingly abandoned their wagons. The three thousand or so soldiers who were left could do no more than break off the spokes of the wagon wheels and carry them in their hands for weapons, while their officers bore their foot-long swords.

When they reached the mountain, they entered its narrow valley, whereupon the *Shan-yü*, blocking their rear, had his men mount the cliffsides and throw heaps of stones down on them. Many of the officers and men were killed and the army was unable to go any farther.

After sundown, Li Ling changed into ordinary dress and walked out of the encampment alone, signaling those about him to stay behind. "Don't come with me," he said. "One good man alone can capture the *Shan-yü!*" After a long while he returned and with a profound sigh said, "Defeat at arms—that means death."

One of his officers said, "The general's might has set the Hsiung-nu to quaking with terror. Though fate does not seem to be with you now, later you will find some trail or bypath by which to make your way back home. If someone like the marquis of Cho-yeh, after he had been captured by the enemy and had escaped and come home, was treated as an honored guest by the Son of Heaven, how much more a man like yourself, general!"

"No more of that, sir!" said Li Ling. "If I do not die, I will not be a man of honor!" Then he broke up all of his flags and pennants and objects of value and buried them in the ground. "If only we had twenty or thirty arrows, we could make our getaway," he said with a sigh. "But now there are no more weapons to fight with, and when dawn comes we'll just be sitting here waiting to be tied up! Each of you must scatter and go your way like birds or beasts —some of you may manage to escape and get back to report to the Son of Heaven." Then he ordered that each soldier be given two pints of dried rations and one chunk of ice, instructing them to rendezvous at the Outpost for Blocking the Enemy and wait there for stragglers.

At midnight he ordered the drums to beat and rouse the soldiers, but the drums would make no sound. Li Ling and Han Yen-nien together mounted their horses and set out with ten or more of their bravest men in attendance. Several thousand of the enemy cavalry set out after them in pursuit and Han Yen-nien died in the fighting. "I could never face His Majesty with a report of this!" said Li Ling, and thereupon surrendered.

The men of his army scattered in all directions and some four hundred or more of them succeeded in escaping and reaching the border. The place where Li Ling met his defeat was a little over a hundred li from the border.

When reports first came from the border, the emperor hoped that Li Ling had died fighting, but when he summoned Li Ling's mother and wife and had them examined by a physiognomizer, the latter could discern no sign of a death in the family. Later, when word came that Li Ling had surrendered, the emperor was enraged. He began to question and berate Ch'en Pu-lo, whereupon Ch'en Pu-lo committed suicide.

The mass of court officials all blamed Li Ling, but when the emperor questioned the grand historian Ssu-ma Ch'ien, he spoke enthusiastically on Li Ling's behalf, declaring that "he is filial to his parents and trustworthy with his associates; constantly he has hastened forward in time of need to sacrifice himself for his country without thought for his own safety. This was always in his mind— his ways marked him as one of the finest men of the nation. Now he has committed one unfortunate act, and the officials who think only to save themselves and protect their own wives and children vie with each other in magnifying his shortcomings. Truly it makes one sick! The infantry that Li Ling commanded did not come up to five thousand. They marched deep into nomad territory, fending off the numberless hosts, so that the enemy did not have time even to rescue their dead or aid their wounded. They called up all their men who could use a bow and together they surrounded and attacked Li Ling's army, which fought its way along for a thousand li, until its arrows were gone and the road was blocked. Then the men stretched out their empty bows and warded off the bare blades of the attackers, facing north and fighting to the death with the foe. Li Ling was able to command the loyalty of his troops in the face of death—even the famous generals of old could do no more! And though he fell into captivity, yet the losses and injury which he has inflicted upon the enemy are worthy to be proclaimed throughout the world. The fact that he did not choose to die must mean that he hopes sometime to find a way to repay his debt to the Han." [12]

When the emperor first dispatched the Sutrishna general at the head of a large army to march beyond the border, he intended to use Li Ling's men merely as an auxiliary force. But later Li Ling came face to face with the *Shan-yü*, while the Sutrishna general accomplished very little. The emperor therefore supposed that Ssu-ma Ch'ien was engaging in slander and deceit, trying to disparage the Sutrishna general and plead a special case for Li Ling. He therefore had Ssu-ma Ch'ien condemned and punished by castration.

Later the emperor felt sorry that he had failed to supply Li Ling with relief troops. "I should have waited until Li Ling was ready to set out from the border before ordering the chief commandant of strong crossbowmen Lu Po-te to follow after him. But because I issued the order ahead of time, I gave the old general a chance to hatch his underhanded schemes!" He then dispatched a messenger to thank and reward those of Li Ling's army who had managed to escape and return to the border.

[12] The section in quotation marks is condensed from the letter which Ssu-ma Ch'ien wrote to his friend Jen Shao-ch'ing explaining how he spoke out in Li Ling's defense. The full text of the letter is recorded in the biography of Ssu-ma Ch'ien, *Han shu* 62, and is translated by J. R. Hightower in *Anthology of Chinese Literature*, Cyril Birch, ed. (New York, Grove Press, 1965), pp. 95–102, and in my *Ssu-ma Ch'ien: Grand Historian of China* (New York, Columbia University Press, 1958), pp. 57–67.

After Li Ling had been among the Hsiung-nu for a year or so, the emperor dispatched the Yin-yü general Kung-sun Ao to lead his troops deep into Hsiung-nu territory and fetch Li Ling. The army, however, returned without having accomplished anything and Kung-sun Ao reported, "I took one of the enemy alive and he informed me that Li Ling is instructing the *Shan-yü* in military matters so he will know how to deal with the Han armies. That was why I could not win any advantage." When the emperor heard this, he had Li Ling's family put to death in punishment; his mother, his younger brothers, his wife and children all bowed before the executioner.[13] The gentlemen and officials of the region of Lung-hsi, where the Li family originated, all felt they had been disgraced by the Lis.

Later when the Han sent an envoy to the Hsiung-nu, Li Ling said to him, "For the sake of the Han I led five thousand foot soldiers in defiant march against the Hsiung-nu, but because of the lack of relief troops, I was defeated. In what way have I ever betrayed the Han, that it should wipe out my family?"

"The emperor heard that Li Shao-ch'ing was instructing the Hsiung-nu in military affairs," explained the envoy.

"That must be Li Hsü," said Li Ling. "It is not I!" (Li Hsü was formerly a chief commandant beyond the border and was stationed in the fortress of Hsi-hou, but when the Hsiung-nu attacked there, he surrendered to them. The *Shan-yü* treated him like a guest and always seated him higher than Li Ling.)

Li Ling, grieved that his family had been wiped out because of Li Hsü, hired a man to stab and kill Li Hsü. The *Shan-yü's* mother in turn tried to kill Li Ling, but the *Shan-yü* hid him in the region to the north. Only after the *Shan-yü's* mother died was he able to return to the *Shan-yü's* camp.

The *Shan-yü* admired Li Ling's spirit and gave him one of his daughters for a wife. He was appointed right company king, while Wei Lü was made king of the Ting-ling tribe; both were honored and given positions of responsibility. (Wei Lü's father was a barbarian who came originally from Ch'ang-shui. Wei Lü was born and raised in Han territory and was very friendly with the chief commandant Li Yen-nien, the Harmonizer of the Tones.[14] Li Yen-

[13] Li Ling's father died before he was born, so he could not have had any younger brothers; the term *ti* here must refer to younger cousins or half brothers.

[14] A force of non-Chinese cavalrymen who had come over to the side of the Han was stationed in Ch'ang-shui, in present-day Honan, and Wei Lü's father

nien recommended that he be sent as envoy to the Hsiung-nu, but
when he returned from this mission, he found that Li Yen-nien and
his family had been arrested. Wei Lü, fearful that he might be
punished along with the members of the Li family, escaped, made
his way back north, and surrendered to the Hsiung-nu, who
treated him with kindness. He was constantly to be found in the
presence of the *Shan-yü*. Li Ling, on the other hand, lived outside
the *Shan-yü's* quarters and was only summoned when there was
some important matter to be discussed.)

When Emperor Chao came to the throne, the general in chief
Ho Kuang and the general of the left Shang-kuan Chieh assisted in
affairs of state. Having been friendly with Li Ling in former times,
they dispatched Jen Li-cheng and two other old friends of Li Ling
from Lung-hsi to go in a party to the Hsiung-nu and invite Li Ling
to return.

When Jen Li-cheng and his companions arrived, the *Shan-yü*
brought out wine and offered it to the Han envoys; Li Ling and
Wei Lü sat with him in attendance. Jen Li-cheng and the others
thus could see Li Ling but had no opportunity to speak with him
in private. Jen stared meaningfully at Li Ling and from time to
time stroked the ring on the head of his sword and grasped his
foot, in this way hoping to convey a hint to Li Ling and indicate
that the time had come for him to return to the Han.[15]

Afterwards Li Ling and Wei Lü brought beef and wine to give
to the Han envoys in recompense for the hardships of their journey, playing dice with them and drinking. Both men wore barbarian dress and had their hair done up in mallet-shaped fashion. Jen
Li-cheng said in a loud voice, "The Han has already proclaimed a
general amnesty. China is happy and peaceful, the sovereign is
young in years, and Ho Tzu-meng and Shang-kuan Shao-shu are in
charge of affairs." [16] By speaking in this way he hoped, without
being explicit, to rouse Li Ling to action. But Li Ling sat silent
and did not respond, staring intently at Jen Li-cheng and running

---

was presumably among them. Li Yen-nien, brother of the Sutrishna general Li
Kuang-li, was made "Harmonizer of the Tones" because of his knowledge of
music. He and his brothers were later tried on charges of immorality and put
to death along with their families.

[15] Because the word for ring (*huan*) is a homophone for the word "return"
(*huan*).

[16] Tzu-meng and Shao-shu are the polite names of Ho Kuang and Shang-
kuan Chieh respectively.

his hands over his hair. Then by way of reply he said, "I have already adopted barbarian dress!"

After a while, Wei Lü got up and left to change his clothes. "Well, Shao-ch'ing!" said Jen Li-cheng. "You have certainly suffered. Ho Tzu-meng and Shang-kuan Shao-shu send you their regards."

"Ho and Shang-kuan—are they well?" asked Li Ling.

"They beg you to come back to your homeland, Shao-ch'ing. You will never have to worry about money or position," said Jen Li-cheng.

Li Ling, addressing Jen Li-cheng by name,[17] said, "Shao-kung, going back is easy enough, but I'm afraid of another humiliation —how could I face it?"

Before they had finished speaking, Wei Lü came back, arriving in time to overhear the last of the conversation. "A worthy man like Li Shao-ch'ing does not have to stay forever in one country!" said Wei Lü. "Fan Li wandered all over the world, Yu Yü left the Jung and went to Ch'in.[18] What is all this chummy talk about!"

With this the party broke up and Wei Lü and Li Ling left. Jen Li-cheng called after Li Ling, "Have you thought about it?" but Li Ling replied, "A brave man cannot suffer humiliation twice."

So Li Ling remained among the Hsiung-nu, and some twenty years later, in the first year of *yüan-p'ing* (74 B.C.) he died of an illness.

SU CHIEN

Su Chien was a native of Tu-ling. As a company commander he accompanied the general in chief Wei Ch'ing in an attack on the Hsiung-nu and was enfeoffed as marquis of P'ing-ling. He was made a general and ordered to build fortifications at So-fang.

---

[17] That is, by his *tzu* or polite name, Shao-kung, a sign of affection. Ordinarily persons of equal standing addressed each other by family name or official title.

[18] The statesman Fan Li of Yüeh aided King Kou-chien (r. 496–465 B.C.) in wiping out a disgrace suffered by the state. This done, he left, changed his name, and went to the state of Ch'i. In time he settled in T'ao, where he made a fortune in trade. Yu Yü was a man of Chinese parents from the state of Chin who lived among the Jung barbarians of the northwest. Having been sent by the Jung leader as an observer to the court of Duke Mu (r. 659–621 B.C.) of Ch'in, he eventually went over to the side of Duke Mu, acting as his adviser in attacks on the barbarians.

Later, when he was a colonel of the guard, he was made scouting and attacking general and joined the general in chief in an expedition out of So-fang. A year later he was made general of the right and once more joined the general in chief, this time in an expedition out of Ting-hsiang. Because he allowed his fellow general Chao Hsin, the marquis of Hsi, to escape, and lost his army, he was condemned to death but was permitted to pay a fine and become a commoner. Later he became governor of Tai Province and died in office. He had three sons, Chia, who was made a chief commandant in charge of carriage; Hsien, who was made a chief commandant of cavalry; and Wu, the middle son, who became the most famous of them all.

SU WU

Su Wu's polite name was Tzu-ch'ing. In his youth he was given an official position because of his father, he and his older and younger brother all being made palace attendants. Gradually he advanced until he had reached the position of superintendent of the I-chung Stables.

At this time the Han was engaged in repeated attacks on the barbarians, and the two sides frequently sent envoys to observe and spy on one another. The Hsiung-nu detained the Han envoys Kuo Chi, Lu Ch'ung-kuo, and others, numbering something over ten persons, and when the Hsiung-nu sent envoys to the Han, the Han in turn detained them by way of retaliation. In the first year of *t'ien-han* (100 B.C.), when Chü-ti-hou first assumed the position of *Shan-yü*, he was afraid that the Han might attack him and so he declared, "The Han Son of Heaven is like a father to me!" and returned Lu Ch'ung-kuo and all the other Han envoys to their homeland.

Emperor Wu, gratified by this display of righteous conduct, thereupon dispatched Su Wu as a general of palace attendants, instructing him to bear the imperial credentials and escort the Hsiung-nu envoys who had been detained at the Han court back to their home. At the same time he was to present generous gifts to the *Shan-yü* in recognition of his act of good will. Su Wu, his subordinate general of palace attendants Chang Sheng, an acting official named Ch'ang Hui, and others gathered together a party of over a hundred soldiers and scouts for the expedition. When the group reached the Hsiung-nu, they laid their gifts before the

Shan-yü, but the *Shan-yü* only grew increasingly arrogant, which was not what the Han had hoped for.

The Hsiung-nu were on the point of dispatching an envoy to escort Su Wu and his party back, when it was discovered that the Kou king, along with Yü Ch'ang of Ch'ang-shui and others, was plotting to raise a revolt among the Hsiung-nu. The Kou king was the son of the elder sister of the Hun-yeh king. He was with the Hun-yeh king and his group when they surrendered to the Han, but later accompanied the marquis of Cho-yeh when the latter was overwhelmed by the barbarians.[19] Later he joined Yü Ch'ang and the men whom Wei Lü had led over to the side of the Hsiung-nu in a plot to threaten the *Shan-yü's* mother and make their way back to China. It was just at this point that Su Wu and his party arrived on the scene. When Yü Ch'ang was living in Han territory, he had been acquainted with the subordinate commander of Su Wu's party Chang Sheng, and he paid a secret call on him and said, "I hear that the Han Son of Heaven harbors a deep resentment against Wei Lü. I could do the Han a favor by lying in wait with a crossbow and shooting him down. My mother and younger brother are still in China—I would be deeply grateful if they could be given whatever reward I might have earned."

Chang Sheng gave his approval and made Yü Chang a present out of the goods at his disposal. A month or so later, the *Shan-yü* went out hunting, leaving his mother alone with his sons and younger brothers. Yü Ch'ang and his group of seventy men decided that this was the time to put their plot into action, but one of the men stole away in the night and reported what was afoot. The *Shan-yü's* sons and younger brothers called out the troops and engaged the conspirators, and the Kou king and others were all killed. Only Yü Ch'ang was taken alive.

The *Shan-yü* put Wei Lü in charge of cleaning up the affair. On hearing this, Chang Sheng became fearful that his earlier conversation with Yü Ch'ang would come to light and he went to Su Wu and informed him of the situation.

"If this is the way things are," said Su Wu, "then I am certain to become implicated. To wait until after one has suffered indignity

[19] The Hun-yeh king, a tribal leader who lived in the western sector of the Hsiung-nu domain, in 121 B.C. led a force of over forty thousand men and surrendered to the Han. Some time later, Chao P'o-nu, the marquis of Cho-yeh, led a force of cavalry in an attack on the Hsiung-nu but was defeated and forced to surrender.

before dying is to do a double disservice to the state!" He was on the point of committing suicide when Chang Sheng and Ch'ang Hui together prevailed on him to stop.

As had been feared, Yü Ch'ang's testimony eventually implicated Chang Sheng. The *Shan-yü*, enraged, summoned the elders of the tribe to a conference, intending to put the Han envoys to death. But the *I-chih-tzu* leader of the left said, "Supposing they had plotted against the *Shan-yü* himself—then what penalty more severe than death would be left to be imposed on them? It is enough that they all be made to surrender!"

The *Shan-yü* ordered Wei Lü to summon Su Wu for the sentencing, but Su Wu said to Ch'ang Hui and the others, "I have betrayed the trust placed in me and brought dishonor to my mission —with what face could I go back and report to the Han?" Then he drew a knife from his girdle and stabbed himself. Wei Lü, startled, picked up Su Wu in his arms and hastened off with him to summon a doctor. They dug a pit in the ground, laid it with glowing embers, and placed Su Wu on top, stamping on his back in order to drive out the blood. Su Wu ceased breathing entirely, but after half a day his breath returned. Ch'ang Hui and the others, lamenting, placed him in a carriage and took him back to their encampment. The *Shan-yü*, struck with admiration for such honorable conduct, sent men morning and evening to inquire about Su Wu's condition. At the same time he had Chang Sheng arrested and bound.

Su Wu gradually recovered and the *Shan-yü* sent one of his men to try to persuade Su Wu to come to terms. When it came time to execute sentence upon Yü Ch'ang, he hoped to use the opportunity to induce Su Wu to come over to the side of the Hsiung-nu. After Yü Ch'ang had been put to death by the sword, Wei Lü announced, "The Han envoy Chang Sheng plotted to kill me, a minister in personal attendance on the *Shan-yü*, and for that he deserves to die! However, the *Shan-yü* encourages men to surrender, and in such cases pardons their crimes." Wei Lü then raised his sword in preparation to strike Chang Sheng, whereupon Chang Sheng begged to be allowed to surrender.

Wei Lü then said to Su Wu, "Since your subordinate is guilty of a crime, you should be held accountable as well!"

"I never had anything to do with the plot, nor is this man a relative of mine!" said Su Wu. "Why do you say that I should be held accountable?"

Again Wei Lü raised his sword, this time making as though to strike Su Wu, but Su Wu did not make a move.

"My lord Su," said Wei Lü, "in the past I turned against the Han and came over to the Hsiung-nu, and I have been treated with the greatest kindness and generosity. The title of king has been bestowed upon me, I command a horde numbering several tens of thousands, my horses and livestock fill the hills—such is the wealth and honor I enjoy! And if you were to surrender today, Lord Su, the same might be yours tomorrow! What good is there in leaving your body to rot and enrich the grassy plain? Who will ever know about it?"

When Su Wu made no reply, Wei Lü continued, "If you surrender with me as your intermediary, then you and I will become brothers. But if you fail to listen to my advice now, then later on, though you may wish to see me, do you think you'll ever get another chance?"

Su Wu began to curse Wei Lü, saying, "You are supposed to be a subject and a son, yet you give no heed to the dictates of gratitude or duty. You have betrayed your sovereign, turned your back on your parents, and given yourself up as a prisoner to these barbarian tribes. Why would I want to see anyone like you! Moreover, the *Shan-yü* trusts you and has given you the power to decide whether men shall live or die. But instead of approaching the task with a fair mind and a respect for justice, you turn around and try to cause dissension between the two rulers so you can sit back and watch the evil and destruction that ensue. When Southern Yüeh dared to kill a Han envoy, its people were slaughtered and its territory carved up into nine provinces. The king of Ta-yüan killed a Han envoy and his head ended up hanging by the north gate of the imperial palace. Ch'ao-hsien killed a Han envoy and in no time at all it was struck down and destroyed. The Hsiung-nu's turn just hasn't come up yet, that's all! You know I have no intention of surrendering—it is clear that you simply want to kill me and set the two countries to fighting. But the downfall of the Hsiung-nu will begin with my death!"

Wei Lü realized that he could never terrify Su Wu into surrendering and he reported this to the *Shan-yü*, but the latter only became more anxious than ever to bring about a surrender. He had Su Wu confined in a large storage pit and deprived of all food and drink, but there was a snowfall and Su Wu, lying on the floor of the pit, chewed up the felt of his garments along with the snow and managed to swallow it down, so that several days passed and he remained alive. The Hsiung-nu thereupon concluded that he must be a god. Eventually he was moved to an uninhabited region along the shores of the Northern Sea [Lake Baikal] where he was set to herding rams. "When your rams give milk, you may return!" he was told. Ch'ang Hui and the others in Su Wu's party were all separated and sent to different places for detention.

When Su Wu reached the Northern Sea, he was too far away to draw grain from the storehouses; instead he dug up the burrows of field mice and ate the seeds of grasses stored in them. The rod identifying him as an imperial envoy he used for a staff when he herded his sheep, asleep or awake holding tight to it, until the hairs of the yak tail that decorated the tip had all dropped out.

Five or six years passed when the *Shan-yü's* younger brother, the Yü-chien king, came to the shores of the lake with his bow and arrows on a shooting expedition. Because Su Wu was good at fashioning nets, twisting cords for stringed arrows, and straightening bows and crossbows, he won favor with the Yü-chien king, who supplied him with food and clothing. Some three years later the king died, leaving Su Wu a gift of horses, livestock, storage jars, and yurts. After the death of the king, his tribesmen all drifted away, and that winter the Ting-ling people stole Su Wu's cattle and sheep. Once more he was reduced to poverty and distress.

In past times Su Wu and Li Ling had both served as attendants of the inner palace. The year after Su Wu went on his mission to the Hsiung-nu, Li Ling surrendered, but he had not dared to seek an interview with Su Wu. After a long time, the *Shan-yü* ordered Li Ling to go to the Northern Sea. There he set out wine for Su Wu, provided music for his entertainment, and used the occasion to speak with Su Wu. "The *Shan-yü* heard that you and I were close friends in the old days and so he has sent me to come and talk to you," said Li Ling. "He is prepared to welcome you with an open heart. In the end you will never be able to return to the Han. Useless as it is, you insist upon making life hard for yourself here in this deserted wilderness. But how is anyone ever going to appreciate such loyalty and devotion to duty?

"Earlier, when your elder brother Chang-chün was in charge of the imperial carriage, he accompanied the emperor to the Yü-yang Palace at Yung. He was helping to carry the emperor's hand-drawn cart down the portico steps when the cart struck a column and broke its axle. He was impeached for extreme lack of reverence and was forced to fall upon his sword and take his own life. The emperor contributed a gift of two million cash to pay for the funeral.

"Your younger brother Ju-ch'ing accompanied the emperor when he went to Ho-tung to sacrifice to the Earth Lord. As they were crossing the river by boat, a eunuch rider began quarreling with the keeper of the emperor's auxiliary horse from the Yellow Gate. The eunuch pushed the keeper of the horse into the river and he drowned. When the eunuch escaped, Ju-ch'ing was commanded by the emperor to pursue and capture him, but he failed to accomplish this and, growing fearful, drank poison and died.

"At the time I came here, your honored mother had already passed away—I accompanied the funeral procession to Yan-ling. Your wife is young and has married again, they tell me. Of your family, only two younger sisters, two daughters, and a son remained, and that was over ten years ago—no one knows if they are still alive or not. Man's life is like the morning dew. Why do you go on torturing yourself like this?

"When I first surrendered, I was as dazed and distraught as a madman, so greatly did it pain me to betray the Han. On top of that, my aged mother was bound and held prisoner in the Detention Room of the palace. Your desire to avoid surrender could not be any greater than was mine! Remember too that the emperor is now well along in years and the laws and regulations are administered with complete lack of consistency. Twenty or thirty high officials have been wiped out along with their families, though they had committed no offense. No one can tell whether he is safe or in danger. For whose sake, then, do you go on like this, Tzu-ch'ing? I hope you will listen to my advice and not make any more objections."

Su Wu replied, "My father, my brothers, and I were without merit or virtue—all we had was bestowed upon us by the emperor. We were placed among the ranks of generals, enfeoffed as marquises, and my brothers permitted to wait upon the emperor in person. Our constant desire was to serve, though it meant spilling our very liver and brains upon the ground! Now if I can prove my loyalty by giving up my life, I will kneel beneath the ax and halberd or face a caldron of boiling water, and do so, I assure you, with resignation and joy. A subject serves his lord as a son serves his father. When a son dies for the sake of his father, he has no regrets. I beg you to say no more of this!"

After Li Ling and Su Wu had spent several days drinking together, Li Ling again said, "Tzu-ch'ing, if you would only listen just once to what I am saying!"

"For a long time I've thought of myself as already dead," said Su Wu. "King that you are, if you are bent upon forcing me to renounce my allegiance to the Han, then when today's festivities are over, I request permission to end my life in your presence."

Li Ling saw that Su Wu was utterly sincere. With a sigh of admiration he said, "Ah, here is a man of honor! The crime which Wei Lü and I have committed must surely be heard all the way to Heaven!" Tears wetting the lapels of his robe, he took leave of Su Wu and went on his way. He did not wish to send gifts to Su Wu in his own name, and so he had his wife send Su Wu thirty or forty head of oxen and sheep.

Later Li Ling once more went to the shores of the Northern Sea. Conversing with Su Wu, he said, "One of the Ou-t'o border patrols captured a man from Yün-chung and he reported that, from the governor on down, all the officials and people of the province were in white mourning robes. 'The sovereign has passed away,' he said."

When Su Wu heard this, he faced to the south and cried and wailed until he spat blood. He continued his ritual lamentations morning and evening for several months.

In the years following Emperor Chao's succession to the throne, the Hsiung-nu established peaceful relations with the Han. The Han asked for the return of Su Wu and his party, but the Hsiung-nu lied and reported that Su Wu was dead. Later, when an envoy from the Han once more journeyed to the territory of the Hsiung-nu, Ch'ang Hui, a member of Su Wu's original party, asked the guard in charge of the visitors if he might join him, and in this way he was able to get to see the Han envoy in the night and give him a full account of what had happened. He instructed the envoy to address the *Shan-yü* and say, "The Son of Heaven, hunting in his Shang-li Park, has shot down a wild goose, and tied to its leg was a letter written on silk which said that Su Wu and the others were to be found in such-and-such a swamp!"

The envoy was delighted and proceeded to do as Ch'ang Hui had advised, berating the *Shan-yü* for his lies. The *Shan-yü* looked to left and right in consternation and then apologized to the Han envoy. "Su Wu and the others are in fact still alive," he said.

Li Ling then set out wine and offered a toast of congratulation to Su Wu. "Now you will be going home," he said. "Your fame has spread abroad among the Hsiung-nu, your achievements reflect glory on the house of Han; those heroes of old whose stories are recorded in books on bamboo and silk, whose portraits are limned in pigments of red and green—even they could not surpass you, Tzu-ch'ing! As for myself, though I may be a tired old horse, and a cowardly one at that, if the Han had been willing to overlook my offense, had left my old mother unharmed, and had given me a chance to fulfill those long-nurtured hopes I had of wiping out the terrible shame I had incurred—then I would have become a veritable Ts'ao Mei at the altar of K'o! [20] All those days the thought of it never left my mind. But they arrested my family and wiped them out—one of the most terrible slaughters of the age! Now who is there left for me to care about? Well, let it be. I wanted you to know what is in my heart, that was all. We are men of different lands—once we part, it must be forever." Then Li Ling rose and danced, singing this song:

> Trekking ten thousand li,
>   crossing desert sands,
> marching in the sovereign's name,
>   I challenged the Hsiung-nu.
> But roads ran out, cut off,
>   arrows and blades were broken;
> armies of men wiped out—
>   my good name perished with them.
> Now that my old mother is dead and gone,
>   though I might wish to repay kindness,
>   where could I turn?

Tears streamed down Li Ling's face as he said farewell to Su Wu.

The *Shan-yü* called together the officials who had been in Su Wu's party, but since some had long ago surrendered to the Hsiung-nu and others had died, only nine men in all were left to accompany Su Wu home.

In the spring of the sixth year of *yüan-shih* (81 B.C.) Su Wu

---

[20] Ts'ao Mei, a general of Lu, participated in a diplomatic meeting at K'o between his sovereign, Duke Chuang of Lu (r. 693–662), and Duke Huan of Ch'i. There he mounted the altar that had been set up for the oath of agreement, seized Duke Huan, and threatened him with a dagger until he agreed to return the lands he had earlier taken away from Lu. Li Ling is suggesting that he might have seized and threatened the *Shan-yü* in the same way.

reached the capital. On instructions from the emperor he paid his respects at the funerary park and temple of Emperor Wu, where he offered a *t'ai-lao* sacrifice.[21] He was appointed director of dependent states, a post drawing the salary of a full two thousand picul official, and was presented with two million in cash, two *ch'ing* of public lands, and a house and grounds. Ch'ang Hui, Hsü Sheng, and Chao Chung-ken were all appointed palace gentlemen and presented with two hundred rolls of silk apiece. The remaining six men who returned with Su Wu, being well along in years, retired to their homes with gifts of 100,000 cash each and exemption from taxes and labor services for life. Ch'ang Hui later rose as high as general of the right and was enfeoffed as a marquis; he has his own biography elsewhere in the history.

Su Wu remained among the Hsiung-nu for nineteen years. When he first set out, he was a vigorous man in the prime of life, but by the time he returned, his hair and beard had turned completely white.

The year after Su Wu's return, Shang-kuan An, the son of Shang-kuan Chieh, joined with Sang Kung-yang, the king of Yen, and the princess of Kai in plotting a revolt.[22] Su Wu's son Yüan had joined with Shang-kuan An in the plot and was tried and condemned to death. Earlier, Shang-kuan Chieh and Shang-kuan An had engaged in a struggle for power with the general in chief Ho Kuang. They had several times made itemized lists of Ho Kuang's offenses which they handed over to the king of Yen, persuading him to submit them to the emperor. They also complained that, although Su Wu had remained as an envoy among the Hsiung-nu for twenty years without surrendering, when he finally returned he was only given the post of director of dependent states. Yang Ch'ang, the chief secretary of the general in chief, on the other hand, though he had won no merit, was appointed chief commandant for requisitioning grain, evidence that Ho Kuang was abusing his authority and doing things in any way he pleased.

After the king of Yen and the others were executed for plotting revolt, a thorough investigation was made of their allies and associates. Since Su Wu had been an old friend of Shang-kuan Chieh and Sang Hung-yang, he was several times brought under accusation in connection with the affair of the king of Yen. In addition, his son had been among the conspirators. The commandant of jus-

---

[21] The most elaborate of sacrifices, consisting of an ox, a sheep, and a pig.

[22] For a detailed account of the plot, see the biography of Ho Kuang, p. 128.

tice submitted a memorial asking that he be allowed to arrest Su Wu, but Ho Kuang saw to it that the memorial never reached the emperor. He did, however, dismiss Su Wu from his post.

Several years later, Emperor Chao passed away. As a former official of the two thousand picul class, Su Wu joined with the others in the strategies and deliberations leading up to the enthronement of Emperor Hsüan. He was rewarded with the title of marquis within the Pass and the revenue from a town of three hundred households.

Some time later, the general of the guard Chang An-shih recommended him as a man who was well informed on matters of precedent, who had carried out his duty as envoy without bringing disgrace to his mission, and who had been mentioned in the testamentary edict of the former emperor. Emperor Hsüan thereupon summoned Su Wu and directed him to await the imperial command at the office of the eunuchs. He was several times called into the presence of the emperor. Once more he was appointed director of dependent states, with the additional title of officer of the right. Also, because he was an elderly official renowned for his integrity, he was allowed to attend court on the first and fifteenth days of the month and was awarded the title of sacrificer of wine, proofs of the great honor and favor that he enjoyed.

Whatever rewards and gifts Su Wu received he gave away to his male relatives and friends so that his own family had nothing put aside in the way of wealth. Hsü Po, the marquis of P'ing-en and father of Empress Hsü; the emperor's maternal uncles Wang Wu-ku, the marquis of P'ing-chang, and Wang Wu, the marquis of Lo-ch'ang; the general of carriage and cavalry Han Tseng; the chancellor Wei Hsiang; and the imperial secretary Ping Chi all treated him with great respect.

The emperor felt sorry for Su Wu because he was old and his son had earlier been condemned and put to death. Questioning his attendants, he asked whether, since Su Wu had lived so long among the Hsiung-nu, he did not perhaps have another son. Su Wu then made a full confession through Hsü Po, the marquis of P'ing-en, reporting that as he was about to leave the land of the Hsiung-nu, his Hsiung-nu wife had borne him a son whom he named T'ung-kuo, "Uniter of Nations." He said that he had had news from the boy and asked if he might send gifts of money and silk to him by way of the Han envoy. The emperor gave his permission, and sometime later T'ung-kuo arrived in the company of the envoy. The emperor appointed him a palace attendant, and also granted the title of officer of the right to the son of Su Wu's younger brother.

Su Wu lived to be over eighty and died of illness in the second year of *shen-chüeh* (60 B.C.).

In the third year of *kan-lu* (51 B.C.) the *Shan-yü* for the first time came to pay his respects at the Han court. The emperor, remem-- bering with admiration the great men who had acted as arms and legs to their sovereign, had portraits of them painted in the Uni- corn Hall. A likeness was made of each man, identified with his of- fice, fief, family name and personal name; only in the case of Ho Kuang was the personal name omitted. These are the names:

1. Grand marshal, general in chief, marquis of Po-lu, family name Ho.
2. General of the guard, marquis of Fu-p'ing, Chang An-shih.
3. General of carriage and cavalry, marquis of Lung-e, Han Tseng.
4. General of the rear, marquis of Ying-p'ing, Chao Ch'ung-kuo.
5. Chancellor, marquis of Kao-p'ing, Wei Hsiang.
6. Chancellor, marquis of Po-yang, Ping Chi.
7. Imperial secretary, marquis of Chien-p'ing, Tu Yen-nien.
8. Director of the imperial clan, marquis of Yang-ch'eng, Liu Te.
9. Privy treasurer Liang Ch'iu-ho.
10. Grand tutor to the heir apparent Hsiao Wang-chih.
11. Director of dependent states Su Wu.

All were men of merit and virtue whose names were known to the world of their time, and in this way they were held up as ex- amples and given further recognition, making clear that they had assisted the ruler in bringing about a renaissance of the state and were worthy to rank beside Fang Shu, Chao Hu, and Chung-shan Fu.[23] These eleven men all have biographies in the history.

Men such as the chancellor Huang Pa, the commandant of jus- tice Yü Ting-kuo, the minister of agriculture Chu Yi, the prefect of the capital Chang Ch'ang, the right prefect of the capital Yin Weng-kuei, or the Confucian scholar Hsia-hou Sheng and others all lived and died well, gaining renown in the age of Emperor

---

[23] Ministers who assisted King Hsüan of the Chou (r. 827–782 B.C.) in his efforts to restore the waning power and glory of the dynasty. Emperor Hsüan was regarded as having done the same thing for the Han, hence his posthu- mous name Hsüan.

Hsüan, and yet they did not qualify to join the gallery of famous officials described above. From this one can see what a select group it is.

In appraisal we say: General Li Kuang was a man so simple and sincere that one would take him for a peasant, and almost incapable of speaking a word. And yet the day he died all the people of the empire, whether they had known him or not, were moved to the profoundest grief, so deeply did men trust his sincerity. There is a proverb which says, "Though the peach tree does not speak, the world wears a path beneath it." It is a small saying, but one which is capable of conveying a great meaning.

To become generals for three generations in succession—this is something that the Taoists have warned against, and in fact the Li family, with its three generations from Li Kuang to Li Ling, eventually met with destruction, alas!

Confucius said, "The gentleman of determination, the man of benevolence, will at times give up his life to fulfill the demands of benevolence; he will not seek to preserve life at the expense of benevolence." [24] Envoy to the four quarters, bringing no shame to the mission his lord had entrusted to him—that was Su Wu!

[24] *Analects* XV, 8.

HAN SHU 63: THE BIOGRAPHIES OF
the Five Sons of Emperor Wu

OF THE SIX SONS of Emperor Wu, Emperor Chao and the king of Ch'i left no heirs. King Tz'u of Yen plotted rebellion, the king of Kuang-ling uttered curses; the king of Ch'ang-i was short-lived, and his son Liu Ho, the marquis of Hai-hun, was given a position he never should have had. The heir apparent Li suffered misfortune, but his grandson Emperor Hsüan succeeded to the Heaven-appointed line. So I have transmitted the Biographies of the Five Sons of Emperor Wu.

Emperor Wu the Filial had six sons: the heir apparent Li, his son by Empress Wei; Emperor Chao the Filial, his son by the Beautiful Companion, Lady Chao; Liu Hung, King Huai of Ch'i, his son by Madam Wang; Liu Tan, King Tz'u of Yen, and Liu Hsü, King Li of Kuang-ling, his sons by Lady Li; and Liu Po, King Ai of Ch'ang-i, his son by Madam Li.

THE HEIR APPARENT LI

The heir apparent Li, whose name was Liu Chü, was appointed heir to the emperor in the first year of *yüan-shou* (122 B.C.), when he was seven years old. Earlier, when the emperor, twenty-nine at the time, first succeeded in siring a son, he was extremely pleased and set up a shrine for the supplication of sons to commemorate the event, ordering Tung-fang Shuo and Mei Kao to compose prayers for the shrine.

When the prince grew older, he was commanded by the emperor

to study the *Kung-yang Commentary* on the *Spring and Autumn Annals,* and he also studied the *Ku-liang Commentary* under Master Chiang of Hsia-ch'iu. After his capping ceremony was completed [1] and he had moved into his own palace, the emperor had the Broad Vista Gardens built for him and allowed him to have his own guests and retainers and to do very much as he pleased. As a result, many men of dubious principles came to him with proposals.

In the fourth year of *yüan-ting* (113 B.C.) the prince took as a concubine one of his consort's ladies in waiting, the Good Companion Shih, and she bore him a son named Chin. He was called the Imperial Grandson Shih.

Toward the end of Emperor Wu's reign, Empress Wei fell from favor and the official Chiang Ch'ung rose to a position of power. Chiang Ch'ung was on bad terms with the prince and the members of the Wei family and he was afraid that, after the emperor's demise, he would be put to death. When the black magic affair occurred, Chiang Ch'ung decided to make use of it for his own evil ends. [2] By this time the emperor was well along in years and had grown highly suspicious, thinking that everyone around him was employing sorcery to put a curse on him. He ordered a thorough investigation of the affair, and as a result the chancellor Kung-sun Ho and his son, the princesses of Yang-shih and Chu-i, [3] and the son of Empress Wei's younger brother, Wei Kang, the marquis of Ch'ang-p'ing, were all tried and put to death. (An account will be found in the biographies of Kung-sun Ho and Chiang Ch'ung.)

Chiang Ch'ung was put in charge of investigating the black magic affair and, knowing the emperor's feelings, he announced that there were "airs of sorcery in the palace" and entered the palace, proceeded to the emperor's private quarters, dismantled the imperial seat and dug up the earth under it. The emperor ordered Han Yüeh, the marquis of An-tao, the imperial secretary Chang Kung, the gentleman of the Yellow Gate Su Wen, and others to assist Chiang Ch'ung. Chiang Ch'ung finally went to the heir appar-

---

[1] The capping ceremony was usually performed around the age of twenty and signaled entry into manhood; the prince, however, seems to have been capped at a rather early age.

[2] Someone accused Kung-sun Ho's son and others of burying a wooden doll in the roadway reserved for the emperor's carriage and trying to put a curse on him.

[3] Daughters of the emperor by Empress Wei.

ent's palace and began digging for evidence of sorcery, coming up with a doll made of paulownia wood. At this time the emperor was ill and had retired to the Palace of Sweet Springs to avoid the heat. Only Empress Wei and the heir apparent were in the capital.

The prince sent for his lesser tutor Shih Te and questioned him as to what to do. Shih Te, fearing that as tutor he would be forced to share punishment with the prince, accordingly replied, "Earlier, the chancellor and his son, two princesses, and a member of the Wei clan were all tried for this offense. Now the shamans and officials have dug up the ground and produced evidence. I don't know whether the shamans planted it there or whether it was actually there to begin with, but in any case we have no way to prove our innocence. It would be best to use your credentials to simulate an imperial order and have Chiang Ch'ung and the others arrested and put in jail. Then you can conduct a thorough investigation into their evil deceits. As it happens, the emperor is now ill at Sweet Springs, and even if an official were sent from the empress or from your household to try to communicate with him, there would be no response. We don't even know whether the emperor will survive this illness, and yet here is this evil minister behaving in such a way—surely you haven't forgotten what happened to Fu-su of the Ch'in, have you?" [4]

The prince, realizing the urgency of the situation, decided to follow Shih Te's advice.

In the second year of *cheng-ho* (91 B.C.), the seventh month, the day *jen-wu* (September 1), the prince finally dispatched his retainers in the guise of imperial messengers to arrest Chiang Ch'ung and the others. Han Yüeh, the marquis of An-tao, suspected that the messengers were impostors and refused to accept the imperial command, whereupon the retainers attacked and killed him. The imperial secretary Chang Kung was wounded but managed to escape and make his way to the Palace of Sweet Springs.

The prince and his steward Wu Chü, bearing credentials, at night entered the Long Autumn Gate of the Eternal Palace and, through a lady in waiting named Yi Hua, reported to the prince's mother Empress Wei all that had happened. They then brought out the carriages from the stable and loaded them with archers, issued weapons from the armory, and called out the guard from the

---

[4] Fu-su was the elder son of the First Emperor of the Ch'in. When the emperor died on a journey, the evil minister Chao Kao forged a will in the emperor's name ordering Fu-su to commit suicide and designating his younger son Hu-hai as his successor.

Palace of Lasting Joy. Issuing an announcement to the various officials that Chiang Ch'ung had revolted, they proceeded to have Ch'ung cut in two to serve as a warning. The foreign shamans who had assisted Ch'ung were roasted over coals in the Shang-lin Park. Then the prince, dividing his retainers into battalions and acting as their leader, engaged the chancellor Liu Ch'ü-li and his associates in battle.

Ch'ang-an was in utter confusion, and because word went around that the heir apparent had revolted, the populace as a whole declined to support him. His soldiers were defeated and he fled, eluding those who tried to capture him. The emperor was enraged and the courtiers, frightened and perplexed, did not know what to do.

Mou, an elder of Hu-kuan,[5] submitted a letter to the throne which read:

"I have heard that the father is like heaven, the mother like earth, and the son like the ten thousand creatures between. Therefore if heaven is calm, earth stable, and the yin and yang in harmony, then all creatures will flourish and mature, and if the father is kind and the mother loving, then within the home the son will be filial and obedient. But if the yin and yang are not in harmony, then the ten thousand creatures will suffer and die young, and if the father and son are not in harmony, then the family will crumble and perish. Hence if the father is not a father, the son will not be a son, and if the ruler is not a ruler, the minister will not be a minister—and then, though there is grain in the country, who will live to eat it?[6]

"In ancient times Shun was the epitome of filial piety, yet he failed to please his father Ku-sou; Yi the Filial suffered calumny and Po-ch'i was banished.[7] Though tied by the closest bonds of kinship, father and son grew suspicious of one another. Why did this come about? Because of a long accumulation of slanders. From this one can see that the son may not necessarily be lacking in filial piety—there are times when the father is lacking in perspicacity.

---

[5] The "elders" or *san-lao* were distinguished men over fifty chosen from among the common people to act as consultants to government officials. Though the present *Han shu* text records only the man's given name, other texts indicate that his family name was Ling-hu.

[6] The latter part of the passage is based on *Analects* XII, 11.

[7] All were paragons of virtue who became estranged from their fathers, in most cases because of the slanders of an evil stepmother.

"Now the crown prince is the rightful heir to the throne of the Han, the successor to an undertaking destined to endure for ten thousand generations, the embodiment of the solemn charge that has come down from the ancestors of the dynasty. In terms of kinship, he is the eldest son of the emperor. Chiang Ch'ung, on the other hand, is no more than a commoner, a petty minister from the back alleys. Your Majesty raised him to distinction and made use of him, but he presumed upon the supreme authority of the ruler to harry and oppress the crown prince, decking himself out in falsehood and deceit and conjuring up a host of evil lies and misunderstandings to block the road of kinship and create barriers that can barely be surmounted. If the prince had attempted to move forward, he still could not have obtained an interview with his sovereign; if he had attempted to move backward, he would have fallen victim to this traitorous minister. Alone in the snares of injustice with no one to appeal to, he could not endure the terrible anger in his heart and so he rose up, killed Chiang Ch'ung, and then fled in fear. It is true that the son stole the father's weapons, but he did so only to save himself from disaster. If I may presume to speak out, I believe there are no evil designs in his heart. The *Book of Odes* says:

> Buzz buzz go the green flies,
> Lighting on the hedge.
> Good and kind gentleman,
> Do not heed words of slander!
> Slanderous words have no end,
> Spreading chaos to the four corners of the state.[8]

"In the past Chiang Ch'ung slandered and brought about the death of the heir apparent of the state of Chao.[9] Everyone in the empire knows of the affair and it is only right that he should have been punished for it. But Your Majesty failed to perceive what kind of a person he is, and instead has laid all the blame on the crown prince, in a frenzy of rage calling out a large body of soldiers to seize him and appointing one of the three highest ministers

[8] Mao #219.

[9] Chiang Ch'ung's sister was married to Liu Tan, the heir apparent of the state of Chao, but when trouble developed between the two men, Chiang Ch'ung fled to the capital and denounced Liu Tan to the emperor, accusing him of incest and various other crimes, for which Liu Tan was tried and put to death.

of the state to command them in person.[10] Yet at that time no wise man was willing to speak out against such action, no eloquent gentleman was willing to offer an explanation—if I may say so, it fills me with grief!

"I have heard that Wu Tzu-hsü displayed the utmost loyalty, forgetting his own reputation, and Pi Kan displayed the utmost benevolence, neglecting his own safety.[11] A loyal minister strives only to be sincere, taking no thought for the executioner's ax. Offering his opinion, poor as it may be, his only wish is to remedy the errors of the ruler and to insure the safety of the altars of the soil and grain.

"The *Odes* says:

> Take that maligning man,
> Throw him to the wolves and tigers! [12]

My only hope is that Your Majesty will open your heart, calm your mind, and give some small thought to the ties of kinship. Do not fear offense from the prince, but quickly recall the armed troops so that he will not be forced to continue fleeing forever. Unable to overcome my feelings of deep concern, I risk this feeble life of mine and await punishment for my audacity at the gate of the Chien-chang Palace."

When the letter was presented to the emperor, he was moved and enlightened by it.

The prince had fled east as far as Hu District and was in hiding in the village of Ch'üan-chiu. The family he was staying with was poor and the head of it had to sell shoes in order to support the prince. The prince had an old friend in Hu who, according to report, had become rich and prosperous, and the prince therefore sent someone to summon him. In the process, the secret of the prince's whereabouts leaked out, and the law officials surrounded the house and prepared to arrest him. Judging that he could not escape, the prince went immediately to his room, bolted the door, and hanged himself. A man from Shan-yang named Chang Fu-

---

10 The chancellor Liu Ch'ü-li.

11 Wu Tzu-hsü tried to warn the king of Wu of danger from the state of Yüeh but was ordered by the king to commit suicide. Pi Kan admonished Chou, the last ruler of the Shang dynasty, for his evil ways, but Chou in anger killed him and cut out his heart.

12 Mao #200.

ch'ang, who was serving as a soldier, kicked down the door with his foot, while Li Shou, the secretary to the magistrate of Hsin-an, rushed in, flung his arms around the prince, and cut him down. The master of the house died in the fighting and the prince's two sons were both killed.

The emperor was grieved by the prince's death, but he handed down an edict saying: "One must give rewards even in doubtful cases in order to show that one's word can be trusted. Therefore let Li Shou be enfeoffed as marquis of Yü, and Chang Fu-ch'ang as marquis of T'i." [13]

After some time it became evident that there were many dubious aspects to the black magic affair. The emperor realized that the prince had acted out of fear and had had no ulterior motives in mind. In addition, Chü Ch'ien-ch'iu submitted an appeal arguing that the prince had been a victim of injustice. The emperor eventually appointed Chü Ch'ien-ch'iu as chancellor, had all of Chiang Ch'ung's family wiped out, and had Su Wen burned to death on the Heng Bridge. The man who had struck the first blow at the prince in Ch'üan-chiu village had earlier been appointed governor of Pei-ti but was eventually executed along with the members of his family.

The emperor, saddened that the prince, though innocent, had met such a fate, built a Shrine of the Beloved Son and Terrace of the Longed-for Return at Hu. When the people of the empire heard of this, they pitied him.

The prince had three sons and one daughter. The daughter married the heir of the marquis of P'ing-yü. When the prince met his downfall, all his children died at the same time. Empress Wei and the prince's concubine the Good Companion Shih were both buried beyond the south wall of Ch'ang-an. The imperial grandson whom Companion Shih bore to the prince, his consort Lady Wang, and their daughter were buried at Kuang-ming. The other two imperial grandsons had accompanied the prince when he fled and hence were buried with him at Hu. The prince had one surviving grandson, the son of the Imperial Grandson Shih and Lady Wang. At the age of eighteen he attained the position of highest honor and is posthumously known as Emperor Hsüan the Filial.

When Emperor Hsüan first came to the throne (73 B.C.), he issued an edict saying, "The late crown prince is buried at Hu but

[13] Evidently the emperor had promised a reward to the men who first seized the prince, though by this time he had little heart for the matter.

he has never received a posthumous name or the customary seasonal sacrifices. Let deliberations begin on a posthumous name and the establishment of a funerary park and village."

The officials in charge of such matters submitted the following proposal: "According to ritual, the successor of a man becomes that man's son. Therefore he must reduce the rank of his real father and mother and may not sacrifice to them. This is done to show respect for the ancestors of the man he succeeds. Now Your Majesty is the official successor to Emperor Chao the Filial and the one who carries on the sacrifices to the founders of the dynasty. It is important not to overstep the bounds of ritual. Having examined with care the precedents set by Emperor Chao the Filial, we believe that an altar should be raised to the late crown prince at Hu, a grave mound to the Good Companion Shih north of the Broad Vista Gardens, and an altar to your father, the Imperial Grandson Shih, north of the outer wall of Kuang-ming. The rules for posthumous names say that the name should reflect the actions of the recipient. Aware of our ignorance, we nevertheless suggest that the appropriate posthumous name for your father would be Tao, The Ill-fated, and for your mother, The Consort of Tao. Their funerary park should be like those of the feudal lords and kings, with a village of three hundred households established to maintain it. The late crown prince should be posthumously named Li, The Perverse, and a park and village of two hundred households set up for him. The Good Companion Shih should be named Lady Li and thirty households set up to guard her grave. Officials should be appointed to supervise the parks, guarding and maintaining them according to the law. The village of Hsi-hsiang-yeh in Hu should be made into the Li Park, the area east of White Pavilion in Ch'ang-an should be made the Li Consort Park, and Ch'eng-hsiang in Kuang-ming should be made the Tao Park. The bodies should all be exhumed and reburied in their appropriate parks."

Eight years later, the officials once more submitted a proposal, saying, "According to ritual, if the father is a gentleman and the son an emperor, the father should be sacrificed to as an emperor. The occupant of the Tao Park should be honored with the title of Imperial Sire. A funerary temple should be built for him, utilizing the present park for the inner chambers, and seasonal offerings presented there. The number of households maintaining the park should be increased to a full 1,600 and the area made into the Feng-ming District. Lady Li should be honored with the title of

Empress Li and a park and village set up for her with three hundred households. The park of the heir apparent Li should also be increased by three hundred households."

LIU HUNG, KING HUAI OF CH'I

Liu Hung, King Huai of Ch'i, was made a king on the same day as Tan, the king of Yen, and Hsü, the king of Kuang-ling. All were presented with tablets instructing and warning them in accordance with the customs of the state to which they were assigned. The tablet of Liu Hung read:

"In the sixth year of *yüan-shou* (117 B.C.), the fourth month, the day *i-ssu* (June 12), the emperor has caused the imperial secretary Chang T'ang here in the ancestral temple to establish Hung as the king of Ch'i, saying: 'Harken, my little son Hung, and receive this sacred green soil! [14] I, who have been chosen by Heaven to carry on the imperial line, have examined the precedents of the past and hereby appoint you the ruler of a kingdom, enfeoffing you in the eastern region, where for generations to come you may serve as a bastion to the Han. Harken and think on it! Honor my command. This charge may not remain with you forever. If a man loves virtue, he will shine in glory, but if he fails to give thought to righteousness, he will cause men of principle to look on him with contempt. Endeavor with all your heart to hold fast to the mean, and the blessings of Heaven will be with you forever. But should there be any error or lack of goodness in your ways, then misfortune will come to your kingdom and disaster to your person. Harken! Guard your state and govern your people well. Do you dare to be disrespectful? King, be warned by this!' "

Hung's mother Madam Wang enjoyed favor with the emperor and Hung was the best loved of all the emperor's sons. Eight years after he was made a king, he passed away. He left no sons and his kingdom was abolished.

LIU TAN, KING TZ'U OF YEN

The tablet presented to Tan, King Tz'u of Yen, read: "Harken, my little son Tan! Receive this sacred black soil. I appoint you the

---

[14] From soils of five different colors the emperor selected the soil which, according to the theory of the Five Elements, corresponds to the color appropri-

ruler of a kingdom, enfeoffing you in the northern region, where for generations to come you may serve as a bastion to the Han. Harken! The Hsün-chu tribes [15] are cruel to their elders and have the hearts of beasts, deceiving and inflicting evil on the people of our frontier. I ordered my generals to lead their troops and go to punish them for their crimes, and thirty-two of their leaders, the heads of bands of a thousand or ten thousand men, lowered their flags and came scurrying to surrender to our armies. The Hsün-chu have now moved to another region and the northern provinces are at peace. Endeavor with all your heart. Do nothing that will arouse hatred, do nothing contrary to virtue. Do not neglect the border defenses; if you do not train your men well, they will be of no use in an emergency. King, be warned by this!"

When Tan reached manhood, he proceeded to his kingdom. As a man he was eloquent and resourceful. He had studied widely both in the Classics and in the works of the various philosophers and was fond of such things as the lore of the stars, matters pertaining to the calendar, arithmatic, entertainers, and hunting, and gathered about him a number of wandering scholars.

When the heir apparent, the son of Empress Wei, met his downfall, and King Huai of Ch'i also passed away, Liu Tan considered that he must be next in line for succession to the throne and so he sent a letter to the emperor asking to become a member of the guard quartered in the palace. The emperor was furious and had the messenger who delivered the letter thrown into jail.[16] Later Tan was accused of hiding refugees from the law and was deprived of the three districts of Liang-hsiang, An-tz'u, and Wen-an.

From this time on, Emperor Wu came to hate Tan. Eventually he appointed his youngest son as heir apparent. When he passed away, this son succeeded to the throne, becoming Emperor Chao the Filial. He dispatched letters bearing the imperial seal to the various feudal lords and kings informing them of the emperor's demise. When Tan received the letter addressed to him, he refused to

---

ate to the direction in which the fief lay, in this case east, the color green. The recipient then took the soil with him to his fief and established a *she* or altar of the soil, which symbolized the existence of the state.

[15] A non-Chinese people of ancient times; here the name refers to the Hsiung-nu.

[16] Because he resented the implication that he could not manage affairs by himself, or because he did not want any of his sons so close to him? I am unclear as to why Emperor Wu reacted so violently.

perform the proper ritual lamentation, but instead said, "The letter is so brief it only requires a small seal—I suspect something peculiar has happened in the capital!"

He dispatched his trusted ministers Shou-hsi Ch'ang, Sun Tsung-chih, Wang Ju, and others to go to Ch'ang-an, ostensibly to make inquiries concerning the funeral. Wang Ju met with Kuo Kuang-i, the chief of the capital police, and asked what illness had brought about the emperor's demise, which of his sons had been made his successor, and how old the successor was. Kuang-i replied that he had been in attendance at the Palace of Five Oaks when he heard a great clamor in the palace and people shouting that the emperor had passed away. The various generals had together set up the heir apparent as the new emperor. According to Kuang-i, the new emperor was eight or nine years old and did not appear at the funeral.

When the ministers from Yen returned and reported this to the king, he said, "The emperor passed from this world without leaving any final words and even Princess Kai [17] was unable to gain an interview with him—it all looks highly suspicious!" He then sent his palace counselor to the capital to present a letter which read:

"In my humble view, Emperor Wu the Filial was the embodiment of the sacred Way, filial in his attendance of the ancestral temples, kind and loving to his kin, bringing together his countless subjects in harmony and peace. His virtue possessed the magnitude of heaven and earth, his wisdom the brightness of the sun and moon. His majesty and awe spread far and wide, so that distant regions, bearing treasures, came to pay him court. He added new provinces to the number of thirty or forty, opened up new territories till he had almost doubled the size of the empire. He performed the Feng sacrifice on Mount T'ai and the Shan sacrifice at Liang-fu, traveling back and forth across the empire. Because of him, the ancestral temple of the founder is filled with rare objects from faraway regions. His virtue was truly vast and wonderful. I request that permission be given to set up temples to him in the provinces and kingdoms as well as the capital."

Word came down from the emperor that he had received the letter and noted its contents.[18] At the time, the general in chief Ho

---

[17] Emperor Wu's eldest daughter.

[18] Evidently the emperor and those about him were not taken in by Liu Tan's sudden burst of filial piety and regarded the suggestion that he be allowed to set up his own temple to Emperor Wu as a breach of imperial prerogative.

Kuang was handling affairs of government and as a reward he sent the king of Yen a gift of thirty million cash and increased his fief by thirteen thousand households. Liu Tan was furious and said, "I ought to be made *emperor*—what do I want with presents!"

Eventually he joined with Liu Ch'ang, the son of King Ai of Chung-shan, Liu Tse, the grandson of Kiang Hsiao of Ch'i, and others of the imperial family in plotting villainy. Liu Tan falsely claimed that in the time of Emperor Wu he had received an imperial command which permitted him to supervise official matters and build up the military defenses in order to be prepared for an emergency.[19] Liu Ch'ang then drew up a proclamation in Tan's name to be issued to the courtiers of the state which read:

"Through the sublime virtue of the former emperor, I have been allowed to serve as ruler of this northern bastion. I have personally received an imperial command to supervise official matters, attend to armaments, and prepare military defenses. The responsibility is grave and the task a great one—morning and evening I tremble with fear. My lords, what counsel and assistance have you to offer me? Though Yen is a small state, it was established in the time of the Chou.[20] From its first ruler, the Duke of Shao, down through later rulers such as King Chao-hsiang, it has continued in existence now for a thousand years. One can hardly believe that it has never produced any worthy men. Yet I have bound up my sash and supervised court affairs for over thirty years and I have yet to hear of one such man. Is it because of some failure on my part, or perhaps because you, my lords, have not given sufficient thought to the matter? Where does the fault lie?

"It is now my desire to remedy error and block the path of evil, to honor men of good repute and spread harmony abroad, to bring solace to the common people and to correct and reform their customs. Tell me, by what road shall I proceed? My lords, let each of you endeavor with all his heart to find an answer and I shall give careful thought to your suggestions."

The courtiers all removed their hats and apologized for their delinquency. The palace attendant Ch'eng Chen said to Liu Tan, "Your Highness has failed to receive the appointment you ex-

---

[19] Ordinarily the Han kings were not allowed to take any part in the actual administration of their territories, all such affairs being handled by the prime minister, the military commander, and other officials sent out from the central government.

[20] King Wu of the Chou (traditional dates 1122–1116 B.C.) enfeoffed the Duke of Shao as ruler of Yen.

pected, but it will never come to you while you remain seated—
the only thing to do is to rise up and seek it! Once you rise up,
everyone in the state down to the women and children will all
wave their arms and follow after you."

Liu Tan replied, "In the past, in the time of Empress Lü, Hung,
who was falsely proclaimed to be a son of Emperor Hui, was put
on the throne and all the feudal lords folded their hands and
served him for eight years. Only after the empress had passed away
and the high ministers had wiped out the members of the Lü clan
and invited Emperor Wen to take the throne did the world for the
first time learn that Hung was not really the son of Emperor Hui
the Filial.[21] Now I am the eldest surviving son of Emperor Wu and
yet I am not allowed to ascend the throne. I have submitted a letter asking for permission to set up an ancestral temple and that too
is denied me. I suspect the man they have made emperor is not of
the Liu clan at all!"

Liu Tan thereupon plotted with Liu Tse. They drew up a nefarious letter claiming that the young emperor was not the son of Emperor Wu but someone whom the great ministers had agreed to
put on the throne, and called on the empire to join in overthrowing him. They sent men to deliver the letter to the various provinces and kingdoms, hoping to stir up the common people. Liu Tse
according to plan then returned to the state of Ch'i, called out the
troops to Lin-tzu, and prepared to join with the king of Yen in
open attack.

Liu Tan invited lawbreakers from the other provinces and kingdoms to join him. Commandeering all the copper and iron he
could get, he made weapons and armor and held repeated reviews
of his carriages, horsemen, bowmen, and soldiers. He supplied his
army with pennons, flags, and a carriage with a war drum, and
had "yak-heads" to act as forerunners.[22] The palace attendants who
accompanied him wore hats trimmed with sable tails and decorated in front with gold ornaments in the shape of cicadas; they
were all referred to as "attendants in the inner palace." [23] Liu Tan

---

[21] The events, which took place after the death of Emperor Hui in 188 B.C.,
when Empress Lü and her clan held power, are described in detail in the annals of Empress Lü, *Shih chi* ch. 9; see my translation, *Records of the Grand
Historian of China*, vol. 1, pp. 321–40.

[22] The "yak-heads," so called because they wore their hair hanging down,
were a corps of select soldiers who acted as forerunners of the guard.

[23] All this was done in deliberate imitation of the emperor's army and equi-
page.

led the prime minister, the military commander, and the other officials of the state, called out his carriage and horsemen, com-
mànded the people to assemble, and held a great hunt in Wen-an
District in order to train his men and horses and there await the
day of departure.[24] The palace attendant Han Yi and others repeatedly admonished Liu Tan, but Tan killed Han Yi and the rest,
fifteen men in all.

It so happened that Liu Ch'ang, the marquis of P'ing, learned
that Liu Tse and the others were plotting together and he reported
it to Ch'üan Pu-i, the provincial director of Ch'ing-chou. Ch'üan
Pu-i had Liu Tse arrested and informed the emperor of the action.
The emperor sent the assistant to the director of foreign vassals to
conduct an investigation, and it was found that the king of Yen
was implicated in the affair. The emperor gave orders that the king
of Yen was not to be charged, but Liu Tse and the others were all
sentenced to death and the fief of the marquis of P'ing was increased.

After some time had passed, Liu Tan's elder sister, Princess Kai
of O-i, and the general of the left Shang-kuan Chieh and his son
became engaged in a struggle for power with Ho Kuang, enmity
arising between the two parties. The princess and the others of her
group all knew that Liu Tan hated Ho Kuang and they therewith
began secret negotiations with Tan. Tan in turn dispatched Sun
Tsung-chih and others, over ten men in all, to go to the capital at
different times and present lavish gifts of gold, jewels, and fast
horses as a bribe to Princess Kai, Shang-kuan Chieh, and the imperial secretary Sang Hung-yang. They all entered into communication with him, sending him various accounts of the mistakes and
oversights which Ho Kuang had committed so that he could report
them to the emperor. Shang-kuan Chieh hoped to use his position
in the palace to have the charges against Ho Kuang turned over
immediately to the law officials for action.

When Liu Tan received the reports, he was delighted and submitted a letter to the throne which read:

"In times past the First Emperor of the Ch'in, relying upon his
position as a supreme ruler who faces south, decreed the fate of a
whole generation. His awe forced the submission of the foreign
tribes on all four sides, but he treated with contempt and weak-

---

[24] Earlier we were told that Liu Tan had been deprived of the district of
Wen-an. Presumably it had subsequently been restored to him, perhaps at the
time when Ho Kuang increased his fief by thirteen thousand households.

ened his own flesh and blood and instead raised to eminence the men of other clans, abandoning the Way, relying upon heavy punishments, and failing to act with generosity toward the members of the imperial family.[25] Subsequently the military commander Chao T'o went south and set himself up as ruler of the barbarians, Ch'en She raised the cry of revolt in the swamps of Ch'u, those close to the ruler turned against him, and rebellion broke out both within the state and abroad, until the ruling family of the Ch'in was wiped out and its sacrificial fires extinguished. Thereupon Emperor Kao-tsu of the Han surveyed the history of what had happened, observed the successes and failures of the Ch'in, and perceived that it had been founded on error. Therefore he proceeded by a different way, measuring out the land, setting up strings of walled cities, and appointing his sons and brothers as kings to rule them, thus insuring that the leaves and branches of his own family should flourish and that men of other surnames should have no avenue to power.

"Now Your Majesty has become the successor to this enlightened and perfected form of rule. But you have entrusted its direction to the high ministers, so that the courtiers have taken to banding together in cliques to villify and undo the members of the imperial family. Accusations that sting the flesh are daily bandied about the court; villainous officials ignore the law and work to build up their personal power, and as a result the ruler's bounty is prevented from reaching down to those on lower levels.

"Now I have heard that Emperor Wu dispatched Su Wu, a general of palace attendants, as his envoy to the Hsiung-nu, and that, though Su Wu was detained for twenty years, he refused to acknowledge sovereignty to them. Yet when he finally returned home, he was given only the post of director of dependent states. On the other hand Yang Ch'ang, who was acting as head secretary to the general in chief Ho Kuang, has been appointed chief commandant for requisitioning grain, though he has done nothing to deserve the post. In addition, when the general in chief Ho Kuang called out the palace attendants and the Feather and Forest Guard for inspection, he had runners to announce his coming and clear the road, and sent the imperial butler ahead to prepare his quar-

[25] Liu Tan's objection is that the First Emperor of the Ch'in refused to enfeoff any of the members of his family, as had been the custom in former dynasties and was again under the Han. This is seen as the reason for the rapid downfall of the Ch'in.

ters.[26] I, your servant Tan, therefore request that I be allowed to return the credentials and seal of the kingdom of Yen and be admitted as a member of the guard quartered in the palace so that I may keep watch on the doings of villainous ministers!"

At this time Emperor Chao was only fourteen years old but he realized there was deception afoot. In the end, therefore, he trusted and continued to be on close terms with Ho Kuang, while treating Shang-kuan Chieh and the others of his party with coldness. Shang-kuan Chieh and his group then plotted to join in killing Ho Kuang and deposing the emperor, intending to set up the king of Yen in his place as Son of Heaven.

Liu Tan had couriers to carry his letters here and there, and after exchanging messages with people in the capital, he agreed to make Shang-kuan Chieh a king after the plot had been carried through. He also communicated with thousands of powerful and influential men in the other provinces and kingdoms to enlist their support. He discussed his plans with P'ing, his prime minister, but P'ing replied, "In the past Your Highness joined with Liu Tse in laying plans, but before the affair could be brought to a successful conclusion, word of it leaked out. That happened because Liu Tse was a habitual braggart and loved to abuse and lord it over others. Now I have heard that the general of the left Shang-kuan Chieh is by nature reckless and unthinking, and his son An, the general of carriage and cavalry, is young and arrogant. I am afraid that, just as in the case of Liu Tse, the affair will never be successful. I am also afraid that even if it is carried out, there will be those who will turn against Your Highness!"

Liu Tan replied, "Some days ago a man appeared at the gate of the imperial palace claiming that he was the late crown prince Li. People from all over Ch'ang-an flocked around him until the clamor got completely out of hand. The general in chief Ho Kuang, frightened, called out troops and had them drawn up in formation, but this was done solely as a measure of self defense.[27] I am the eldest son of Emperor Wu and have the trust of the entire nation—why should I worry about being betrayed!"

[26] Such procedures were reserved for the emperor when he went abroad. The Feather and Forest guards who served in the palace were supposedly so named because they were as swift as arrows and as numerous as trees in a forest.

[27] Liu Tan is implying that the troops were called out only because of the excitement over the false "prince" and not because Shang-kuan Chieh and his son had done anything to betray the plot. On the false prince, see p. 160.

Later he said to his courtiers, "According to the reports I have had from Princess Kai, the only persons we had to worry about were the general in chief Ho Kuang and the general of the right Wang Mang. Now the general of the right has died and the chancellor Chü Ch'ien-ch'iu is ill. She says the affair is certain to succeed. Before long, they will be summoning me to the throne!" He then ordered his courtiers all to make preparations for the journey.

At this time rain fell from the sky and a rainbow came straight down to the palace of Yen and drank up the water in the wells until they all went dry.[28] The pigs broke out of the privy in a herd and smashed the stove of the royal butler. Crows and magpies fought to the death and a rat danced in the main gate of the palace. The doors of the hall shut by themselves and could not be opened; fire from the sky burned up the city gate and a great wind destroyed the walls and towers of the palace and broke and uprooted trees. Falling stars descended in streams. Everyone from the queen and the royal concubines on down was terrified and the king was so alarmed he fell ill. He sent men to offer sacrifices to the Chia and T'ai rivers. Lü Kuang and others of the king's entourage who knew how to read the stars spoke to the king, saying, "There will be soldiers who will come and surround the city. This will happen in the ninth or tenth month. A great minister of the Han will be put to death!" (A discussion will be found in the Treatise on the Five Elements.)

The king, increasingly worried and frightened, said to Lü Kuang and the others, "The plot has not been brought to completion and all these portents and weird objects have appeared. Now you say there are signs that soldiers are on the way. What shall I do?"

As it happened, Yen Ts'ang, the father of one of Princess Kai's retainers, had learned of the plot and reported it, and thus the whole affair came to light. The chancellor dispatched letters bearing the imperial seal to the officials of the two thousand picul class, ordering them to arrest Sun Tsung-chih as well as the general of the left Shang-kuan Chieh and the others. All were put to death.

When Liu Tan heard of this, he summoned his prime minister P'ing and said, "The plot has failed! Shall I go ahead and call out the troops?"

[28] The character for "rainbow" contains the radical indicating an insect or reptile, which is apparently what the ancient Chinese conceived a rainbow to be; hence it could be imagined as drinking up the water of the wells.

P'ing replied, "The general of the left is already dead and all the common people know it—it will not do to call out the troops!"

The king, filled with anguish and foreboding, had wine set out in the Palace of Ten Thousand Years and summoned his guests and courtiers and his consort and concubines to sit and drink with him. The king sang this song:

> In the end an empty city,
> No dogs barking,
> No chickens crowing.
> Angling streets broad and bare—
> How well I know there's no one left alive in my land!

Then Lady Hua-yung rose and danced, singing:

> Hair knotted and tangled, clotting the moat,
> Bones heaped about, nowhere to lay them—
> The mother seeks her dead son,
> The wife seeks her dead husband,
> Wandering back and forth between the two moats.[29]
> Can you alone, my lord, find a place to rest?

All those present wept.

A letter of pardon arrived from the capital, but when the king read it, he said, "Alas, it pardons only my officials and the people—it does not pardon me!" Accordingly he summoned his consort and his various concubines and ladies in waiting and said, "Those miserable old wretches in the capital have done it! They will have me and my whole family put to death." He then prepared to commit suicide, but those about him said, "Perhaps you will only be deprived of your kingdom and will not have to die!" The consort and concubines and ladies in waiting joined their voices in weeping and moaning, begging the king to desist.

At that point a messenger arrived from the Son of Heaven and presented the king of Yen with a letter bearing the imperial seal. It read:

"Long ago, when Emperor Kao-tsu became Son of Heaven, the ruler of the empire, he enfeoffed his sons and brothers so that they might act as bastions and protectors of the nation's altars of the soil and grain. But the day arrived when the members of the Lü

---

[29] The moats on either side of the palace garden. The songs are visions of the destruction that is about to befall the state.

clan plotted high treason and the Liu family came within a hair's breadth of extinction. It fell to the marquis of Chiang, Chou P'o, and the others to attack and wipe out the traitors and place Emperor Wen the Filial on the throne so that he could insure the safety of the ancestral temples. They were able to do this, were they not, because there were qualified men both at court and in the provinces, and because both parties worked together?

"Fan K'uai, Li Shang, Ts'ao Ts'an, and Kuan Ying [30] grasped their swords, raised their spears, and followed after Kao-tsu, cutting down evil, clearing away what was harmful, plowing and cultivating the entire area within the four seas. They labored hard and long, yet in reward they received ranks no higher than that of marquis. Now the sons and grandsons of the imperial family, though they have never had to bare their robes to the sun and their caps to the dew and endure the hardships of battle, have been given territory and been made kings; they have had wealth handed out to them as a gift. In their case, when the father dies the son is allowed to succeed him, when the elder brother passes away, his younger brother becomes his heir.

"You, king, are my own flesh and blood, as close to me as kin can be, a very part of my body. And yet you join with men of different surnames and other clans to plot injury to the altars of the soil and grain. You draw close to those who are most distant, and behave distantly to those who should be most close. You have a heart filled with treachery and betrayal, one in which there is no thought of loyalty or love. If our forefathers could learn of this, with what face would you once more bear offerings of wine and present them in the ancestral temple of Kao-tsu?"

When Liu Tan received the letter, he handed over his credentials and seal to the palace physician and apologized to the prime minister and other officials of the two thousand picul class, saying, "I have failed to perform my duties with care and I must die for it." Thereupon he hanged himself with the cord that had been attached to the seal. His consort and ladies in waiting followed him, over twenty of them committing suicide. As a special act of mercy, the emperor pardoned the king's heir, Liu Chien, and allowed him to become a commoner.

Liu Tan was given the posthumous name of Tz'u, the "Piercing King." He had held his position for thirty-eight years when he was

---

[30] Generals who assisted Kao-tsu in overthrowing his rivals and founding the Han.

sentenced to die. His kingdom was abolished. Six years later, when Emperor Hsüan came to the throne, he enfeoffed Liu Tan's two surviving sons, making Liu Ch'ing the marquis of Hsin-ch'ang and Liu Hsien the marquis of Ting-an. He also enfeoffed the son of Liu Tan's heir, Liu Chien, who had died; he is posthumously known as King Ch'ing of Kuang-yang. After twenty-nine years, he passed away and was succeeded by his son Liu Shun, King Mu. He passed away after twenty-one years and was succeeded by his son Liu Huang, King Ssu. He passed away after twenty years and was succeeded by his son Liu Chia. In the time of Wang Mang all the Han kings were deprived of their titles and were made commoners. Only Liu Chia, because he had presented a list of auspicious omens indicating that Wang Mang should become ruler, was exempted and instead was enfeoffed as marquis of Fu-mei and given the surname Wang.

LIU HSÜ, KING LI OF KUANG-LING

Liu Hsü, King Li of Kuang-ling, was presented with a tablet of enfeoffment that read:

"Harken, my little son Hsü, and receive this sacred red soil. I appoint you the ruler of a kingdom, enfeoffing you in the southern region, where for generations to come you may serve as a bastion to the Han. From ancient times men have said that the people in the area south of the Yangtze and around the Five Lakes are reckless in heart, believing that they are safe from punishment in their far-off land of Yang-chou. In the time of the Three Dynasties, this was one of the outlying areas and the influence of the government did not reach this far.[31] Harken! Endeavor with all your heart to be respectful, to be cautious, to practice kindness and obedience. Do not spend time with the pleasure seekers, do not become the companion of little men. Do only what is lawful, what is prescribed by the rules. The *Book of Documents* says: 'The minister may not on his own authority hand out benefits or apply punishment.'[32] Do nothing that you will be ashamed of later. King, be warned by this!"

[31] The Three Dynasties are the Hsia, Shang, and Chou, the earliest dynasties of Chinese history. The regions of China and the territories beyond were divided into five areas depending upon their distance from the capital. The region referred to here fell into the area known as *yao-fu*, the next to the farthest region from the center of Chinese civilization.

[32] The *Hung-fan* or "Great Plan" section of the *Documents*.

When Liu Hsü grew to manhood he proved to be very fond of entertainers, musicians, and idle pastimes. He was so strong he could lift a metal caldron and would wrestle barehanded with bears, swine, and other fierce beasts. Nothing he did was according to law or regulation, and therefore he was never permitted to succeed to the throne.

When Emperor Chao came to the throne, he increased Liu Hsü's fief by thirteen thousand households. During the *yüan-feng* era (80–75 B.C.) Liu Hsü came to court and his fief was once more increased by ten thousand households. He was presented with a gift of twenty million cash, two thousand catties of yellow gold, a "comfortable carriage," [33] a team of four horses, and a precious sword. When Emperor Hsüan came to the throne, he enfeoffed Liu Hsü's four sons, appointing Sheng, Tseng, and Ch'ang as marquises and the youngest son Hung as king of Kao-mi.[34] Thus it may be seen that Liu Hsü was treated very generously in the way of gifts and rewards.

Earlier, in the time of Emperor Chao, Liu Hsü, observing that the emperor was young and had no sons, began to nourish hopes and ambitions for his own position and, since the region of Ch'u, where his kingdom was situated, is much given to shamanism and spirit worship, he summoned a shamaness named Li Nü-hsü and ordered her to call down the spirits and utter curses and imprecations. Li Nü-hsü, weeping, announced, "Emperor Wu the Filial has descended and taken possession of me!" whereupon all those about her bowed down to the ground. Then the spirit of Emperor Wu spoke through her, saying, "I will without fail cause Hsü to become the Son of Heaven!" Liu Hsü presented Li Nü-hsü with generous gifts of cash and sent her to offer prayers on Shaman Mountain.

Just at that time, Emperor Chao passed away. "Li Nü-hsü is an excellent shaman!" said Liu Hsü, and killed an ox and offered it with prayers of thanks.

When the king of Ch'ang-i was called to the capital to take the throne, Liu Hsü summoned the shamaness once more and had her put a curse on him. Later, when the king of Ch'ang-i was deprived of the position of emperor, Liu Hsü had greater faith than ever in Li Nü-hsü and the other shamans and frequently rewarded them with gifts of cash and valuables.

[33] A carriage in which one rode sitting down, suitable for women or elderly persons. In the ordinary Chinese carriage one always rode standing up.
[34] Following Wang Hsien-ch'ien, I omit the name Pao.

When Emperor Hsüan came to the throne, Liu Hsü said, "He is only a grandson of the heir apparent Li—how does he get to become emperor instead of me!" Once more he put Li Nü-hsü to work uttering curses as before. In addition, Liu Hsü's daughter was married to the younger son of the consort of Liu Yen-shou, the king of Ch'u, and there were frequent exchanges of gifts and secret communications between the two courts. Later, Liu Yen-shou was accused of plotting rebellion and was put to death. In the course of the investigation Liu Hsü became implicated as well, but an order came from the emperor that he was not to be brought to trial. All in all, he received five thousand catties of yellow gold in gifts from the emperor, as well as vessels and other valuable objects.

When Liu Hsü heard that Emperor Hsüan had appointed his son as heir apparent to the throne, he said to Lady Nan and his other concubines, "I will never get to be emperor!" and he had the cursing brought to an end.

Later, Hsü's son Ch'ang, the marquis of Nan-li, was charged with murder and was deprived of his title.[35] After he had come home to Kuang-ling, he carried on a secret affair with his father's concubine Tso-hsiu, and when the matter came to light, he was imprisoned in chains and later executed and his body exposed in the market place. Sheng-chih, the prime minister of Kuang-ling, submitted a memorial to the throne asking that the king be deprived of the grassy meadows of She-pei so that they could be turned over to the poor people. The emperor approved the memorial, whereupon Liu Hsü set his shamans to cursing as in the past.

The jujube tree in the garden of Liu Hsü's palace put out over ten shoots, all bright red with leaves as white as undyed silk. The water in the garden pond turned red and the fish died. There was a rat that in the middle of the day stood on its hind legs and danced in the courtyard of the king's consort. Liu Hsü said to Lady Nan and the others, "These strange happenings with the jujube and the pond, the fish and the rat—they portend something truly terrible!"

A few months later, the cursing affair came to light. The officials began examining the evidence, whereupon Liu Hsü, confused and frightened, poisoned the shamans and the women of his palace, killing over twenty persons in order to prevent them from speaking out. The high ministers requested that Liu Hsü be put to death, but the emperor instead dispatched the commandant of justice and

[35] Following Wang Hsien-ch'ien, I read Ch'ang instead of Pao.

the director of foreign vassals to go to Kuang-ling and look into the affair.

Liu Hsü admitted his guilt, saying, "Even the death penalty would not be severe enough for one like me. All the charges brought against me are true, but many of them relate to matters far in the past. If I may, I would like to return to my quarters and think back carefully over what has happened before formally replying to them."

After meeting with the emperor's envoys, Liu Hsü returned to his quarters and had wine set out in the Palace of Manifest Brightness where, summoning the heir apparent Pa, as well as his daughters Tung-tzu, Hu-sheng, and others, he spent the evening drinking. He ordered his favorites, the palace lady Kuo Chao-chün, the lady in waiting Chao Tso-chün, and others to play the lute and dance and sing. The king composed this song:

> I wanted to live forever,
> Never dying,
> But long life without joy—
> How is it worth pursuing?
> I honor the Heaven-appointed time,
> No moment's delay.
> Thousand li horses of the envoys
> Wait by the roadside.
> The Yellow Springs below
> Are dark and far away.
> A man, once born, is destined to die—
> Why should it pain my heart?
> Where does one find joy?
> In what pleases the heart.
> But I come and go in sorrow,
> My joys only fleeting.
> The land of the dead calls me,
> Graveyard gates unfold.
> No one can do the dying for me—
> I am the one who must go.

Those in attendance took turns pouring wine for him, all of them in tears. At cockcrow the party ended.

Liu Hsü said to the heir apparent Pa, "The emperor has treated me generously and yet I have turned against him in a terrible way. When I die, my bones will probably be left to bleach in the field, but if the emperor should be merciful enough to permit my burial, you must make it a simple one, not lavish!" Then he used his seal cord to hang himself. The ladies Kuo Chao-chün and Chao Tso-chün both committed suicide.

The emperor as an act of special mercy pardoned all the king's sons and allowed them to become commoners. Liu Hsü was given the posthumous name Li, the "Cruel King." He had held his position for sixty-four years when he was sentenced to death and his kingdom abolished.

Seven years later Emperor Yüan reestablished it and set up Liu Hsü's heir Liu Pa as ruler; he is known as King Hsiao. After thirteen years he passed away and was succeeded by his son Liu Yi, King Kung. Three years later, Liu Yi passed away and was succeeded by his son Liu Hu, King Ai. Sixteen years later he passed away, and since he had no sons, the line came to an end. Six years later Emperor Ch'eng reestablished the kingdom, setting up King Hsiao's son Liu Shou as ruler; he is known as King Ching. He passed away two years later and was succeeded by his son Liu Hung. In Wang Mang's time the line was discontinued.

Earlier, Liu Hung, King Ai of Kao-mi, was made a king in the first year of the *pen-shih* era (73 B.C.), being the youngest son of Liu Hsü, the king of Kuang-ling. Nine years later he passed away and was succeeded by his son Liu Chang, King Ch'ing. Thirty-three years later Liu Chang passed away and was succeeded by his son Liu K'uan, King Huai. Eleven years later Liu K'uan passed away and was succeeded by his son Liu Shen, but in the time of Wang Mang the line was discontinued.

LIU PO, KING AI OF CH'ANG-I

Liu Po, King Ai of Ch'ang-i, was made a king in the fourth year of the *t'ien-han* era (97 B.C.). With his demise eleven years later, his son Liu Ho succeeded to the title. He had been king for thirteen years when Emperor Chao passed away, leaving no heir to the throne. The general in chief Ho Kuang summoned Liu Ho to come to the capital and take charge of the funeral. The letter, sealed with the imperial seal, read: [36]

"Imperial command to the king of Ch'ang-i: the privy treasurer

[36] The seal was that of the consort of Emperor Chao, Empress Shang-kuan, who with the emperor's death became empress dowager; she was about fifteen at the time.

Shih Lo-ch'eng, who is also acting for the director of foreign vassals; the director of the imperial clan Liu Te; the counselor to the keeper of the palace gate Ping Chi; and the general of palace attendants Li-han are to summon the king to come to the capital by seven-horse relay carriage and proceed to his residence in Ch'ang-an."

When the letter reached Ch'ang-i, the water clock showed that the end of the night was still one notch away, but the letter was opened by torchlight, and by noon Liu Ho had set out on his journey. He reached Ting-t'ao at sundown, a distance of 135 li, though the road was veritably strewn with the dead horses of his followers and attendants, so hard did they ride. His chief of palace attendants Kung Sui admonished him against such conduct and managed to have fifty or more of the king's palace attendants and masters of guests sent back.

When Liu Ho reached Chi-yang, he asked for the long-crowing chickens, and along the road he bought some canes made of laminated bamboo.[37]

When the party passed through Hung-nung, Liu Ho ordered Shan, his chief slave, to hide some women in the clothes cart. At Hu the imperial envoys, having found out about the women, berated the king's prime minister An Lo, who in turn reported the matter to Kung Sui. Kung Sui requested an interview with the king and asked if the charge were true. "I never ordered any such thing!" said Liu Ho. "If the charge is not true," said Kung Sui, "then why spare the life of this one slave and risk ruining your reputation for good conduct? I beg to have him turned over to the law officials so that Your Highness's name may be fully cleared of guilt." He thereupon seized Shan by the hair of the head and handed him over to the chief of the palace guard for the law to deal with.

When Liu Ho reached Pa-shang, the director of foreign vassals came out to the suburbs of the capital to greet him, offering him a carriage and driver to take him the remaining distance. Liu Ho ordered his own master of carriage Shou Ch'eng to act as driver and had his chief of palace attendants Kung Sui accompany him. At dawn they reached the Eastern Capital Gate in the outer wall at

[37] The long-crowing chickens were a rare variety brought from Indochina; the canes, made of strips of green bamboo glued together, were prized for their strength and pliability. The historian mentions these actions to show Liu Ho's lack of gravity in such a time of mourning and crisis.

Kuang-ming. Kung Sui said, "According to ritual, when one is has-tening to a funeral, he should cry out in lamentation when he first comes within sight of the capital. This is the eastern gate of the outer wall of Ch'ang-an."

"My throat is sore—I can't do any crying," said Liu Ho.

When they reached the inner wall gate, Kung Sui repeated his suggestion, but Liu Ho replied, "The gate of the inner wall is no different from the gate of the outer wall!"

When they were about to arrive at the eastern gate of the Eter-nal Palace, Kung Sui said, "The mourning tent for the king of Ch'ang-i is beyond this gate, north of the imperial highway. There is a road running north and south leading to it. When the horses are still several paces from the road, Your Highness should get down from the carriage, face west toward the palace gate, bow down and lament with the utmost show of grief."

"I understand," said the king, and when they reached the spot, he cried out in lamentation as prescribed.

Liu Ho received the imperial seal and seal cord and succeeded to the position and title of emperor, but twenty-seven days after he was set up, because his conduct was so disorderly and scandalous, the general in chief Ho Kuang consulted with the other ministers and requested the empress of Emperor Chao the Filial to remove him from the position and send him back to his former kingdom. He was to receive a bath-town of two thousand households, and all the houses, valuables, and other private possessions that had be-longed to him as king of Ch'ang-i were to be turned over to him.[38] In addition, the four daughters of his father King Ai were each to be given a bath-town of a thousand households. (A discussion will be found in the biography of Ho Kuang.) The kingdom of Ch'ang-i was abolished and made into the province of Shan-yang.

Earlier, while Li Ho was still in his kingdom, there were several strange occurrences. Once the king saw a white dog three feet high that had no tail; from the neck down, it looked like a man and it was wearing a Fang-shan hat.[39] Later he saw a bear. None of those

---

[38] The bath-towns did not pay taxes to the government, their revenues going instead to provide "bath and hair-washing water," i.e., private funds, for the holder.

[39] The text here says that the dog had no head, but the correct reading is found in the Treatise on the Five Elements, ch. 27B1. Liu Ho customarily wore a Fang-shan hat made of gauze of five colors. The dog probably symbol-izes Liu Ho, half man, half beast, and the fact that it has no tail indicates that he will have no heir.

about him could see these beasts. In addition, a number of large birds came and roosted on the palace.

The king knew that these things portended evil and he forthwith asked his chief of palace attendants Kung Sui about them. Kung Sui explained to him their meaning.[40] (A discussion will be found in the Treatise on the Five Elements.) The king looked up to the heavens and sighed, saying, "Why do these inauspicious omens keep occurring?"

Kung Sui knocked his head on the ground and replied, "When I have loyal advice to give, I have never dared to hide it. Several times I have warned of impending danger, though Your Highness was not pleased. But how could the survival or downfall of the state depend on any words of mine? I beg you rather to look within yourself. Your Highness has committed to memory the 305 songs of the *Book of Odes*, which record all that is proper in human affairs, all that is to be known of the ways of a king. But conduct such as yours—to which of the odes does it correspond? Your Highness holds the position of a king among the feudal lords, yet your actions are viler than those of a commoner. Under such circumstances, it is difficult to survive but very easy to perish. It would be well to ponder deeply on this!"

Later, blood was found on the mat where the king customarily sat. When the king questioned Kung Sui about it, the latter gave a loud cry and said, "Before long the palace will be empty! These evil portents keep appearing. Blood is the sign of hidden sorrow. The time has come to look into oneself with fear and circumspection."

But in the end Liu Ho failed to change his ways, and not long afterwards, he was summoned to the capital. After he had ascended the throne, he dreamed that the dirt of green flies was piled up on the east side of the western stairway, as much as five or six piculs of it. It was covered over with concave roof tiles and only after he had removed the tiles and examined it did he realize that it was the dirt of green flies. He asked Kung Sui what the dream meant and Kung Sui replied, "Does it not say in Your majesty's copy of the *Book of Odes*,

> Buzz buzz go the green flies,
> Lighting on the hedge.

[40] Kung Sui said that the dog symbolized Liu Ho's familiars, beasts disguised as men, who must be banished if the king is to survive.

Good and kind gentleman,
Do not heed words of slander! [41]

There are many slanderous men at Your Majesty's side—they are like the filth of green flies. You should appoint to office the sons and grandsons of the former emperor's high ministers, confide in them, and make them your companions. If you cannot bring yourself to dismiss your old followers from Ch'ang-i but continue to listen to their slanders and flatteries, some fearful calamity is bound to occur. I beg you to turn disaster into good fortune by banishing all of them from your side—and if you wish, I will be the first to go!"

But Liu Ho would not listen to his advice and in the end he was removed from the position of emperor. The general in chief Ho Kuang put in his place the great-grandson of Emperor Wu, who is posthumously known as Emperor Hsüan the Filial. After he came to the throne, he began to feel uneasy in his heart about Liu Ho. In the second year of *yüan-k'ang* (64 B.C.) he dispatched an envoy with a letter bearing the imperial seal addressed to Chang Ch'ang, the governor of Shan-yang, where Liu Ho was residing. It read, "Imperial command to the governor of Shan-yang: you will be careful to be prepared to deal with thieves and rebels and will keep a watch on travelers passing back and forth. Do not show this letter to your subordinates."

Chang Ch'ang thereupon submitted a memorial describing in detail Liu Ho's activities and way of life, making clear that he deserved only to be cast aside and left to perish. It read:

"Your servant Ch'ang took up administrative duties in the fifth month of the third year of *ti-chieh* (67 B.C.). The former king of Ch'ang-i lives in what used to be the palace. There are 183 male and female slaves in the palace. The main gate is closed but there is a small gate open. An overseer handles matters of money and property and goes to the market each morning to buy food, but other goods are not allowed to go in or come out of the house. There is a thief inspector whose particular duty is to patrol the grounds and examine persons coming and going. The king uses his household funds to hire guards to keep the palace clean and protect it from thieves and rebels.

"I have several times sent my assistants to conduct inspections, and in the ninth month of the fourth year, I myself went to see

[41] Mao #219.

what kind of life he leads. At that time the former king was twenty-six or twenty-seven. He has a grayish complexion, small eyes, a pointed low-bridged nose, and thin whiskers and eyebrows. He is a large, tall man and suffers from a palsy that makes it difficult for him to walk. He was wearing a short jacket, large trousers, and a military cap. His girdle was hung with jade disc ornaments. He had a writing brush stuck in his hair and carried a writing tablet as he hurried forward to greet his guest.

"I sat and talked with him in the middle courtyard and inspected his wife, children, and slaves. In hopes of finding out what was in his mind, I tried to see if I could rouse him by mentioning a bird of ill omen, saying, 'Ch'ang-i has many owls.' [42] But the former king merely replied, 'Yes, indeed. Earlier, when I went west to Ch'ang-an, there were hardly any owls there, but when I came back and had gotten as far as Chi-yang I could hear their cries once more.'

"I inspected his children and when I reached the daughter named Ch'ih-p'ei, the former king knelt and said, 'Ch'ih-p'ei's mother is the daughter of Yen Ch'ang-sun.' I had previously been told that Lo-fu, the daughter of Yen Yen-nien, whose polite name is Ch'ang-sun and who is chief of the capital police, had become a wife of the former king.

"Observing the former king's dress, speech, and actions, I would say that he is harmlessly insane—he does not seem to be blessed with normal intelligence. He has sixteen wives and twenty-two children, eleven boys and eleven girls. Aware of the gravity of my responsibility, I herewith present a list of their names along with an inventory of the former king's male and female slaves and other goods and property.

"Some time ago, I submitted a letter concerning Chang Hsiu and the others, ten singers and dancers who had belonged to the former king's father, King Ai of Ch'ang-i. They were all childless and had no official titles, being not of the *chi* but of the *liang-jen* class of attendants. When the king passed away, they should have been discharged and allowed to return to their homes, but the grand tutor Pao and others willfully detained them and assigned them to the funerary park of King Ai. Since this was contrary to the law, I requested that they be sent home. When the former king

[42] The owl is said to eat its mother. Chang Ch'ang is implying that Liu Ho is as evil as an owl in a deliberate attempt to anger him and make him disclose his inner feelings.

heard of this, he said, 'The women are assigned to look after the park. If they fall ill, they should not be treated, and anyone who injures or kills any of them should not be punished by law. One would like to see them dead as soon as possible.[43] I don't know why you are trying to send them home!' From this it is apparent that the former king is by nature given to violence and destruction and will never show any evidence of benevolence and righteousness. Later the chancellor and the imperial secretary submitted my letter to the throne and it was approved. I have accordingly sent all the women home."

When the emperor received this letter, he realized that there was no need to worry about Liu Ho.

In the spring of the following year the emperor handed down an edict which read: "It is said that the sage ruler Shun enfeoffed his younger brother Hsiang, though Hsiang was guilty of evil. Those of the same flesh and blood may be parted, yet the ties of kinship that bind them can never be undone. Let Liu Ho, the former king of Ch'ang-i, be enfeoffed as marquis of Hai-hun with the revenue from a town of four thousand households."

The attendant of the inner palace and colonel of the guard Chin An-shang submitted a letter to the throne which read: "Though Liu Ho has been cast aside by Heaven, Your Majesty in infinite benevolence has enfeoffed him once more as a marquis. But Liu Ho is a perverse and unprincipled man who, having been rejected, behaves in any manner he pleases. It is not proper that he should be allowed to serve in the ancestral temples of the founders or to take part in the rituals of the court." The suggestion was approved. Liu Ho proceeded to his fief, the city of Yü-chang.

A few years later, K'o, the provincial director of Yang-chou, submitted a memorial which said:

"Liu Ho is friendly with Sun Wan-shih, a secretary to the late governor, and Sun Wan-shih once said to him, 'When you were about to be deprived of the position of emperor, why didn't you strengthen your guard, refuse to leave the palace, and cut down the general in chief with a sword instead of tamely letting people take away the imperial seal and seal cord from you?' Liu Ho replied, 'I should have done that! That's where I went wrong!' Sun Wan-shih also said to Liu Ho that the latter would soon be made king of Yü-chang and would not have to remain a marquis much

[43] Liu Ho apparently felt that the women should die and join their former lord, his father Liu Po, in the afterworld.

longer, whereupon Liu Ho replied, 'I expect that is what will happen.' Neither of these remarks was proper for Liu Ho to have uttered."

The officials examined the evidence and requested that Liu Ho be arrested, but the emperor commanded that he be deprived of three thousand households instead.

After Liu Ho passed away, Liao, the governor of Yü-chang, submitted a memorial which read:

"Shun enfeoffed Hsiang at Yu-pi, but after Hsiang died, no heir was appointed to succeed him. This was because he was a cruel and violent man and it was not proper that he should become the founder of a line. When Liu Ho, the marquis of Hai-hun, died, his son Liu Ch'ung-kuo was named to succeed him, and when Liu Ch'ung-kuo died, his younger brother Liu Feng-ch'in was named to carry on the line. Now Liu Feng-ch'in has also died. It is clear that Heaven intends the line to end. Your Majesty out of holy benevolence has been extremely generous to Liu Ho—even Shun's treatment of Hsiang cannot excel what you have done. But it is proper that Liu Ho's line be treated according to the rituals of a line that has ended, in this way complying with the will of Heaven. I ask that this letter be handed down to the proper officials for discussion."

All of the officials were of the opinion that no successor to the line should be appointed and the fief was accordingly abolished. When Emperor Yüan came to the throne, he enfeoffed Liu Ho's son Tai-tsung as marquis of Hai-hun, and the fief has descended to his son and grandson and is still in existence today.

In appraisal we say: How tragic was the suffering caused by the black magic affair! Yet it was not only the work of one man, Chiang Ch'ung. Human power alone could not have brought it about—rather it was decreed by the seasons of Heaven. In the sixth year of *chien-yüan* (135 B.C.) the banner of Ch'ih Yu appeared, so long that it stretched all the way across the sky.[44] Later the generals were ordered to march north, seizing the region of Ho-nan and setting up the province of So-fang, and in the spring of that year the heir apparent Li was born. From this time on there were thirty years of military campaigns, and those who were killed, wiped out and destroyed by the weapons of war, were too

[44] Ch'ih Yu is a warrior of legendary times and the god of war. The banner of Ch'ih Yu is a comet that portends the outbreak of war.

numerous even to count. When the black magic affair occurred, the streets of the capital ran with blood and the fallen corpses numbered in the tens of thousands. The heir apparent and his sons all perished. Thus the heir apparent grew up amid weapons and met his end by them. His downfall was not due solely to the machinations of one minister who had wormed his way into favor with the ruler.

The First Emperor of the Ch'in in the course of his thirty-nine years on the throne [45] conquered all the six feudal states within the borders of the empire and abroad drove back the barbarians of the four quarters, until the dead were heaped about like tangled hemp, their bones left to bleach at the foot of the Long Wall, their skulls lying strewn along the road. Not a day went by without the clash of weapons, and as a result, uprisings broke out east of the mountains and the lands in the four directions broke their bonds of loyalty and turned against the Ch'in. The Ch'in generals and officers plotted rebellion abroad, traitorious ministers infiltrated the court, treason did its work behind the very screens of the throne room, and disaster reached its climax in the time of the Second Emperor.[46]

Therefore it is said, "Weapons are like fire—if not suppressed, they are bound to burn the user." [47] This is the reason that, when Ts'ang Chieh invented writing, he took the characters for "stop" and "spear" and combined them to form the character for "military." The sage uses military power to do away with violence and correct disorder, to suppress and put an end to shields and spears. He does not resort to it whenever he pleases merely to inflict injury.

The *Book of Changes* says, "The man whom Heaven aids is an obedient one; the man whom other men aid is a trustworthy one. The gentleman practices trustworthiness and gives his thoughts to obedience, and Heaven assists him. He enjoys good fortune and nothing that is not profitable." [48] Thus Chü Ch'ien-ch'iu pointed out to the emperor the true facts of the black magic affair and made it clear that the heir apparent had been the victim of injus-

---

[45] Either Pan Ku has counted wrong or the text is faulty; the First Emperor of the Ch'in reigned for 37 years.

[46] The dynasty was overthrown in the third year of the Second Emperor's reign, 207 B.C.

[47] *Tso chuan*, Duke Yin fourth year.

[48] *I ching, Hsi-tz'u*, part 1.

tice. In talent and wisdom, Chü Ch'ien-ch'iu did not necessarily surpass other men. But because he put an end to the cycle of evil and blocked the springs of rebellion, happening along at a time when deterioration had reached its lowest point and opening the way for new forces of good, he is spoken of as a man who enjoyed the assistance and aid of both Heaven and men.

HAN SHU 65: THE BIOGRAPHY OF
Tung-fang Shuo

TUNG-FANG SHUO WAS RICH IN WORDS, a man of jests and witticisms, an actor and a buffoon. In condemning the Shang-lin Park and blocking Tung Yen's entrance into the hall of state, he voiced a just reprimand and exposed error, yet he thrust the meat into the breast of his robe and dirtied the palace. He had his stiff moods and his relaxed ones, his bobbings and his sinkings. So I have transmitted the Biography of Tung-fang Shuo.

Tung-fang Shuo, whose polite name was Man-ch'ien, was a native of Yen-tz'u in Yüan-p'ing. When Emperor Wu first came to the throne, he sent out a call to the empire for the promotion of men who were "honest and upright," "worthy and good," or noted for scholarly or literary talents or unusual strength, offering to assign them to posts without requiring them to advance in the ordinary fashion. As a result, many men from all quarters submitted letters to the throne with their suggestions on policy; thousands came forward to peddle and parade their abilities in this way. Those who did not seem worthy of selection were summarily informed that their papers had been examined and were then dismissed.

When Tung-fang Shuo first came forward, he submitted a letter to the throne which said: "When I was young, I lost my father and mother and was brought up by my older brother and his wife. At the age of twelve I began to study writing, and after three winters I knew enough to handle ordinary texts and records. At fifteen I studied fencing; at sixteen, the *Odes* and *Documents;* and soon I had memorized 220,000 words. At nineteen I studied the works on military science by Masters Sun and Wu, the equipment pertaining to battle and encampment, and the regulations concerning drum and gong.[1] Once more I memorized 220,000 words, so that in all I could recite 440,000 words. In addition, I always kept in mind Tzu-lu's words.[2] I am twenty-two years in age, measure nine feet three inches,[3] have eyes like pendant pearls, teeth like ranged shells, and am as brave as Meng Pen, nimble as Ch'ing-chi, scrupulous as Pao Chu, and loyal as Wei Sheng. I am fit to become a great minister to the Son of Heaven. Daring death, I bow twice and submit this report."

Tung-fang Shuo's words were so lacking in humility and he praised himself so extravagantly that the emperor, concluding that he was no ordinary man, ordered him to await the imperial command in the office of public carriage. His stipend was meager, however, and he had not yet been granted an audience with the emperor.

After some time, Shuo played a trick on the dwarfs who worked in the stable, telling them, "His Majesty has decided that you fellows are of no benefit to the government. In plowing fields and raising crops you are surely no match for ordinary men. Given official posts and put in charge of the multitude, you would never be able to bring order to the people. Assigned to the army and dispatched to attack the barbarians, you would be incapable of handling weapons. You contribute nothing to the business of the state —all you do is use up food and clothing! So now he has decided to have you killed."

The dwarfs, thoroughly terrified, began weeping and moaning, whereupon Shuo instructed them, saying, "When His Majesty passes by, knock your heads on the ground and beg for mercy." After a while, word came that the emperor was on his way. The dwarfs all wailed and bowed their heads, and when the emperor asked them why they were doing that, they replied, "Tung-fang Shuo told us Your Majesty was going to have us all executed!"

The emperor, knowing that Shuo was a man of many devices, summoned him and asked him what he meant by terrifying the

[1] In battle the drum sounded the call to advance, the gong that to retreat.

[2] *Analects* XI, 25: "Tzu-lu briskly replied, 'Give me a country of a thousand war chariots, ... and I can make the people do brave deeds, and furthermore understand the right direction to go in!' "

[3] The Han foot was about three fourths of an English foot.

dwarfs in this fashion. Shuo replied, "I will speak out, whether it means life or death for me! The dwarfs are somewhat over three feet in height, and as a stipend they receive one sack of grain and 240 cash each. I am somewhat over nine feet in height, and as a stipend I too receive one sack of grain and 240 cash. The dwarfs are about to die of overeating, I am about to die of hunger. If my words are of any use, I hope I may be treated differently from them. If my words are of no use, then dismiss me. There's no point in merely keeping me around to eat up the rice of Ch'ang-an!"

The emperor roared with laughter and accordingly assigned him to await command at the Golden Horse Gate. Little by little, Shuo gained the confidence of the emperor.

Once the emperor ordered his various tricksters to play "guess-what's-under-it."[4] He placed a gecko lizard under the cup and asked them to guess, but no one was able to get the answer. Shuo then volunteered his services, saying "I have received instruction in the *I Ching*—let me try guessing." He then divided up the milfoil stalks, laid out the hexagrams, and announced, "I would take it for a dragon but it has no horns. I'd say it was a snake except that it has legs. Creeping, crawling, peering here and there, good at moving along the wall—if it's not a gecko, it's bound to be a skink!"

"Splendid!" said the emperor, and presented him with ten rolls of silk. Then he ordered him to guess some other objects. Again and again Shuo guessed correctly, and was immediately presented with more silk.

At this time there was an actor named Courtier Kuo who enjoyed great favor with the emperor for his never-ending fund of waggery and was constantly in attendance at the ruler's side. "Shuo just happened to make a few lucky hits!" he asserted. "This is not true art. I would like to have Shuo guess again. If he guesses correctly, I am willing to accept a hundred blows of the cane; but if he fails, I am to be given all the presents of silk!" Then he put a round tree fungus under the cup and ordered Shuo to guess. Shuo replied, "It's a saucer."

"There!" said the actor. "I knew he couldn't guess it!" But Shuo replied, "Fresh meat—you call it a stew; dried meat—you call it jerky. Growing on a tree, you call it a fungus; under a cup, you

---

[4] A game in which an object is placed under an overturned cup or bowl and the participants try to guess what it is.

call it a saucer!" The emperor ordered the official in charge of actors to have Kuo beaten. Unable to bear the pain, Kuo squealed in
anguish, but Shuo only laughed at him and said, "Ugh! Mouth
with no hair—voice all ablare—rear end in the air!"

Infuriated, the actor screamed, "Shuo is brazenly trying to hood-
wink and humiliate an attendant of the Son of Heaven! His corpse
ought to be exposed in the market place!"

The emperor then asked Shuo why he was trying to humiliate
the man, but Shuo replied, "How would I dare humiliate anyone?
I was just making up some riddles for him, that's all."

"What riddles?" asked the emperor.

" 'Mouth with no hair,' " said Shuo, "that's the dog's private
door.[5] 'Voices all ablare'—fledglings at supper, calling for more.
'Rear end in the air'—a crane, bending over, pecking at the floor."

But Kuo refused to acknowledge defeat. Instead, he said, "Now I
would like to ask Shuo some riddles. If he can't solve them, he too
ought to be given the cane!" Then he put together this absurd jingle:

> "Law pot snaggle-toothed
> age cypress mud-grooved
> *yi-yu-ya*
> *ngi-ngu-nga*

What does that mean?"

Shuo replied, "Law—an ordination. Pot—to store your ration.
Snaggle-toothed—non-conformation. Age—what all men hail.
Cypress—the spirits' vale. Mud-grooved—a soggy trail. *Yi-yu-ya*
—words merely jangling. *Ngi-ngu-nga*—two dogs tangling!" Whatever Kuo asked, Shuo would immediately come back with an answer in rhyme, twisting things around, distorting, popping out in
any number of weird ways so that no one could pin him down.
The company was reduced to utter astonishment.

The emperor appointed Shuo a gentleman in constant attendance and eventually bestowed great affection and favor on him.

Some time later, during the hottest days of summer, the emperor
ordered that a gift of meat be given to his attendants. But, although the day grew late, the assistant to the imperial butler did
not appear to distribute the gift. Shuo then took it upon himself to
draw his sword and cut off a portion of meat, saying to his fellow

[5] The small opening in a gate or wall for dogs to go in and out; the word
"mouth" may also mean "door."

officials, "In these hot days one ought to go home early. With your permission, therefore, I will take my gift." Then he put the meat into the breast of his robe and went off. The imperial butler reported him to the emperor, and when Shuo appeared at court, the emperor said, "Yesterday when the gift of meat was being given out, you did not wait for the imperial command but cut off a piece of the meat with your sword and made away with it. What do you mean by such behavior!"

Shuo doffed his cap and apologized, but the emperor said, "Stand up, sir, and confess your faults!"

Shuo bowed twice and said, "All right now, Shuo! You accepted the gift without waiting for the imperial command—what a breach of etiquette! You drew your sword and cut the meat—what singular daring! When you carved it up, you didn't take much—how abstemious of you! You took it home and gave it to the little lady —how big-hearted!"

The emperor laughed and said, "I told you to confess your faults and here you are praising yourself!" Then he presented him with a further gift of a gallon of wine and a hundred catties of meat and told him to take them home to "the little lady."

Some time before this, in the third year of the *chien-yüan* era (138 B.C.), the emperor first began going out on incognito expeditions, venturing north as far as Ch'ih-yang, west to Yellow Mountain, south on hunting trips to Long Willows, and east on excursions to I-ch'un. Such incognito expeditions were customarily carried out in the eighth or ninth month, after the offerings of rich wine had been presented in the ancestral temples. The emperor was accompanied by the gentlemen in constant attendance and armed riders, along with the sons of good families from Lung-hsi and Pei-ti who had been assigned to await his command and who were skilled at horsemanship and archery. They were instructed to rendezvous at the gate of a particular palace; it was at this time that the term *ch'i-men* or "rendezvous gate" first came into use. The group would set out in the evening, at the tenth notch of the water clock, announcing themselves as the party of the marquis of P'ing-yang, and by dawn would reach the foot of the Southern Mountains.[6] There they would pursue and shoot at deer, boar, fox, and rabbit, and wrestle bare-handed with black and tawny bears,

[6] The "tenth notch of the water clock" was about eight-thirty in the evening. The marquis of P'ing-yang was the husband of Emperor Wu's eldest sister; he enjoyed great honor at this time and hence was not likely to be challenged by the officials.

galloping wildly through the fields of rice and grain while the common people all shouted and screamed curses at them. Once the people got together and reported the matter to the magistrate of Hu-tu, who went and asked for an interview with the marquis of P'ing-yang. The horsemen were about to set upon the magistrate with their whips, but the magistrate in a rage instructed his clerks to shout at the hunters and command them to halt. Several of the horsemen were accordingly detained, and it was only after they had shown him the carriages and other equipment and revealed the true nature of the expedition that they were at last able to obtain release. Sometimes the parties would leave at night and return on the evening of the following day, but later they began taking along rations enough for a five day outing, returning in time for the emperor to pay his respects to his grandmother at the Palace of Lasting Trust.[7] The emperor found all this highly enjoyable. After this, the people in the region of the Southern Mountains became aware that it was the ruler who was making these expeditions. The emperor went on a number of such trips, but he was still somewhat intimidated by his grandmother, the empress dowager, and did not dare to venture very far away.

The chancellor and the imperial secretary, aware of the emperor's wishes, instructed the chief commandant in charge of the western area of the capital to inspect and alert the area from Long Willows east. They also had the prefect in charge of the western area muster a force of commoners and assign them to appropriate places for the staffing and attendance of the imperial party. Later, arrangements were quietly made for the setting up of "clothes-changing" places—twelve of them, ranging south from the Hsüan-ch'ü Palace. In the daytime the imperial party would stop at such places to rest and change clothes; in the evening it would put up in the various palaces until morning. Of these, the Long Willows, Five Oaks, Pei-yang, and Hsüan-ch'ü palaces were most favored.

But the emperor found the journey to these places long and wearisome, and he was aware of the trouble he was causing the common people. He therefore ordered the palace counselor Wu-ch'iu Shou-wang, along with two men in the imperial service who were good at calculations, to make a survey of the area south of the A-fang walls, east of Chou-chih, and west of I-ch'un, detailing the exact amount of acreage contained within these boundaries and

[7] Custom required him to visit his grandmother, Empress Dowager Tou, once every five days. She died in 135 B.C.

the market price of the lands there. His aim was to take over the area for the creation of the Shang-lin Park, which would extend as far as the Southern Mountains. He also ordered the commanders and prefects in charge of the eastern and western areas of the capital to draw up a report on unused grasslands in nearby districts, intending to use such lands to reimburse the people of Hu-tu whose fields would be confiscated. Wu-ch'iu Shou-wang submitted his report and the emperor was very pleased, calling it an excellent job.

At this time Tung-fang Shuo was in attendance, and he stepped forward with the following remonstrance: "I have heard that Heaven responds to humility and quietude—responds by sending down good fortune. It likewise responds to pride and extravagance —by sending down prodigies! Now Your Majesty has built story on story of verandahs and terraces, fearful only that they would not be high enough; has marked off lands for shooting and hunting, fearful only that they would not be vast enough. If Heaven manifests no unusual change in the face of this, then why not take over the entire capital area and make it into a park? Why confine yourself to the region of Hu-tu? But if such luxury and extravagance, such overstepping of bounds, should draw a response from Heaven, then, small though the Shang-lin area may be, I fear it will still be too big!

"The Southern Mountains are the bastion of the empire. South of them flow the Yangtze and the Huai, north of them the Yellow River and the Wei. The region they occupy stretches east from the Ch'ien River and Lung and west from the districts of Shang and Lo, a land both fertile and rich. When the Han dynasty arose, it abandoned the old area of the Three Rivers and moved to the region west of Pa and Ch'an, founding its own capital south of the Ching and Wei rivers. A veritable sea of blessings within the dry land, unparalleled throughout the world—such is this region. The Ch'in dynasty because of it was able to conquer the Jung barbarians to the west and gain mastery of the entire area east of the mountains!

"From its hills come jade and other stones, gold, silver, copper, and iron, camphor trees, sandalwood, boxwood, and other rare products too numerous to be recounted, such as provide raw materials for a hundred different types of artisans and ample livelihood for ten thousand people. In addition, it brings forth bountiful harvests of glutinous and non-glutinous rice, pears, chestnuts, mulberry, hemp, and different varieties of bamboo. Its soil is well suited to ginger and taro, its waters teem with fish and frogs, so that the poor may supply their whole households with plenty and never need worry about hunger and cold. That is why the area of the old cities of Feng and Hao has always been known as a fertile region and its lands are valued at one gold piece per *mou*.

"Now the plan is to make all of this into a park, wiping out the profits of dike and pond, lake and swamp, taking away from the people these rich and bountiful lands. On the higher level, this will impoverish the resources of the state; on the lower, it will strike a blow to the undertakings of agriculture and sericulture. A rejection of success and accomplishment, a deliberate move in the direction and failure, a diminution in the harvests of the five grains—this is the first reason why it will not do!

"Moreover, while we encourage the growth of these forests of thorn and bramble, while we nourish deer and elk, enlarge our fox and rabbit parks, and magnify the wastes where tiger and wolf dwell, we will also be destroying men's tombs and grave mounds, leveling their homes and cottages, causing children and young ones to think longingly of their native lands and the old folk to weep and wail with sorrow. This is the second reason why it will not do!

"And when we have cleared the land and marked it off, fenced it and enclosed it, then horsemen will race east to west, carriages will speed headlong north to south, and there will be deep ditches and huge conduits to contend with. Is one day of such pleasure sufficient reason to endanger the boundless blessings that reside in the person of Your Majesty? This is the third reason why it will not do!

"Therefore, to strive only for bigger gardens and parks, not caring what this may do to the farmers and their crops—this is no way to strengthen the nation and enrich the people. The Yin dynasty built its 'palace the size of nine market places,' and the feudal lords rose up in revolt. King Ling built his Bright Flower Terrace and the people of Ch'u turned away from him. The Ch'in raised up the halls of the A-fang Palace and the whole world was plunged into disorder.

"Worthless and stupid as I am, forgetful of life, courting death, I have called into question this exalted proposal and dared to defy the august will, for which I deserve to die ten thousand deaths. But I have one great desire which I cannot suppress—a desire to present a report on the Great Stairway and the Six Verifications.[8] Therein are revealed the changes of Heaven; one must not fail to examine them!" On the same day, Tung-fang Shuo accordingly submitted to the throne his report on the Great Stairway.

The emperor honored Shuo by making him a palace counselor, with the additional title of steward of the palace, presenting him with a gift of a hundred catties of gold. But in the end he went ahead with the construction of the Shang-lin Park just as Wu-ch'iu Shou-wang had recommended.

Sometime later, Lord Chao-p'ing, the son of Princess Lung-lu, married a daughter of the emperor, Princess I-an.[9] Princess Lung-lu fell ill and, thinking of the future, took a thousand catties of gold and ten million cash and asked if she might buy commutation of the death sentence in case her son should ever commit a capital offense. The emperor gave his permission, and the princess passed away. Lord Chao-p'ing grew more overbearing each day, and in a fit of drunkenness killed his wife's duenna. He was arrested and held in confinement in the Inner Office. Since he was the son of a princess, the commandant of justice submitted the case to the emperor, asking him to pronounce sentence. Various people close to the emperor spoke on the young man's behalf, and there was also the fact that his mother had previously paid for commutation of the death sentence and the emperor had given his approval. "My sister had only this one son, born in her old age, and on her death she entrusted him to me," said the emperor. He wept and sighed for the young man, and then, after a long time, continued. "Our laws and regulations were created by the former emperor. If I should do violence to the former emperor's law just because of my sister, what face could I put on when I enter the ancestral temple of Kao-tsu? Moreover, I would be betraying the common people below me!" Thereupon he gave his approval to the death sentence as it had been recommended.

The emperor could not shake off his grief, and those about him all were moved to sorrow. Tung-fang Shuo, however, stepped for-

---

[8] The Great Stairway is one of three sets of two stars each, whose movements provide six omens or "Verifications" indicating the fate of human society. Evidently Tung-fang Shuo intended to reinforce his warning on the creation of the Shang-lin Park by some report on the omens indicated by these stars, the "response of Heaven" which he mentions in his reprimand.

[9] Princess Lung-lu was Emperor Wu's younger sister.

ward and proposed a toast to the emperor's long life, saying, "I have heard that when the sage kings conducted their rule, in handing out awards they did not pass over their enemies, and in inflicting punishment they did not spare their own flesh and blood. The *Book of Documents* says, 'Neither partial nor partisan, but broad and fair is the way of the king.' [10] To punish and to reward impartially—these two tasks are something that the Five Emperors of antiquity found very difficult, that the kings of the Three Dynasties could hardly bear to do—and yet Your Majesty has carried them out! So it is that, within the area of the four seas, each member of the vast multitude of mankind is able to obtain his rightful place, and the whole world is blessed in abundance. Your servant offers this cup, braving death and bowing twice, wishing Your Majesty a life of ten thousand years!"

The emperor rose and withdrew to his inner apartments. When evening came, he sent for Tung-fang Shuo and berated him, saying, "The book says, 'If you wait till the proper time to speak, people will not be repelled by your words.' [11] Now when you offered your toast, was that the proper time?"

Shuo doffed his hat, bowed his head and said, "I have heard that when joy is too great, then the yang element overflows, and when grief is too great, then the yin element causes havoc. If yin and yang become unbalanced, then the heart and breath will be moved, and if the heart and breath are moved, the energy and spirit will be scattered and malignant vapors will pour in. For dispelling melancholy, there is nothing like wine. I proposed a toast because I wished to make clear that Your Majesty is upright and without favoritism, and at the same time to put a stop to grief. In my stupidity I did not know that I was violating a taboo. I deserve to die." [12]

Once in the past, Tung-fang Shuo had come into the palace drunk and had pissed in the upper part of the hall. He had been indicted on charges of irreverence, but the emperor had ordered that he be spared the death penalty, merely dismissing him from

[10] From the *Hung-fan* or "Great Plan" section of the *Book of Documents*.
[11] *Analects* XIV, 14.
[12] I take Tung-fang Shuo's toast and praise of the emperor's impartiality to be ironic, and the talk of yin and yang merely a device to save the emperor's face, though other interpretations are surely possible. One wishes at such times that the historian would give some indication of how he himself viewed the incident.

office and reducing him to the rank of commoner. Because of the reply he gave to the emperor concerning the toast, however, he was restored to the post of palace attendant and rewarded with a hundred bolts of silk.

Earlier, the emperor's aunt Princess Kuan-t'ao, known as the Elder Princess Tou, had married Ch'en Wu, the marquis of T'ang-i. Ch'en Wu died and the princess remained a widow; at this time she was over fifty. She had, however, grown intimate with one Tung Yen.

Tung Yen and his mother had originally made their living selling pearls. When Yen was thirteen years old, he began to accompany his mother in her goings and comings in the princess's household. The attendants of the princesses remarked on how good looking he was, whereupon the princess summoned him to an interview. "I will be a mother to you and bring you up," she said, and accordingly kept him in her household. He was taught to read, write, do accounts, judge horses, drive a carriage, and shoot a bow; he read rather widely in various books and records. When he reached the age of eighteen he was capped; abroad, he would hold the reins for his mistress, at home, he would attend her in her inner apartments. He was by nature a warm, gentle person who loved others, and because of the princess's influence, he was accepted by the members of the nobility. His name became known throughout the capital and he was addressed as Lord Tung. The princess then urged him to dole out money in order to attract friends. She gave instructions to the manager of her household, saying, "So long as Lord Tung does not call on you for more than a hundred catties of gold, a million cash, or a thousand bolts of cloth in one day, you need not bother to report to me."

Yüan Shu of An-ling was the son of Yüan Ang's elder brother.[13] He was very friendly with Tung Yen, and said to him, "You are carrying on a secret alliance with a princess of the Han, a crime that could involve you in incalculable trouble! How do you propose to insure your safety?"

Tung Yen, looking frightened, replied, "I've been worrying about this for a long time but I don't know what to do!"

Yüan Shu said, "The Ku-ch'eng ancestral temple is a long way from the capital and there is no palace in the vicinity where the

[13] Yüan Ang was a high official under Emperor Wu's predecessor, Emperor Ching.

emperor may spend the night when he visits there.[14] Moreover, there are groves of catalpa and bamboo there, and the sacred field that the emperor plows in person. Why don't you suggest to the princess that she present her Long Gate Gardens to the emperor as a gift. It is precisely what the emperor wants, and when he learns that the idea originated with you, then you will be able to sleep easy at night and will not have anything to fear or fret about for a long time to come. But if you allow things to drag on without taking any action, then eventually the emperor will ask for the estate himself. Then what good will you get out of it?"

Tung Yen bowed his head and said, "I am only too happy to follow your instructions." Then he went and told the princess of the plan, and she immediately submitted a letter to the throne making the presentation. The emperor was higly pleased and renamed the princess's garden estate, calling it the Long Gate Palace. The princess, delighted, instructed Tung Yen to take a hundred catties of gold and present it to Yüan Shu as a birthday gift.

Yüan Shu thereupon began devising a plan for Tung Yen whereby he might gain an actual audience with the emperor. He had the princess say that she was ill and could not appear at court. The emperor came to visit her, inquiring how her illness was and asking if there was anything she desired. The princess thanked him politely. "Because of the generosity and kindness which Your Majesty has showered upon me," she said, "and because of the sacred memory of my brother, the late emperor, I have been allowed to pay my respects at court at the spring and autumn receptions and to fulfill the duties of a loyal subject. I have been ranked among the princesses of the imperial house, have received gifts, and enjoyed the revenue from a fief assigned to me. Loftier than heaven, weightier than earth is the debt I owe, one that to my death I can never hope to repay. Now if one day I should become incapable of performing my womanly duties of sweeping and sprinkling, if I should precede you to my humble death, like a dog or horse tumbled in a ditch, I would, I confess, go with regret. For I have this irrepressible wish. I wish that Your Majesty, forgetting the ten thousand affairs of state, would at times nourish your vitality and let your spirit wander free; that you would emerge from your private apartments, turn aside your carriage, follow this out-of-the-

[14] The Ku-ch'eng temple, which enshrined the ancestral spirit of Emperor Wen, was situated south of Ch'ang-an, near the Long Gate country estate of Princess Tou.

way road and come to look over my hills and forests, where I may offer you the wine cup, toast your health, and provide entertainment and diversion for those attending you. If this were to come about before I die, then what regrets would I have?"

"You must not worry about this," said the emperor. "Hopefully you will recover. But I'm afraid my officers and attendants will be too many and will put you to too much expense."

The emperor returned to the capital, and shortly afterwards, the princess recovered from her illness, rose from her bed and went to call upon him. The emperor gave her ten million cash and expressed a desire to join with her in drinking. A few days later, he went to "look over her hills and forests." The princess prepared the meal with her own hand and, wearing the knee-worn smock of a menial, led him into the hall, up the steps, and to his seat. Before they had settled in their seats, the emperor said, "I would like to have a look at your husband."

The princess at once stepped down to the lower part of the hall, removed her hairpins, earrings, and footgear, and bowed her head to the floor. "There is no excuse," she said in apology. "I have betrayed Your Majesty's trust and I deserve to kneel before the executioner, though Your Majesty might perhaps refrain from applying the law. I bow my head, confessing that my fault deserves death."

The emperor ordered that she be pardoned. She donned her hairpins and footgear, rose, went to the eastern apartments, and came back leading Lord Tung. Lord Tung was wearing the green headcloth and leather sleeve-guards of a cook; following the princess, he came forward and prostrated himself in the lower part of the hall. The princess pronounced the words of introduction: "Your servant Yen, cook to the Kuan-t'ao Princess, braving death, bows twice and presents himself for an interview." Then he struck his head on the floor in apology. The emperor rose from his seat in acknowledgment, and then ordered that he be presented with a robe and hat and allowed into the upper part of the hall. Tung Yen rose and hurried to put on the robe and hat.

The princess in person served the food and presented the wine cup. During the proceedings, the emperor showed special favor to Tung Yen by refraining from calling him by his personal name, addressing him instead as "husband of the princess." When the drinking had induced a state of general joy and merriment, the princess requested that she be allowed to present gifts of gold, cash, and assorted silks in appropriate quantities to the generals, marquises, and officers in attendance.

As a result of this, there was no one throughout the empire who did not hear of Lord Tung's eminence and favor. From the various provinces and kingdoms, fencing masters and those involved with horses, dogs, and football flocked about him like spokes about a hub. Tung Yen constantly attended the emperor in his outings and entertainments in the northern palace; he raced in pursuit of game at the Tower of Peaceful Joy, watched cock fights and football matches, observed tests of swiftness among dogs and horses. The emperor found his company highly enjoyable.

The emperor thereupon arranged to hold a feast for Elder Princess Tou, setting out wine in the Proclamation Chamber of the palace and instructing the master of guests to have Lord Tung conducted into the hall. At this time Tung-fang Shuo was among the lance-bearers who flanked the steps in the lower part of the hall. Dipping his lance, he stepped forward and said, "Tung Yen has committed three crimes deserving of the death sentence—what right has he to come in here?"

"What are you talking about?" asked the emperor.

Shuo replied, "A commoner, he has been carrying on a secret alliance with a princess of the imperial family—that is his first crime. He has violated the teachings that govern man and woman, and has subverted the rites of matrimony, injuring the royal statutes—that is his second crime. Now, when Your Majesty is still young in years, when you are turning all your thoughts to the Six Classics, concentrating your spirit upon kingly affairs, racing in pursuit of the principles of Yao and Shun, bending joints in service of the ideals of the Three Dynasties, Tung Yen shows no respect for the Classics, no wish to encourage learning. On the contrary, vain show is what commands his respect, luxury and extravagance are all he strives for, giving himself wholly to the joys of dog and horse, pursuing to the extreme the delights of ear and eye. He walks the path of evil and perversion, follows the road of wantonness and sin. He is in fact a great threatener of state and family, a major plague to the ruler of men. Yen is the chief of evildoers— this is his third crime. Long ago, Princess Po burned to death and all the feudal lords were awed.[15] What do you say to that, Your Majesty?"

[15] Princess Po was a daughter of the ducal family of Lu and wife of the ruler of Sung. One night in 543 B.C., when she was a widow of about sixty, fire broke out in her apartments, but she chose to burn to death rather than to

The emperor was silent and did not answer. After a long time, he said, "I've already had everything put out for the banquet. Wait until later and I'll correct the situation myself."

But Shuo said, "That will not do! The Proclamation Chamber is the hall of state of the former emperors, and no one who is not concerned with the rule of law and ordinance is permitted to enter it. If wantonness and disorder continue unchecked, they may turn into usurpation. This is how Shu-tiao came to work his evil and I-ya to create havoc. When Uncle Ch'ing died, the state of Lu was saved; when Kuan and Ts'ai were punished, the house of Chou was made secure." [16]

"Very well," said the emperor. He then ordered that the plan be abandoned and the banquet moved to the northern palace. He had Lord Tung escorted there through the Eastern Gate of the Marshal, changing the name of the gate to the Eastern Friendship Gate. He rewarded Tung-fang Shuo with thirty catties of yellow gold.

From this time on, the favor enjoyed by Lord Tung began to wane day by day; he died at the age of thirty. Several years later, the Elder Princess Tou passed away and was buried with Lord Tung at Pa-ling. Subsequently, many of the princesses and nobles took to overstepping the rites and regulations—it all began with Tung Yen!

At this time luxury and vain show filled the empire. Pursuing lesser occupations, many of the common people abandoned their fields and farms. The emperor in a moment of leisure questioned Tung-fang Shuo, saying, "I want to reform the people—how should I go about it?"

Shuo replied, "The affairs of Yao, Shun, Yü, T'ang, Wen, Wu, Ch'eng, and K'ang belong to high antiquity; they took place several thousand years ago and are difficult to speak about. I for one would not venture to describe them. Instead I wish to talk of re-

---

violate the rules of propriety by venturing out without a chaperone. Tung-fang Shuo is implying a contrast between her chaste behavior and that of the Elder Princess Tou and her paramour.

[16] Shu-tiao and I-ya were evil ministers to Duke Huan of Ch'i; the former had himself made a eunuch in order to gain power in the duke's household; the latter killed his own son and served up the flesh to the duke. Both later led a revolt against the duke. Uncle Ch'ing was a member of the ruling family of Lu who murdered one of the dukes of Lu and for a while threatened the security of the state. Kuan and Ts'ai were brothers of King Wu of Chou who, after his death, plotted to overthrow his heir; they were punished by the Duke of Chou.

cent times, the age of Emperor Wen the Filial, which was seen and experienced in person by all the older men of today. At that time, though the ruler enjoyed all the honor of a Son of Heaven, all the wealth to be found within the four seas, he dressed himself in coarse black silk, wore on his feet shoes of untanned leather, and buckled on his sword with a simple thong. Sedge and rushes served for his mat, his weapons were of wood without any blades, his robes were stuffed with wadding and innocent of design. He gathered up the old bags that had been used to submit memorials to the throne and had them made into curtains for his hall, for he regarded the Way and its Virtue as his adornment, benevolence and righteousness as his standard. So it was that the whole world looked to his example and shaped its customs on this basis. With brilliant effectiveness he reformed the people.

"But now Your Majesty, regarding the area within the capital walls as too small, plans to build the Chien-chang Palace. To the left your Phoenix Portals, to the right your Spirit Bright Tower—'a thousand gates, ten thousand doors' is the way men speak of them. Even trees and earth mounds wear rich brocade, dogs and horses go draped in five-colored felt. Your palace people sport tortoise-shell combs and drip with round and oval pearls. You train stunt-riders in their chariots and set them racing and chasing; you adorn with hue and pattern, collect what is rare and strange. You strike bells that weigh ten thousand piculs, pound on drums that roll like thunder, command your actors and entertainers to perform, your women of Cheng to do dances. If a ruler indulges in such luxury and excess, and still hopes to persuade the common people not to be wasteful and extravagant, not to give up farming, I am afraid he will have a difficult time of it.

"But if Your Majesty would only follow my plan, would tear down the elegant draperies and burn them in the street where the avenues cross, then you could create an age of order worthy to stand beside the greatest days of Yao and Shun! The *Book of Changes* says, 'Make the base upright and ten thousand affairs will be ordered. An error of one inch can make a thousand miles' difference.' [17] I hope Your Majesty will consider the matter and give it careful thought."

Though Shuo was given to jests and buffoonery, he would on occasion observe the emperor's mood and, if he found it right, would

[17] No such quotation is found in the present text of the *Changes*.

speak out boldly in severe reprimand. The emperor always listened
to what he had to say. From the highest nobles and office-holders
on down, Shuo would bait and banter with everyone, betraying no
hint of subservience. Because of his glib and witty responses, the
emperor was fond of asking him questions. Once he said to Shuo,
"Look at me, sir—what kind of ruler am I?"

"From the golden days of Yao and Shun, the times of Ch'eng and
K'ang, there has never been anything to match the present age,"
replied Shuo. "When from my lowly position I observe Your Majesty's merit and virtue, I find it ranged above that of the Five Emperors, more estimable than that of the kings of the Three Dynasties. And that is not all. You have also succeeded in attracting to
your service the most worthy gentlemen of the world. Every high
post has been filled with exactly the right man. It is as though you
had the dukes of Chou and Shao for your chancellors, Confucius as
your imperial secretary, T'ai-kung Wang as your general, and Pi-
kung Kao to follow after and correct oversights. Pien Chuang-tzu
is your colonel of the guard, Kao Yao your chief coordinator, Hou
Chi your minister of agriculture, Yi Yin your privy treasurer. Tzu-
kung conducts missions to foreign countries, Yen Hui and Min
Tzu-ch'ien act as erudits, Tzu-hsia is master of ritual, Yi oversees
the western reaches of the capital, Tzu-lu is chief of capital police,
Hsieh is director of vassals, Kuan Lung-feng heads the imperial
clan, Po-i serves as prefect of the capital, while Kuan Chung oversees the eastern reaches of the capital. Lu Pan is your master car-
penter, Chung-shan Fu your censor, Shen Po your master of carriage, Chi Tzu of Yen-ling your director of water works, Po-li Hsi
your director of dependent states, Hui of Liu-hsia the supervisor of
your harem, Shih Yü your director of rectitude, and Ch'ü Po-yü
your grand tutor. K'ung Fu manages the heir apparent's household,
Sun-shu Ao is chancellor at the court of the feudal lords, Tzu-ch'an
governs your provinces, Prince Ch'ing-chi is keeper of the Rendezvous Gate, Hsia Yü is officer of caldrons, Yi carries the flag at the
head of the procession, and Sung Wan makes certain that the road
has been cleared." [18] The emperor laughed uproariously.

At this time there were many talented and worthy men at court.
The emperor continued to question Shuo, saying, "Nowadays we
have men like Prime Minister Kung-sun, Lord Ni, Tung Chung-

---

[18] Needless to say, these ancient worthies are all in one way or another pe-
culiarly suited to the tasks and offices to which Tung-fang Shuo assigns them.

shu, Hsia-hou Shih-ch'ang, Ssu-ma Hsiang-ju, Wu-ch'iu Shou-wang, Chu-fu Yen, Chu Mai-ch'en, Chuang Chu, Chi An, Chiao Ts'ang, Chung Chün, Yen An, Hsü Yüeh, and Ssu-ma Ch'ien, all of great wisdom and understanding, with superlative talent in letters and learning. Looking at yourself, how do you think you compare?"

Shuo replied, "When I see them clacking teeth and fangs, puffing out jowls, spluttering from the mouth, craning necks and chins, lining up flank by thigh, pairing off buttock bones, snaking their way along, mincing side by side in crook-backed ranks, then I say to myself, Shuo, you may not be much, but you're still equal to all these gentlemen put together!"

Shuo answered all the emperor's queries in this deft and nimble manner.

Emperor Wu, having sent out his call for men of unusual stature, was busy weighing talents and abilities and alloting posts as though he would never get around to everyone. At this time he was engaged abroad in campaigns against the Hsiung-nu and the inhabitants of Yüeh, while at home he was putting into effect his new laws and statutes. The government was involved in numerous undertakings, and from Kung-sun Hung down to Ssu-ma Ch'ien, the men mentioned above were all dispatched as ambassadors abroad, employed as governors of provinces or prime ministers of feudal states, or assigned to important posts at court. Tung-fang Shuo had once risen as high as palace counselor, but afterwards he remained a palace attendant, waiting on the emperor along with Mei Kao and the courtier Kuo, playing the jester and nothing more. After a long time, Shuo submitted a memorial in which he set forth a plan to improve agriculture and warfare and strengthen the state, at the same time complaining that he alone had failed to attain any important office. He petitioned that his proposal be given a trial, quoting mainly from the Legalist philosophers Shang Yang and Han Fei Tzu, but his reasoning was vague and far-fetched, and much of the memorial, which ran to thirty or forty thousand words, was taken up with jests and witticisms; in the end it went unheeded.

As a result of this experience, Shuo wrote a discussion in which an imaginary friend poses criticisms, and the author replies by explaining the consolations deriving from a low position such as his. The piece went as follows:

Someone criticized Tung-fang Shuo, saying, "Su Ch'in and Chang Yi, once they had met up with a lord of ten thousand chariots, won the position of highest ministers, and their blessings passed down to their heirs in ages after.[19] Now you, sir, study the arts of the former kings, and pursue the ideals of the sages. You intone the *Odes* and *Documents* and the sayings of the hundred schools of philosophy; too numerous to count are the books you read, written on bamboo and silk, until your lips rot and your teeth fall out, taking their doctrines to heart and never neglecting them. The fervency of your devotion to learning, your love of the Way, is evident for all to see. And since you suppose that no one within the four seas is your equal in wisdom and ability, you expect to be dubbed a man of broad learning and perfect understanding. Yet, though you have exhausted your strength and put forth the utmost loyalty in the service of our sage emperor, though you have piled up days and persisted for a long time, your rank does not exceed palace attendant, your post is no more than that of lance-bearer! I wonder, is it because there is still some action you have failed to perform? Your kinfolk enjoy not the slightest preferment. What is the reason for this?"

Master Tung-fang gave a long, heart-felt sigh, looked up at the sky and replied, "This of course is the sort of thing you would never be able to comprehend! *That* was one age, *this* is another—how can you possibly compare them?

"In the time of Su Ch'in and Chang Yi, the royal house of Chou was in complete collapse. The feudal lords no longer paid allegiance at its court, but ruled by force and vied for authority, taking one another prisoner by dint of arms. The feudal domains had through annexation been reduced to twelve states, but as yet it was uncertain which would emerge the victor. States that were able to attract men to their service became powerful; those that lost them were doomed. Therefore men like Su Ch'in and Chang Yi were able to put their theories and proposals into practice. They themselves came to occupy the most lucrative positions, their apartments crammed with jewels and treasures, their grounds dotted with barns and storehouses, and their bounty extended to ages after, for the endless enjoyment of sons and grandsons.

"Now, however, things are different. The virtue of our sage emperor overflows and the whole world quakes with awe. The feudal lords come as guests to speak their submission; regions beyond the

19 Su Ch'in and Chang Yi were political advisers of the 4th century B.C., proponents of the Vertical and Horizontal alliances respectively, who wandered from state to state until they found a ruler who was sympathetic to their ideas and who would employ them. Both in time rose to high office.

four seas he binds about him like a girdle—all is as steady as a bowl turned face down. And should he choose to move, he does so as easily as one revolving an object in the palm of his hand. What difference is there now between the worthy man and the fool? Our ruler honors the Way of Heaven, abides by the principles of earth, and there is nothing that does not find its proper place. Should he choose to leave men in peace, they will rest easy; should he move against them, they will be troubled. Should he honor them, they may be his generals; should he degrade them, they will become slaves. Raised up, they may soar above the blue clouds; thrust down, they will find themselves beneath the deepest springs. Chosen for office, they turn into tigers; unchosen, they remain mice. So, although one might strive to exert the utmost fidelity and put forth the greatest effort, how can he tell what the future may hold?

"Now from out of the vastness of heaven and earth, and the multitude of men within it, those who exhaust their energies in counsels and expositions, advancing upon the ruler and surrounding him like spokes about a hub, are too numerous to be counted. They spare no effort in their pursuit of him, doing without food or clothing, perhaps even sacrificing home and dwelling. If Su Ch'in and Chang Yi were living today and should join with me in this struggle, they would never even get to be a clerk in charge of precedents, much less could they ever dare hope to become a palace attendant! So it is said, times change, and circumstances with them.

"Nevertheless, this does not mean that one should not strive to improve himself. The *Odes* says:

> Strike bells in the palace,
> Their sound will reach to the wilds.
> Cranes call in the nine swamps,
> Their voices heard to heaven.[20]

If one succeeds in improving himself, why should he worry about lack of recognition? T'ai-kung Wang in his conduct was the embodiment of benevolence and righteousness, yet he was seventy-two before he at last gained employment under kings Wen and Wu. He got the chance to expound his ideas and was enfeoffed in the state of Ch'i, and for seven hundred years his line continued unbroken. This is why the gentleman will strive wholeheartedly

[20] The couplets are quoted from Mao nos. 229 and 184 respectively.

day and night to be diligent in conduct, and will not dare to be remiss. He is like the little wagtail that twitters all the while it flies.

"There is a book that says, 'Heaven does not suspend the winter because men dislike cold; earth does not cease being wide because men dislike difficult terrain; the gentleman does not stop acting because petty men carp and clamor. Heaven has its constant way; earth has its constant dimensions; the gentleman has his constant demeanor. The gentleman follows what is constant; the petty man reckons up his achievements. This is what the *Odes* means when it says:

> If you have no faults of conduct,
> Why be distressed at what others say? [21]

"The saying goes, if the water is too clear, no fish will gather there; if a man is too perceptive, he will have no companions. The ruler's ceremonial hat with the curtain of tassels in front is designed to dim his keen sight; the yellow fringe that dangles over his ears is meant to muffle his keen hearing. They signify that sight should have things it does not see; that hearing should have things it does not hear; that one should applaud outstanding virtue, forgive minor faults, and not look for everything in one man.

"Make it straight by bending—let it do its own mending. Treat it gently and condone—let it find its way alone. Judge and weigh its nature—let it follow its own venture. This indeed is the way the sage teaches and transforms others. He wants them to find what is right for themselves, for when they find it for themselves, they will proceed with alacrity and breadth of understanding.

"Nowadays our gentlemen in retirement sit lumplike and companionless, dwell all alone in vacuity, their eyes fixed on the recluse Hsü Yu of high antiquity, on the madman Chieh Yü of later times. In planning they regard themselves as equal to Fan Li; in loyalty, as one with Wu Tzu-hsü.[22] But now the world is at peace and righteousness has no lack of adherents to support it. Therefore it is only natural that these men should find few employers, should have a dearth of disciples. Why, then, do you wonder at my own low position?

"When Yen employed Yüeh Yi as its general, when Ch'in raised

---

[21] The passage is quoted from *Hsün Tzu*, sec. 17; no such poem is found in the present text of the *Odes*.

[22] On Fan Li and Wu Tzu-hsü, see pages 33 and 51.

Li Ssu to the post of prime minister, when Li I-chi went and talked the state of Ch'i into submission, their ideas were put into practice with the smoothness of streams, agreement surrounded them as a bracelet crooks a wrist. What they hoped for, they obtained; achievement piled up like hills and mountains, the area within the seas was at rest, and the nation found peace—all because these men met up with the proper time. Why do you find anything strange about this? [23]

"The saying goes, if you use a tube to scan the heavens, a calabash to measure the sea, or a twig to strike a bell, how can you possibly see through all its parts and divisions, study its patterns and lineaments, or hope to produce any sound? Consider such a procedure and you will see that it is like a tiny mouse trying to assault a dog, a solitary pig grunting at a tiger. Such creatures would advance only to be annihilated—what success could they achieve? Similarly, if some stupid, inferior person should set out to criticize gentlemen in retirement, though he might hope to avoid difficulties, he will never succeed. His efforts wil! serve only to make clear how ignorant he is of circumstances and the way they shift, and the extent to which in the end he has mistaken the true nature of the Way!" [24]

Tung-fang Shuo also composed the "Discussion on Mr. Nobody." It went as follows:

Mr. Nobody held office in the state of Wu. But when he entered the presence of the ruler, he did not laud the ways of antiquity in order to waken his master's ambitions; and when he retired from court he seemed incapable of praising his lord's good points and publicizing his accomplishment. Instead, he went along silent and unspeaking for three years. The king of Wu, thinking this strange,

[23] There is a certain irony in these examples of "successful" men. Yüeh Yi, a native of Chao, was employed by the king of Yen to launch an attack on Ch'i in 284 B.C. He almost succeeded in conquering all of Ch'i, but later fell out of favor and was dismissed. Li Ssu likewise, though he rose to become prime minister to the First Emperor of the Ch'in, lost power after the emperor's death and was executed in 208 B.C. Li I-chi, acting as envoy from Kao-tsu, in 204 B.C. persuaded the ruler of Ch'i to come over to the side of the Han, but he was shortly afterwards accused of treachery and was boiled alive.

[24] Commentators are divided as to whether the "stupid, inferior person" is Shuo's modest way of referring to himself, or an epithet for his opponent. The latter seems the more likely interpretation.

questioned him, saying, "Thanks to the merit of my ancestors, I find myself placed in a position at the head of this multitude of worthy men. I rise early and retire late, never daring to be remiss in my efforts. Now you, sir, soaring swiftly on high, have come from far away and alighted in this land of Wu, presumably to repair deficiencies in my rule. Truly I congratulate myself on such an undeserved honor. My limbs find no rest on their mat, at meals I do not savor my food; my eyes behold no rich or seductive beauties, my ears do not listen to the tones of bell or drum. Instead, I have emptied my head and steadied my will, hoping to hear some scrap of wise counsel—it has been three years now! Yet, sir, when you come before me you do nothing to repair shortcomings in government, and when you retire you do not spread abroad your lord's reputation. If I may say so, such conduct is not to your advantage. If you harbor talents in your breast but fail to display them, this shows a lack of devotion in you as a minister. And if you display them but they are given no outlet in action, this bespeaks a lack of enlightenment in me as a ruler. Are we to assume, then, that I am indeed such an unenlightened ruler?"

"Just as you say, just as you say!" said Mr. Nobody, prostrating himself.

"You may explain yourself, then," said the king of Wu, "and I will pay strict attention and see what I think of your explanation."

"Alas," said Mr. Nobody. "I may explain, I may explain, you say? But how could it be easy to give an explanation? When it comes to explanations, there are those that are trying to the eye, offensive to the ear, vexing to the mind, and yet beneficial to the body. And then there are those that are attractive to the eye, ingratiating to the ear, stimulating to the mind, and yet ruinous to the conduct. If one is not a truly enlightened and sage-like ruler, how will he be able to tell the difference?"

"Why do you say that?" said the king of Wu. "'Those whose talents are above mediocrity may be told of the highest things.' [25] You just try telling me and I will listen the best way I know how."

"Long ago," replied Mr. Nobody, "Kuan Lung-feng severely reprimanded his sovereign Chieh, and Prince Pi Kan spoke up frankly to his ruler Chou. Both these two ministers, straining their faculties and evincing the utmost loyalty, grieved that the blessings of the ruler did not flow down to those below and that the ten

[25] *Analects* XI, 19.

thousand people were restive and defiant. Therefore they spoke out frankly of their rulers' faults, reprimanding them for their misdoings, hoping thereby to bring glory to their lords and to shield them from disaster.

"But now the situation is quite different. If one behaved as they did, he would on the contrary be regarded as slandering and maligning his lord's conduct, as lacking the etiquette proper to a minister. In the end a storm of injuries would be forced upon him, disgrace would extend even to his forebears, and he would become the laughing stock of the world. Therefore I say, how can it be an easy matter to give explanations?

"This, then, is the reason that ministers who might aid and assist you fall away like broken tiles, while vicious and sycophantic men crowd forward side by side, and in the end you will be faced with a Fei Lien or an E Lai-ko! [26] These two men both resorted to lies and deceits, clever words and facile arguments to advance themselves in favor. On the sly they supplied their ruler with the rarest of carved and inlaid objects in order to win his heart; they strove to gladden the desires of ear and eye, acceptance at any price their only goal. In the end, pursuing their course without taking warning, they fell victim to punishment and execution, the ancestral temples were overturned and destroyed, and the nation was reduced to a wasteland. To banish and slaughter worthy ministers and instead surround oneself with slanderers—is this not what the *Odes* means when it says:

> Slandering men know no limits;
> Together they bring confusion to the lands of the four quarters! [27]

Thus it is that those who humble themselves and assume a lowly posture, who put on pleasing looks and speak in subtle phrases, softly smiling, meekly murmuring, in the end are of no help to the ruler in his government. Hence no gentleman of principle or benevolent man could ever bring himself to act in this way.

"But if one solemnly puts on his sternest countenance and speaks out in bold and cutting reprimand, hoping to rid the sovereign of evil and dispel harm from the common people, then he runs the risk of enraging an evil ruler's heart and falling afoul of the laws of a decadent age. Therefore those gentlemen who are intent upon

[26] Both were evil ministers to Chou, the last ruler of the Shang dynasty, and helped to bring about his downfall.

[27] Mao #219.

nourishing life and longevity are never willing to come forward. They end up instead dwelling among the deep mountains, heaping earth to build their huts, planting raspberry vines for a door, strumming a lute in the midst of it all and singing the airs of the ancient kings. This way they are able to enjoy themselves and forget about death. So it is that Po Yi and Shu Ch'i fled the Chou regime and starved to death at the foot of Shou-yang Mountain, and later ages have praised them for their benevolence. As we can see from this, the actions of an evil ruler are truly to be feared. Therefore I say, how can it be an easy thing to give explanations?"

With this the king of Wu's face took on a look of alarm. Moving off his mat and brushing the arm-rest aside, he sat up very straight and listened.

Mr. Nobody continued, "Chieh Yü shunned the world, Chi Tzu let down his hair and feigned madness. Both fled from a muddy age in order to save their skins. But if they had met up with an enlightened king, a sage ruler; if they had been granted a moment of their lord's leisure, a benign and sympathetic glance, so that they might exert their efforts and demonstrate their loyalty in planning for the safety of the state, weighing and calculating its best interests, above insuring rest to the ruler's person, below bringing benefit to the ten thousand people, then the ideals of the Five Emperors and the Three Dynasties might have been realized once more! Yi Yin took on the humble duties of a cook, bearing caldron and cutting board and blending the five flavors in order to attract the attention of King T'ang; T'ai-kung fished on the sunny side of the Wei in order to gain an interview with King Wen; ruler and minister found hearts in agreement, minds alike, so that none of the ministers' plans failed to win success, none of their strategies were left untried. Truly they encountered the lords they deserved.

"To ponder deeply and plan far ahead, enlisting righteousness to help him rectify himself, extending kindness to ease the lot of those below him; to make benevolence his root and righteousness his ancestor, praising the possessors of virtue, enriching worth and ability, punishing evil and disorder, drawing together the distant regions, unifying his laws and precedents, beautifying his ways and customs—this is the way for an emperor or a king to gain glory. If on the higher plane he does not pervert the nature of Heaven, nor on the lower rob men of their proper relationships, then Heaven and earth will attain peace and harmony, far off lands will turn to him in longing, and he will earn the epithet of sage king.

"When the ministers to such a ruler have likewise fulfilled their duties, then domains are carved out and fiefs assigned to them. They are ennobled as dukes and marquises, their states pass down to their sons and grandsons, their names are well known to later ages, and people to the present day remember them. Yi Yin and T'ai-kung, because they were lucky enough to meet up with kings T'ang and Wen, were able to achieve this. Yet Kuan Lung-feng and Pi Kan alone suffered the fate we have seen—can one help pitying them? Therefore I say, how can it be an easy thing to give explanations?"

The king of Wu fell silent, his head bowed in deep thought. Then he looked up, the streams of tears coursing down his cheeks. "To think my state was on the verge of perishing!" he said. "Its fate hung by a thread, a tiny filament, its generations all but cut off!"

Then he set about holding audience in his Bright Hall, fixing the proper position of lord and minister. He promoted worth and talent, spread virtue and charity abroad, practiced benevolence and righteousness, and rewarded men of merit. He set a personal example of prudence and frugality, reducing the expenditures of his harem, cutting costs on horse and carriage, banning the licentious music of Cheng, putting flatterers far from himself. He had his kitchens more simply run, eliminating waste and luxury; he settled for humbler halls and palaces, abandoned his parks and gardens, filled in the lakes and moats, giving what was saved to those who were poor and without livelihood. He threw open his inner treasuries, succoring the poor and destitute, rescuing the aged, pitying the orphaned and lonely. He lightened the burden of taxes and levies, reduced fines and punishments, and when he had done this for three years, the entire region within the four seas was at peace. The world enjoyed a profound harmony, yin and yang were balanced and in accord, and all the ten thousand things found their proper place. The nation was free of the kind of change that brings harm and disaster, the people no longer wore the look of hunger and cold. Families had a sufficiency, men were well supplied, and stores and provisions piled up to overflowing. The jails stood empty and deserted, while phoenixes gathered about and unicorns were seen in the fields beyond the city. Sweet dew no sooner fell than red auspicious grasses began to sprout. Men of distant regions and strange customs, drawn to such ways, thirsting for righteousness, came to offer what services they were capable of and to pay homage at his court.

The way leading to order or disorder, the signs of survival or destruction, are as easy as this to discern. Yet those who act as the rulers of men are unwilling to do anything about them. May I venture to say I think this is a mistake? This is what the *Odes* means when it says:

> The kingdom was able to breed them,
> They are the very pillars of Chou.
> Stately, stately are these many gentlemen;
> To King Wen they bring repose.[28]

Of Tung-fang Shuo's writings, these two pieces quoted above are the finest. In addition, there is his "Feng Sacrifice on Mount T'ai" and "The Blame for Mr. Ho's Jade," along with the "Thanksgiving on the Birth of an Imperial Prince," [29] "The Screen," "The Cypress Pillars of the Palace," "The Tower of Peaceful Joy," "The *Fu* on the Hunt," eight-character and seven-character poetry in two sections, and "Borrowing a Carriage from Kung-sun Hung." All the writings which Liu Hsiang lists in his bibliography under Tung-fang Shuo's name are genuine, but the other pieces that are passed around these days are completely spurious.[30]

In appraisal we say: Liu Hsiang said that when he was young he several times questioned elder men of good character who had a knowledge of such affairs and who had been living at the same time as Tung-fang Shuo, and they all told him that Shuo was deft in speech and knew how to play the clown, but that he was incapable of sustaining an argument. He loved to make speeches for the benefit of mediocre men, and that is why in later generations there are so many stories handed around about him.

Yang Hsiung also has said that he "does not consider Shuo's words to be entirely worthy of imitation, nor his actions entirely exemplary. The manners attributed to him and writings that have been handed down are rather trivial. However, the fact that Shuo's reputation is greater than he really deserves is due to his masterly

---

[28] Mao #235.

[29] Presumably the piece composed to celebrate the birth of Emperor Wu's son by Empress Wei, the heir apparent Li; see page 46.

[30] The bibliography referred to is the *Ch'i-lüeh* or "Seven Summaries" by Liu Hsiang and his son Liu Hsin, which formed the basis of the *Han shu's* "Treatise on Literature."

wit and his many devices—it is not a reputation based upon one type of action alone. In the aptness of his replies he resembles a professional entertainer. His inexhaustible wit resembles wisdom, his frank remonstrances have the look of candor, his untidy ways are like those of a recluse.[31] He criticized Po Yi and Shu Ch'i and applauded Hui of Liu-hsia.[32] He cautioned his son that getting by is the most important thing. To starve on Shou-yang Mountain like Po Yi and Shu Ch'i he considered stupid, to serve like Lao Tzu as a 'clerk-at-the-foot-of-the-pillar' in the palace he considered clever.[33] 'Eat your fill, walk in safety, work for the government instead of down on the farm, stay in the shade and make sport of the world, be wary of the times and don't get caught,' he said. Was he not the chief of wits and wags?" [34]

Shuo's jokes and sallies, his divinations and guesses, shallow and inconsequential though they are, were passed around among the ordinary run of people, and there was no stripling or cowherd who failed to be quite dazzled by them. In later times, men who fancy such matters have invented all sorts of odd sayings and outlandish tales and attached Shuo's name to them. That is the reason I have written of him in such detail.

[31] Commentators cite the piece of meat carried home in the breast of his robe and the pissing in the palace as examples of Shuo's "untidy ways."

[32] Hui of Liu-hsia was a man of Lu who, unlike the fastidious recluses Po Yi and Shu Ch'i, did not hesitate to take government office even in troubled times.

[33] Lao Tzu, far from retiring to the wilderness, is supposed to have held office at the Chou court. He is thus, like Shuo, an example of a man who knows how to "get by" in the world rather than fleeing from it.

[34] The passage is quoted from *Fa yen*, ch. 8, by Yang Hsiung (53 B.C.–A.D. 18).

Yang Wang-sun, Hu Chien, Chu Yün, Mei Fu, and Yün Ch'ang

YANG WANG-SUN INSISTED upon being buried naked, Hu Chien cut down a general, Chu Yün accused Chang Yü in the very presence of the court, and Mei Fu indirectly criticized the conduct of Wang Feng. They may be said to have been somewhat too impassioned and stubborn; Yün Ch'ang came nearer to the middle way. So I have transmitted the Biographies of Yang Wang-sun, Hu Chien, Chu Yün, Mei Fu, and Yün Ch'ang.

YANG WANG-SUN

Yang Wang-sun lived in the time of Emperor Wu and studied the arts of the Yellow Emperor and Lao Tzu [Taoism]. With his family fortune of a thousand measures of gold he provided for himself very generously, and there was no food or drug calculated to prolong life that he did not procure. Eventually, however, he fell ill and when he was on the point of death, he gave orders to his son, saying, "I want you to bury me naked so that I may return to my true home. You must not go against my wishes! When I am dead, put my corpse in a hemp bag, dig a hole in the ground seven feet deep, and lower me into it. Then take hold of the bag at the end where my feet are and pull it off so that my body will rest directly on the ground."

The son thought perhaps it would be best merely to remain si-

lent and ignore these instructions, yet he hated to disobey his father's order. On the other hand, he felt he could never bring himself to carry out such a procedure. In the end he went to visit his
father's friend the marquis of Ch'i, and the marquis wrote a letter
to Yang Wang-sun saying:

"Though I had heard of your grave illness, I was obliged to accompany the emperor to the sacrifices at Yung and therefore have
not yet had an opportunity to call on you. I hope, however, that
you will keep up your spirits, set aside all worries, do as the doctor
prescribes, and take good care of yourself. I have heard some talk
of you leaving orders to be buried naked. If the dead have no consciousness, then that will be the end of the matter. But if they do,
I'm afraid you will be subjecting your corpse to humiliation in the
world below. Do you intend to appear naked in front of your
ancestors? Personally I don't think you are the kind who would do
such a thing. Moreover, the *Classic of Filial Piety* says: 'Let
clothes, coverlets, and inner and outer coffins be provided for the
dead,' and these after all represent the rules handed down from the
sages. Why must you alone be different and insist upon following
some private procedure of your own? I hope you will give careful
thought to the matter."

Yang Wang-sun replied as follows:

"I have heard that, because human nature will not allow a man
simply to cast his parents aside when they die, the sage kings in
ancient times devised certain rules and rituals for their burial. But
people nowadays far overstep the rules and that is why I want to
be buried naked—so that I may reform the times.

"A lavish burial is of absolutely no benefit to the dead man, and
yet foolish people strive to outdo each other in extravagance, wast-
ing their money, exhausting their resources, putting it all into the
ground to rot. In some cases they bury it today only to have it dug
up tomorrow, so that the result is the same as if they had left the
corpse lying out in the open fields.

"Now death is the transformation that comes at the end of life,
the final return of all things. That which returns reaches its goal,
that which is transformed undergoes a change. Thus each thing returns to its true home, its true home in blackest darkness, where
there is neither form nor sound. Then it may achieve union with
the essense of the Way. Outward decoration may dazzle the mob,
but lavish burial erects a barrier to truth, for it prevents that
which is returning from reaching its goal, prevents that which is to

be transformed from undergoing change. In doing so, it makes it impossible for each thing to find its proper place.

"I have heard that the spirit belongs to Heaven and the bodily form belongs to earth. After the spirit has left the form, then each returns to its true home. Therefore the spirits of the dead are called *kuei*, which is to say that they have 'returned' (*kuei*). As for the body, it lies there all alone like a clod—how could it possibly have consciousness? You may swathe it in silks, enclose it in inner and outer coffins, truss up its limbs, and stuff its mouth with pieces of jade, hoping to prevent it from undergoing change, but in the musty darkness it will shrivel and dry up, and after a thousand years, when the coffins have decayed and rotted away, it will at last return to the earth and find its way to its true home. And if this is the end of its journey, why must it be made to spend so much time as a traveler along the way?

"In ancient times when the sage ruler Yao conducted his burials, he hollowed out a piece of wood for a casket, tied it shut with strands of kudzu vine, and dug a grave deep enough so that the foul odor would not leak out above ground but not so deep as to disturb the underground springs. Therefore the sage kings were easy to serve while they were alive and easy to bury when they died, for they did not expend effort on useless activities or throw away wealth in ways that bring no profit. To spend money on a lavish burial is to delay the return of the body, to prevent it from reaching its goal. The dead man has no consciousness of such expenditures, the living gain nothing by them—hence they represent a double delusion. Alas, you will never persuade me to follow such ways!"

"Very well," said the marquis of Ch'i, and in the end Yang Wang-sun was buried naked.

HU CHIEN

Hu Chien, whose polite name was Tzu-meng, was a native of Ho-tung. During the *t'ien-han* era (100–97 B.C.) of Emperor Wu's reign, he was provisionally appointed as aide to the inspector of the garrisons guarding the capital. He was too poor to afford a horse or carriage but constantly went about on foot, living like a common soldier of the lowest rank. In this way he comforted and encouraged the soldiers under him, and they in turn were intensely loyal to him.

At this time the clerk of the censorate who had been appointed as superintendent of the garrison was engaged in underhanded activities, cutting a hole in the wall surrounding the northern garrison and setting up a small store. Hu Chien decided to punish him and therefore called his soldiers together and made them take an oath, saying, "When I tell you to arrest someone, arrest him, and when I tell you to cut someone down, cut him down!"

When the day came around for inspection of men and horses, the superintendent of the garrison took his seat on the reviewing platform along with the various company commanders attached to the garrison. Hu Chien, followed by his band of soldiers, hurried forward to the foot of the platform and bowed in salute. Then he ascended the platform, his men all accompanying him, pointed to the superintendent of the garrison, and said, "Arrest this man!" The soldiers stepped forward and dragged the superintendent from the platform. "Cut him down!" ordered Hu Chien, and they summarily executed the superintendent.

The company commanders of the garrison, being ignorant of the reasons for such action, were thrown into a state of complete bewilderment, but Hu Chien produced from the breast of his robe a memorial to the throne which he had prepared in advance and forthwith submitted it. The memorial read:

"I have heard that according to the rules of the army, one should make a display of military force in order to inspire awe, and one should punish evildoers in order to prevent malefaction. Now the clerk of the censorate superintending the garrison has brazenly cut a hole in the garrison wall in order to seek commercial gain, privately buying and selling goods and carrying on business transactions with the people. He has shown no evidence of a firm and stalwart heart, of a brave and passionate sense of honor, and lacks the qualities that would entitle him to be a leader of officers and gentlemen. If he were turned over to the civil officials for trial, his case might not be regarded as a very serious one, but the *Yellow Emperor's Rules of the Adjudicator* [1] states, 'Once the walls and battlements of the camp have been fixed, anyone who pierces or cuts through them instead of going by way of the gate shall be regarded as an offender, and offenders shall be put to death.' I would venture to point out that, according to the rules governing the garrison, 'The inspector of the garrison is not subject to the authority of the general. If the general is guilty of a crime, the

---

[1] A work on military affairs, like the *Rules of the Marshal* mentioned below.

inspector shall report it to the authorities, and if any of his subordinate commanders of the two thousand picul rank or lower is guilty, the inspector shall himself administer punishment.' As aide to the inspector, I am in some doubt as to how the law should be administered, but since I did not feel I should trouble the higher authorities with every case that arises, I have respectfully executed the offender. Braving death, I make this report."

The emperor responded with an edict that read:

"The *Rules of the Marshal* states, 'The procedures of civil government shall not be applied to the army, and the procedures of the army shall not be applied to the civil government.' Why would there be any reason to refer the case to the civil officials? The kings of the Three Dynasties of ancient times sometimes took the oath of battle in the midst of the army, hoping that the people would first of all decide what strategy they would follow. Sometimes they took the oath outside the gate of the army, hoping that the people would first of all steel their spirits and in that frame of mind await the action to follow. And sometimes they took the oath just before going into battle to cross swords with the enemy, in this way strengthening the determination of the people.[2] Why should you have any doubts about what you have done?"

As a result of this incident, Hu Chien's name became well known. Later he was appointed magistrate of the district of Wei-ch'eng in the capital area and was widely praised for the way he managed administrative affairs. At this time Emperor Chao was still very young, and the father of his empress, General Shang-kuan An, was very friendly with Ting Wai-jen, a secret lover of Princess Kai, Emperor Chao's eldest sister. Ting Wai-jen was very arrogant and unruly and, bearing a grudge against the former prefect of the capital Fan Fu, he dispatched one of his retainers to shoot and kill Fan Fu. The assassin then went into hiding in the home of Princess Kai where the law officials could not get at him. Hu Chien, the magistrate of the district of Wei-ch'eng in which the princess's house was located, led his officials and soldiers and surrounded the house, demanding the man's arrest. When the princess was informed of this, she, Ting Wai-jen, and General Shang-kuan An, accompanied by a large body of slaves and retainers, fled from the house, shooting as they went along at the law officials who pursued them, until the officials were obliged to scatter and run.

---

[2] I fail to see how these latter remarks, which are also based on a passage in the *Rules of the Marshal*, apply to Hu Chien's case.

The princess then had her archery captain submit a letter of complaint against the magistrate of Wei-ch'eng, claiming that his patrols had inflicted injury on some of the slaves in her household. Hu Chien replied to the charges by stating that his men had merely been carrying out their duties and were guilty of no offense.

The princess, enraged, then had someone submit a memorial to the throne accusing Hu Chien of insulting and mistreating an imperial princess, the eldest daughter of Emperor Wu, and shooting arrows into the gate of her mansion. The memorial further claimed that, though Hu Chien was fully aware that his law officials had inflicted injury on the princess's slaves, he was attempting to put people off with excuses and deliberately refusing to make a thorough investigation of the affair. The general in chief Ho Kuang intercepted the memorial and put it aside before it could reach the emperor, but later, when Ho Kuang fell ill and his duties were taken over by Shang-kuan An's father, Shang-kuan Chieh, the matter was referred to the law officials for action and Hu Chien was arrested. Hu Chien committed suicide. The officials and people of the area, insisting that Hu Chien had been the victim of injustice, set up a shrine to him in Wei-ch'eng which is still in existence today.

CHU YÜN

Chu Yün, whose polite name was Yu, was born in Lu but moved to P'ing-ling.[3] In his youth he was friendly with lawless knights and would assist them in carrying out private vengeance. He was over eight feet tall, with a very impressive face and bearing, and famed for his strength and daring. When he reached the age of forty he eventually reformed and turned to virtuous ways, studying under the erudit Po Tzu-yu and receiving instruction in the *Book of Changes* from him. He also studied with the general of the vanguard Hsiao Wang-chih, receiving instruction in the *Analects*. Both men considered him fully qualified to hand down their teachings. He liked to behave in a very lofty and imperturbable manner, car-

[3] P'ing-ling, in the suburbs of Ch'ang-an, was the site of Emperor Chao's mausoleum. Families were often forcibly moved from the provinces in order to populate these newly founded mausoleum towns, and this may have been the case with Chu Yün.

ing only for the larger concerns of honor, and for this the people of the time admired him greatly.

During the reign of Emperor Yüan (48–33 B.C.), Kung Yü of Lang-ya served as imperial secretary. At this time a certain man named Chia, who was temporarily acting as aide to the magistrate of Hua-yin, submitted a sealed letter to the throne which stated: "The way to good government lies in selecting worthy men. The man who occupies the post of imperial secretary acts as assistant to the chancellor and superior to the nine high ministers and it is therefore important to select the proper person for the post. Chu Yün of P'ing-ling is qualified to handle both civil and military affairs, a loyal and upright man endowed with wisdom and resourcefulness. It would be well to raise him to the six hundred picul rank and try him out temporarily in the post of imperial secretary, where he may have an opportunity to show the extent of his ability."

The emperor referred the matter to his ministers, asking for their advice. The lesser tutor to the heir apparent K'uang Heng replied as follows: "The chief officials are the arms and legs of the nation, men whom the myriad commoners look up to with awe and whom the enlightened sovereign chooses with care. An old text says, 'If inferiors look lightly on those of high rank and mean men lay schemes to control the positions of power, then the state will seethe with agitation and the common people will know no rest.' [4] Now this Chia, who is only an acting aide to a magistrate, is scheming to control the post of a high official, proposing to take a petty commoner, the kind of man who goes about on foot, and promote him over the heads of the nine high ministers. This is no way to show concern for the nation and bring honor to the altars of the soil and grain. In ancient times when Emperor Yao promoted Shun to office and King Wen promoted T'ai-kung, they first tried these men out before actually assigning them a rank—how much more, then, should this be the case with Chu Yün! Chu Yün was originally noted for his love of daring, a man who has frequently broken the law and fled into hiding. Since receiving instruction in the *Changes* he has taken on some of the manners of a schoolmaster, but there is still nothing particularly distinguished about his conduct. The present imperial secretary Kung Yü, on the other hand, is a man of impeccable principles and absolute honesty, thoroughly

---

[4] The source of the quotation is unknown.

versed in the teachings of the Classics, a match for such ancient paragons of virtue as Po Yi and Shih Yü—there is no one within the four seas who does not know of his reputation. And yet this man Chia bestows extravagant praise on Chu Yün, insisting that he should be made imperial secretary. Behind such wild praise and recommendation I fear there may be sinister designs that should not be left to flourish unchecked. It would be well to refer the matter to the authorities for investigation so that they may determine the right and wrong of it."

In the end charges were brought against Chia for his part in the affair.

At this time the privy treasurer Wu-lu Ch'ung-tsung enjoyed great favor with the emperor, being an expert in the Liang-ch'iu interpretation of the *Book of Changes*.[5] From the time of Emperor Hsüan the Liang-ch'iu school had enjoyed considerable popularity, and Emperor Yüan in particular favored it. Wishing to determine how its interpretations differed from those of other schools, Emperor Yüan ordered Wu-lu Ch'ung-tsung to hold a debate with representatives of the various schools of the *Changes*. Since Wu-lu Ch'ung-tsung enjoyed a position of special favor and was a very eloquent speaker, the other Confucian scholars decided they were no match for him; instead they all pleaded illness, none having courage enough to attend the meeting. Someone then recommended Chu Yün and the emperor had him summoned to the palace. Straightening the hems of his robe, he ascended the hall, lifted up his head, and boomed out his questions in a voice that shook the onlookers. When the two men turned to a debate of difficult points, Chu Yün time and again refuted Master Wu-lu's arguments, and as a result the Confucian scholars made up a saying that went:

> Dandy antlers had Wu-lu (Five Deer)
> But Chu Yün broke them all in two!

Because of his performance, Chu Yün was made an erudit, and later was transferred to the post of magistrate of Tu-ling. He was accused of deliberately allowing fugitives from justice to escape, but just at that time a general amnesty was proclaimed and the

---

[5] The interpretation of the *I Ching* or *Book of Changes* expounded by Liang-ch'iu Ho, a scholar of the time of Emperor Hsüan.

charges were dropped. Instead he was chosen as a man of honesty and uprightness and was made magistrate of Huai-li.

At this time the eunuch Shih Hsien, who was chief of palace writers, exercised great influence in the government, and Wu-lu Ch'ung-tsung was a member of his group. All the men who held public office stood in awe of him; only Ch'en Hsien, the middle aide to the imperial secretary, though a relatively young man, dared to stand up against him, refusing to ally himself with Shih Hsien and his group and instead forming close ties with Chu Yün. Chu Yün several times submitted memorials to the throne claiming that the chancellor Wei Hsüan-ch'eng was concerned only in looking out for himself and preserving his position and had nothing to contribute to the good of the state. Ch'en Hsien in like manner frequently voiced criticisms of Shih Hsien.

Some time later, the authorities began investigating Chu Yün on the suspicion of having indirectly incited one of his officials to commit murder. When the various ministers were attending audience in the palace, the emperor asked the chancellor Wei Hsüan-ch'eng what he thought of Chu Yün's performance as an administrator. Wei Hsüan-ch'eng replied that Chu Yün was a violent and tyrannical man who had achieved nothing of worth. Ch'en Hsien, who was present at the time, overheard his remark and reported it to Chu Yün. Chu Yün then decided to submit a letter to the throne arguing in his own defense. Ch'en Hsien prepared the rough draft of the letter, in it requesting that the matter be referred to the middle aide to the imperial secretary—that is, to himself—for action. When the letter was submitted, however, the matter was referred instead to the chancellor, whose assistants conducted an investigation and summarily produced evidence to support the charge that Chu Yün had incited murder. Chu Yün fled into hiding in Ch'ang-an and once more consulted with Ch'en Hsien as to how best to proceed.

The chancellor learned of this and brought the entire matter to light, submitting a report to the emperor saying: "Ch'en Hsien, a member of the palace guard and an official charged with the administration of the law, having graciously been permitted to enter the imperial presence, has let word leak out of what he heard there, secretly reporting the proceedings to Chu Yün. He prepared the draft of a memorial for Chu Yün, hoping that the matter would be referred back to himself for action. Later, when he learned that

Chu Yün was a criminal in hiding from the law, he continued to have communication with him, and it is for this reason that the officials were unable to find Chu Yü and arrest him."

The emperor thereupon had Ch'en Hsien and Chu Yün sent to prison. They were spared the death penalty and instead were sentenced to convict labor building and repairing walls. During the remainder of Emperor Yüan's reign they remained out of office, being barred from public service.

Later, in the time of Emperor Ch'eng (32–7 B.C.), the former chancellor Chang Yü, the marquis of An-ch'ang, because he was the emperor's teacher, was given special promotion to office and treated with great respect and honor. Chu Yün submitted a letter requesting an audience with the emperor, and when it was granted and he stood in the presence of the ruler and the high ministers, he said, "The chief officials in the court today are incapable of correcting the faults of the sovereign above or of bringing benefit to the common people below. All they do is hold on to their posts and draw their pay for nothing. That is why Confucius said that it is impossible to serve one's ruler in company with worthless fellows—if they think there is a danger they will lose their positions, there is nothing they will not hesitate to do![6] I hope you will instruct your master of implements to lend me his 'sword sharp enough to cut a horse in two' so that I may strike down one of these mealymouthed ministers and let that serve as a warning to the rest!"

When the emperor asked who it was he had in mind, Chu Yün replied, "Chang Yü, the marquis of An-ch'ang!"

The emperor was outraged. "A petty official at the bottom of the ranks slandering his superiors and insulting the imperial tutor in the presence of the court—you won't escape the death penalty for this!" he cried.

The clerks of the censorate tried to hurry Chu Yün out of the hall but he held on to the railing of the steps until it broke, shouting, "I'm perfectly content to go to the world below and consort with men like Kuan Lung-feng and Pi Kan—but I don't know what this will do to the reputation of our sacred dynasty!"[7]

When the clerks of the censorate had removed Chu Yün from the

[6] A paraphrase of *Analects* XVII, 13.

[7] Kuan Lung-feng and Pi Kan were virtuous ministers of ancient times who were put to death by their sovereigns for speaking out in frank remonstrance.

hall, the general of the left Hsin Ch'ing-chi doffed his cap, untied his seals of office, and struck his head on the floor at the foot of the throne, saying, "This man has always been known for his insane frankness. If what he says is right, he should not be punished, and even if what he says is wrong, it would surely be best to overlook it. I venture to risk death to plead on his behalf!" He continued to strike his head on the ground until the blood flowed, and finally the emperor's anger subsided and he let the matter rest.

Later, when preparations were being made to repair the railing, the emperor said, "Don't replace it—just put in something to close the gap and let it stand as a memorial to an outspoken minister!" [8]

After this, Chu Yün no longer held office but made his home in the countryside in Hu, from time to time climbing into an ox cart and going off to visit various scholars. Wherever he visited, he was treated with honor. When Hsüeh Hsüan became chancellor, Chu Yün went to call on him. Hsüeh Hsüan received him with all the ceremony due an honored guest and, having persuaded him to spend the night, remarked to him casually, "It must be rather quiet in the country. Why don't you stay a while in my eastern lodge—I can introduce you to the most unusual men in the whole empire."

"See here, young man," said Chu Yün, "are you trying to make me one of your officials?"

After that, Hsüeh Hsüan did not venture to say anything further.

In giving instruction, Chu Yün would choose carefully from among the various students before allowing any of them to become his disciple. Yen Wang of Chiu-chiang and his elder brother's son Yen Yüan, whose polite name was Chung, were considered qualified to hand on Chu Yün's teachings. Both became erudits, and Yen Wang advanced as high as the post of governor of T'ai-shan.

Chu Yün died at home at an age something over seventy. When he fell ill, he refused to send for a doctor or drink any medicine. He left instructions that he was to be buried in his ordinary clothes, in an inner coffin no larger than was necessary to contain the body. A grave was to be dug just big enough to hold the outer coffin, with a mound five *chang* in height erected over it. He was buried beyond the outer wall east of P'ing-ling.[9]

---

[8] It is said that in later ages palaces were fitted with a "broken railing;" i.e., a section of the railing was purposely left out in memory of this incident.

[9] I have at this point omitted the biography of Mei Fu, a scholar of the time of Emperor Ch'eng. The biography consists almost entirely of the texts of two long-winded memorials, one warning of the excessive power of Emperor

YÜN CH'ANG

Yün Ch'ang, whose polite name was Yu-ju, was a native of P'ing-ling. He studied under Wu Chang of the same district, an expert in the *Book of Documents* who became an erudit. When Emperor P'ing, who had previously held the title of king of Chung-shan, was summoned to the throne (A.D. 1), he was still very young and all power was in the hands of Wang Mang, who had bestowed upon himself the title An-han-kung, The Duke Who Brings Safety to the Han. Because Emperor P'ing was regarded as the heir of Emperor Ch'eng, he was not permitted to look after his own blood relatives, and his mother and the other members of the Wei clan were all obliged to remain in Chung-shan and were not permitted to come to the capital.

Wang Mang's eldest son Wang Yü disapproved of this attempt by his father to estrange the emperor from his maternal relatives of the Wei clan, fearing that when the emperor grew older he would bear a grudge against the Wang family because of it. Wang Yü joined with Wu Chang, Yün Ch'ang's teacher, in a plot whereby they would have the gate of Wang Mang's house smeared with blood, as though it were a warning from the ghosts and spirits, hoping in this way to frighten Wang Mang. Wu Chang would then submit an interpretation of the warning, tracing the blame to Wang Mang's treatment of the Wei family. The plot was discovered, however, and Wang Mang put his son Yü to death and wiped out the entire Wei clan. Over a hundred persons were executed because of their involvement in the plot. Wu Chang was tried and cut in two at the waist, after which his corpse was displayed at the gate to the eastern market.

Wu Chang, who was one of the most famous Confucian scholars of the time, had been very active in earlier days as a teacher and his disciples numbered over a thousand. Wang Mang, looking upon them as the followers of an evildoer, placed them all under a ban and would not permit them to hold public office. Meanwhile they had all ceased to acknowledge themselves as Wu Chang's disciples and used some other teacher's name instead. At this time Yün Ch'ang was a clerk in the office of the minister of education.

Ch'eng's maternal uncles of the Wang clan, particularly Wang Feng, the other urging the enfeoffment of Confucius' descendants. Pan Ku apparently regarded Mei Fu as an "outspoken minister" who belonged in the same category as Chu Yün.

Openly proclaiming himself a disciple of Wu Chang, he gathered up his teacher's body in his arms, carried it home, laid it in a coffin, and buried it. The people of the capital praised him for his action. The carriage and cavalry general Wang Shun, admiring such idealism and devotion to honor and comparing it to that of Lüan Pu,[10] submitted a memorial asking that Yün Ch'ang be made a clerk in the general's office and recommending him as a palace attendant and admonisher.

When Wang Mang usurped the throne, Wang Shun was made grand commandant and once again recommended Yün Ch'ang as a man who was capable of assisting the government, but Yün Ch'ang retired on grounds of illness. T'ang Lin then suggested that he would be suitable as administrator of a province and he was chosen to become governor of Lu. In the *keng-shih* era (A.D. 23–24) a comfortable carriage was sent to fetch him and he was summoned to the post of imperial secretary but he once more retired on grounds of illness. He died at his home.

In appraisal we say: Confucius has said that if one cannot find a man who is absolutely equitable in his behavior, it is best to look for one who is a little too impassioned or stubborn in his pursuit of the ideal.[11] Observing Yang Wang-sun's principles, one can see how much worthier a man he was than the First Emperor of the Ch'in! [12]

Nowadays when people talk about Chu Yün, many of them exaggerate the truth. There are those who write about things they know nothing of, though I am not one of them.[13]

Hu Chien was decisive in the face of the foe, making a display of military discipline for the world to see, striking down the evildoer and saving the army from corruption.

---

[10] A friend of P'eng Yüeh, who was enfeoffed as king of Liang by Emperor Kao-tsu, the founder of the Han. Later P'eng Yüeh was executed on charges of treason and his head exposed in Lo-yang. Lüan Pu defied Kao-tsu's orders by sacrificing and lamenting before his old friend's head, a deed for which he was much admired.

[11] A paraphrase of *Analects* XIII, 21.

[12] The First Emperor of the Ch'in was famous, among other things, for the amount of wealth and labor he expended on the building of his mausoleum; the historian, though he does not mention them, no doubt intends his censures to apply to the lavish burials of the Han rulers as well.

[13] The last remark is based on *Analects* VII, 28.

Mei Fu's words accord with the passage in the *Ta-ya* section of the *Odes:*

> Though the elders are no longer with us,
> Still we have their canons and laws.

The mirror of Yin was not far away, but was to be found in the affairs of the ruler of Hsia.[14] Later Mei Fu followed his desires and lived out his days at the gate of the market.[15]

Yün Ch'ang fulfilled his duty to Wu Chang in a way that was clear for all to see. He began by practicing benevolence himself and twice served as a clerk in the offices of the military. They say when the water is clear you should wash your hat strings—that's not far from what Yün Ch'ang did.[16]

---

[14] The passage is quoted and paraphrased from Mao #255; the Yin dynasty should have taken warning from the history of the preceding Hsia dynasty and avoided its mistakes. In similar fashion, Mei Fu warned the Han against repeating the mistakes of previous dynasties.

[15] When Wang Mang usurped the throne, Mei Fu abandoned his family and went off to Chiu-chiang where, according to legend, he became an immortal spirit. Men reported having seen him in K'uai-chi, in the region of Wu, where he had changed his name and was serving as a guard at the gate to the market place.

[16] *Ch'u Tz'u,* "The Fisherman:" "When the waters of the Ts'ang-lang are clear, I can wash my hat strings; when the waters of the Ts'ang-lang are muddy, I can wash my feet"—i.e., in times of good government one may hold public office, but in times of disorder one should retire. Here the reference is to the fact that Yün Ch'ang for the most part declined to hold office during the Wang Mang and *keng-shih* periods.

Ho Kuang and Chin Mi-ti

AUSTERE AND IMPOSING, Ho Kuang, the marquis of Po-lu, received the deathbed charge of Emperor Wu, protecting and nourishing Emperor Chao the Filial, guiding and raising him to eminence in keeping with his father's last command. When Emperor Chao passed away, Ho Kuang deposed the king of Ch'ang-i and set up Emperor Hsüan, his authority bringing stability to the altars of the soil and grain, his loyalty matching that of Yi Yin of old. But he was so greedy for gain, so addicted to favor, that gradually he turned to wicked ways, shielding his wife's foul deeds, and in the time of his sons, the family perished. Chin Mi-ti, the marquis of Tu, was the offspring of a barbarian, but he was reverent and respectful, loyal and trustworthy, and for many generations he and his family practiced virtue, even down to the time of his sons and grandsons. So I have transmitted the Biographies of Ho Kuang and Chin Mi-ti.

HO KUANG

Ho Kuang, whose polite name was Tzu-meng, was a younger brother of the general of swift cavalry Ho Ch'ü-ping. His father was Ho Chung-ju, a native of P'ing-yang in Ho-tung. As a clerk in the district office, Ho Chung-ju was assigned to service in the household of the marquis of P'ing-yang, where he carried on a clandestine affair with Wei Shao-erh, one of the maids, from which union Ho Ch'ü-ping was born. When Ho Chung-ju's term of service was ended, he returned home, married, and had a son named Ho Kuang. He had meanwhile ceased to maintain any contact with

Wei Shao-erh, and for a long time the two heard nothing of one another.

Shao-erh's younger sister Tzu-fu won favor with Emperor Wu and was made empress, and Ho Ch'ü-ping, as a son of the empress's elder sister, was treated with honor. When he grew to manhood, he learned for the first time that his father was Ho Chung-ju, but he made no attempt to contact him. Later, when he had been appointed general of swift cavalry, he had occasion to march against the Hsiung-nu, proceeding by way of Ho-tung. The governor of Ho-tung came out to the suburbs of the provincial capital to greet him, bearing a crossbow and arrows on his back and riding ahead of him as his herald. When Ho Ch'ü-ping reached the post station of P'ing-yang, he sent clerks to go and fetch Ho Chung-ju. Chung-ju hurried into the general's presence, bowing as to a superior, but Ch'ü-ping in turn greeted him with bows and, kneeling before him, said, "Sire, for a long time I did not know that I was your offspring."

Ho Chung-ju, crawling forward on his knees and striking his head on the ground, replied, "To think that your old servant may be allowed to entrust his remaining years to you, general—it is the work of Heaven!"

Ho Ch'ü-ping bought numerous lands, houses, and male and female servants for his father and then resumed his march. On his return from the campaign he stopped once more for a visit and then, taking his half brother Ho Kuang with him, proceeded west to Ch'ang-an. Ho Kuang was a little over ten at the time.

Ho Kuang was made a palace attendant and gradually advanced until he held a position among the attendants of the inner palace in charge of handling memorials. After Ho Ch'ü-ping died, Ho Kuang became chief commandant in charge of the imperial carriage and counselor to the keeper of the palace gate. Abroad he attended the emperor's carriage, within the palace he was constantly at the emperor's side, coming and going in the inner quarters of the palace for over twenty years. He was extremely cautious and circumspect, never once committing an error, and enjoyed a position of great intimacy and trust with the emperor.

In the second year of *cheng-ho* (91 B.C.), the heir apparent, the emperor's son by Empress Wei, was driven to his downfall by Chiang Ch'ung, and the emperor's other sons, Liu Tan, the king of Yen, and Liu Hsü, the king of Kuang-ling, were both guilty of numerous faults and shortcomings. By this time the emperor was well along in years and reserved all his favor for Lady Chao, the

Beautiful Companion of the Hook and Dart Palace. He had a son by her whom he wished to designate as his heir, intending to appoint one of the high ministers to assist the boy in governing. But when he looked over the various officials he found that only Ho Kuang could be entrusted with such a grave responsibility and counted on to protect the altars of the soil and grain. The emperor then had one of the painters of the Yellow Gate paint a picture of the Duke of Chou bearing on his back the infant King Ch'eng and receiving the feudal lords in audience, which he presented to Ho Kuang.[1]

In the spring of the second year of *hou-yüan* (87 B.C.), the emperor went on an outing to the Palace of Five Oaks, where he fell gravely ill. Ho Kuang, in tears, said, "If that which I dare not speak about should occur, who ought to be appointed as successor?"

The emperor replied, "Have you not yet perceived the meaning of the picture I gave you? I want my youngest son set up, with you to act the part of the Duke of Chou."

Ho Kuang bowed his head and begged to be excused, saying, "I would not be as good as Chin Mi-ti," but Chin Mi-ti in turn said, "I am a foreigner—Ho Kuang would be better!"

The emperor thereupon appointed Ho Kuang grand marshal general in chief, and appointed Chin Mi-ti general of carriage and cavalry; he also promoted the master of the carriage, Shang-kuan Chieh, to the position of general of the left, and promoted the chief commandant for requisitioning grain, Sang Hung-yang, to the position of imperial secretary. All bowed down at the foot of the bed in the inner chamber and received the emperor's dying command to assist the child successor.

The following day (March 29), Emperor Wu passed away and his heir succeeded to the position of highest honor, being known posthumously as Emperor Chao the Filial. He was eight years old at the time and all affairs of government were left to the sole decision of Ho Kuang.

Sometime earlier, during the *hou-yüan* era (88–87 B.C.), the archery captain of the inner palace attendants Ma[2] Ho-lo and his younger brother Ma T'ung, the marquis of Ch'ung-ho, had together plotted to rebel. At that time Ho Kuang joined with Chin Mi-ti, Shang-kuan Chieh, and the others in putting the brothers to death,

---

[1] King Ch'eng was an infant when his father King Wu, the founder of the Chou dynasty died. His uncle the Duke of Chou acted as regent for him until he grew to manhood.

[2] I follow Dubs in the romanization of this surname.

but they had as yet received no reward for their meritorious deed. When Emperor Wu fell ill, he prepared a letter sealed with the imperial seal and marked: "On the demise of the emperor, open this letter and carry out the instructions." In it was a testamentary edict enfeoffing Chin Mi-ti as marquis of Tu, Shang-kuah Chieh as marquis of An-yang, and Ho Kuang as marquis of Po-lu. All the enfeoffments were in recognition of the merit achieved earlier in apprehending the insurrectionists.

At this time Wang Hu, the son of the colonel of the guard Wang Mang, was an attendant in the inner palace and he began to spread word around, saying, "When the emperor was ill, I was constantly at his side. How could he have written a testamentary edict enfeoffing the three men? Those fellows are just handing out honors to each other!"

When Ho Kuang heard of this, he severely berated Wang Mang, who in turn forced his son to drink poison and die.

As a person, Ho Kuang was reserved and quiet and gave great attention to details. He was barely seven feet three inches tall,[3] pale in complexion, with wide-set eyes and eyebrows and beautiful whiskers and sideburns. Whenever he was going up and down the steps of the palace or in and out of the gate, he would always walk and halt his steps in exactly the same places each time.[4] The attendants and archery captains, observing him surreptitiously, made a mental note of the places and found that he never varied so much as a foot or an inch. This was the kind of passion for correctness and precision that marked his personality. When he began to act as assistant to the young ruler and all government decisions proceeded from him, the whole world watched with anticipation to see what his behavior would be like.

One night there was a suspicious occurrence in the palace and all the officials were in a state of alarm. Ho Kuang, fearing that something was afoot, summoned the palace attendant who had charge of the imperial credentials and seals and asked him to hand them over.[5] When the attendant refused to do so, Ho Kuang tried to snatch them away from him. The attendant, his hand on his sword, said, "You can have my head but you can't have the seals!"

Ho Kuang was much impressed with the attendant's devotion to

---

[3] A little over five feet.

[4] Presumably he halted to perform a bow or other ceremonial act.

[5] The sentence has been slightly expanded in the light of Yen Shih-ku's note and the parallel passage in the *Tzu-chih t'ung-chien*, ch. 22, end.

duty and the following day an imperial command was issued raising him two steps in rank. Everyone thought highly of Ho Kuang for this.

Ho Kuang and the general of the left Shang-kuan Chieh were related by marriage and on very intimate terms. Ho Kuang's eldest daughter was married to Shang-kuan Chieh's son Shang-kuan An, and the couple had a daughter who was of a suitable age to become a consort of the emperor. Shang-kuan Chieh, through the help of the emperor's elder sister Princess Kai of O-i, had the girl entered in the women's quarters of the palace with the rank of Beautiful Companion.[6] After a few months she was made empress and her father Shang-kuan An was appointed general of swift cavalry and enfeoffed as marquis of Sang-lo. Whenever Ho Kuang left the palace and went home for his hair-washing day, Shang-kuan Chieh would enter the palace and take charge of government affairs in his place.[7]

Both Shang-kuan Chieh and his son An thus enjoyed positions of great honor and felt much indebted to Princess Kai. The princess was far from correct in her private behavior, carrying on an affair with a man of Ho-chien named Ting Wai-jen. Shang-kuan Chieh and his son tried to procure a fief for Ting Wai-jen, arguing that it had been the custom in the past for the emperor to favor the spouses of princesses by making them marquises, but Ho Kuang refused to give his approval. They then asked that Ting Wai-jen be made a counselor to the keeper of the palace gate so that he could be summoned into the emperor's presence, but again Ho Kuang refused. Because of this, the princess came to hate Ho Kuang intensely, and Shang-kuan Chieh and his son, having failed repeatedly in their attempts to obtain a post or title for Ting Wai-jen, likewise felt humiliated.

Shang-kuan Chieh had from the time of the former emperor occupied a post among the nine highest ministers and in rank had been superior to Ho Kuang.[8] Later, both Chieh and his son An were made generals, and also enjoyed a position of honor because

---

[6] *Chieh-yü*, at this time the highest rank among the palace ladies.

[7] Every five days Han officials were allowed to leave court and return to their homes for a day. The holiday was known as the "bath and hair-washing" day.

[8] Under Emperor Wu, Shang-kuan Chieh had been master of carriage, one of the nine high ministers, while Ho Kuang had held the slightly inferior post of chief commandant in charge of the imperial carriage.

of the Pepper Room Palace, the emperor having grown very fond of Shang-kuan An's daughter.[9] Ho Kuang was only the grandfather of the empress on her mother's side, and yet he exercised sole authority in matters of government. The outcome of all this was that Shang-kuan became engaged in a struggle for power with Ho Kuang.

Liu Tan, the king of Yen, being the elder brother of Emperor Chao, harbored constant resentment at the way he had been treated. In addition, the imperial secretary Sang Hung-yang had worked to set up the government monopolies in wine, salt, and iron in order to benefit the state and, puffed up with pride by his achievements, had tried to obtain posts for his sons and younger brothers, though without success. He too felt great resentment toward Ho Kuang. Thereupon Princess Kai, Shang-kuan Chieh and his son An, and Sang Hung-yang all joined with Liu Tan, the king of Yen, in plotting deception. They arranged to have a man submit a letter to the throne in the name of the king of Yen reporting that when Ho Kuang went out to hold an inspection and drill of the palace attendants and the Feather and Forest Guard, he had runners to announce his coming and clear the road and sent the imperial butler ahead to prepare his quarters.[10] It also cited the case of Su Wu who had been sent as envoy to the Hsiung-nu and detained by them for twenty years, during which he refused to acknowledge sovereignty to them. When he returned home, he was given only the post of director of dependent states, while Yang Ch'ang, head secretary to the general in chief Ho Kuang, though he had done nothing to deserve the post, was appointed chief commandant for requisitioning grain. Finally, it asserted that Ho Kuang had increased the number of company commanders in his staff without asking permission and was exercising authority in such a willful and arbitrary manner as to raise the suspicion that he was plotting some drastic move. "I, your servant Tan," it ended, "therefore request that I be allowed to return the credentials and seal of the kingdom of Yen and be admitted as a member of the guard quar-

[9] The Pepper Room Palace, the residence of the empress, was so called because the walls were painted with crushed pepper to scent them.

[10] This would appear to contradict the account given in the biography of Liu Tan, p. 59. Apparently Liu Tan agreed to have the letter sent in his name but left the drafting of the contents to Shang-kuan Chieh and the others in the capital.

tered in the palace so that I may keep watch on the doings of villainous ministers!"

Shang-kuan Chieh waited until Ho Kuang was absent from the palace on his hair-washing day to have the letter presented to the emperor, hoping to use his authority in the palace to have the matter turned over to the officials immediately for action. Sang Hung-yang would then join with the other high ministers in seizing Ho Kuang and stripping him of authority.

But when the letter was submitted, the emperor refused to give permission to act on it. Early the following morning Ho Kuang, hearing of the matter, remained in the Hall of Paintings and did not enter the throne room.[11] The emperor asked where the general in chief was, whereupon the general of the left Shang-kuan Chieh replied, "The king of Yen has submitted a report of his offenses and for that reason he does not dare enter."

The emperor then ordered that the general in chief be summoned. When Ho Kuang entered the room, he removed his cap and bowed his head in apology. The emperor said, "Put on your cap, general! I know the letter is a fraud and that you are not guilty."

"How does Your Majesty know?" asked Ho Kuang.

"It was only a short while ago when you went to Kuang-ming to hold inspection of the palace attendants," replied the emperor, "and less than ten days have gone by since you transferred the company commanders to your staff. How could the king of Yen possibly have gotten word of such things? Moreover, if you were really plotting evil, it wouldn't matter to you whether you had a few more company commanders or not." At this time the emperor was only fourteen years old; the chief of palace writers and others who were in attendance were all amazed at the way he handled the matter.

The man who had submitted the letter, as might be expected, fled into hiding, but the emperor ordered that every effort be made to seize him. Shang-kuan Chieh and the others, alarmed, advised the emperor that it was a trifling affair that was not worth investigating further, but the emperor refused to listen to them. Later, when one of Shang-kuan Chieh's party spoke slanderously of Ho Kuang, the emperor flew into a rage. "The general in chief is a

---

[11] The hall, to the west of the throne room, was decorated with paintings of various famous rulers of antiquity.

loyal minister who was requested by the former emperor to assist me! Anyone who dares to speak ill of him will be charged as a criminal!"

From this time on, Shang-kuan Chieh and the others no longer ventured to speak out. Instead they devised a plot whereby Princess Kai was to set out wine and invite Ho Kuang to drink, whereupon soldiers lying in wait would attack and kill him. After that, they would depose the emperor and summon the king of Yen to take his place as Son of Heaven. The plot came to light and Ho Kuang had Shang-kuan Chieh, his son An, Sang Hung-yang, and Ting Wai-jen put to death along with the members of their families. The king of Yen and Princess Kai both committed suicide.

Ho Kuang's authority made all within the four seas tremble. Even after Emperor Chao had undergone his capping ceremony, he continued to leave all affairs in the hands of Ho Kuang, and in this way ended his thirteen years of rule. The common people enjoyed a life of abundance and the barbarians of the four quarters came as guests to pay allegiance to the Han.

In the first year of *yüan-p'ing* (74 B.C.), Emperor Chao passed away, leaving no heir. Of the six sons of Emperor Wu, only Liu Hsü, the king of Kuang-ling, was still alive, and when the court officials discussed the question of who should be made successor to the throne, they all favored the king of Kuang-ling. But the king had from times past been guilty of erroneous conduct, which was why Emperor Wu had never considered appointing him his heir, and Ho Kuang was very uneasy about the choice. At this point one of the palace attendants submitted a letter saying: "T'ai-wang of the Chou passed over his eldest son T'ai-po and made his youngest son Wang-chi his heir. King Wen put aside his eldest son Po-i K'ao and set up his younger son King Wu. It is simply a question of who is most suitable. There is no objection to setting aside an older person in favor of a younger one. The king of Kuang-ling is not the right man to carry on the service of the ancestral temples!"

The contents of the letter matched Ho Kuang's views exactly. He showed it to the chancellor Yang Ch'ang and had the palace attendant who had submitted it appointed governor of Chiu-chiang. The same day he received a command from the empress dowager [12] ordering the privy treasurer Shih Lo-ch'eng, who was

---

[12] The consort of Emperor Chao, daughter of Shang-kuan An and granddaughter of Ho Kuang on her mother's side; she was fourteen at the time.

acting for the director of foreign vassals, the director of the imperial clan Liu Te, the counselor to the keeper of the palace gate
Ping Chi, and the general of palace attendants Li-han to go and
fetch Liu Ho, the king of Ch'ang-i. Liu Ho was the grandson of
Emperor Wu, the son of the late King Ai of Ch'ang-i.

But after he had assumed the position of emperor, Liu Ho behaved in scandalous and disorderly fashion. Ho Kuang, deeply distressed, discussed the matter in private with the minister of agriculture T'ien Yen-nien, a close friend who had once been attached
to Ho Kuang's staff. T'ien Yen-nien said, "General, you are the pil-
lar and foundation stone of the state. If it appears to you that this
man will not do, why don't you propose to the empress dowager
that a more worthy person be selected and set up in his place?"

"That is just what I would like to do," replied Ho Kuang, "but
are there any precedents in antiquity for such an action?"

T'ien Yen-nien said, "When Yi Yin was prime minister of the Yin
dynasty, he deposed T'ai-chia in order to insure the safety of the
ancestral temples, and later ages have all praised him for his loyalty.[13] If you are able to carry this out, you will become the Yi Yin
of the Han!"

Ho Kuang recommended T'ien Yen-nien for the honorary rank
of steward of the palace. After meeting in secret with the general
of carriage and cavalry Chang An-shih to plan the course of
action, he summoned the chancellor, the imperial secretary, the
generals, marquises, officials of the middle two thousand picul
class, the counselors, and the erudits to come together for deliberation in the Eternal Palace. Ho Kuang announced, "The king of
Ch'ang-i behaves in a benighted and disorderly fashion and I fear
for the safety of the altars of the soil and grain! What is your
opinion?"

The various officials all turned pale in astonishment. No one
ventured to speak out, but all merely mumbled their agreement.
T'ien Yen-nien then stepped forward from his seat and, with his
hand on his sword, said, "The former emperor charged the general
in chief to look after his young heir, entrusting the fate of the em-

---

Until a new emperor was appointed, she was titular head of the state, though
she was of course acting under the direction of Ho Kuang.

[13] T'ai-chia, the traditional dates for whose reign are 1753–1721 B.C., was
the son of the founder of the Yin dynasty. He proved to be such an evil ruler
that after three years he was banished, Yi Yin taking over the direction of the
government. Later he reformed his ways and was called back to the throne.

pire to him, because he knew that the general was a loyal and worthy man who could be counted on to insure the safety of the Liu clan. Now the lower officials are seething with unrest like a boiling caldron and the altars of the soil and grain are in danger of being overthrown. It is the custom of the Han to assign the posthumous name of 'Filial' to its rulers because they have maintained possession of the empire down through the years and have seen to it that the blood of sacrifice is offered in the ancestral temples. Should you cause the sacrifices of the house of Han to be cut off, then when you die, general, how will you face the former emperor in the world below? Today's deliberations should not be prolonged an instant more. If any of the officials is tardy in voicing his agreement, I beg permission to cut him down with my sword!"

Ho Kuang apologized to the assembly, saying, "It is right for the high ministers to berate me. If the empire is filled with clamor and unrest, I am the one who should bear the blame."

Thereupon the members of the assembly all knocked their heads on the ground and said, "The fate of the ten thousand families rests with you, general. We will obey your order alone!"

Ho Kuang and the other officials all went in a group to see the empress dowager and report to her, explaining in detail the reasons why the king of Ch'ang-i was unfit to carry on the service of the ancestral temples. The empress dowager then ordered a carriage and went to the Hall of Inherited Brilliance in the Eternal Palace, where she issued an order that all the gates be closed and that the followers whom the king had brought with him from Ch'ang-i were not to be admitted.

The king had been to the empress dowager's palace to pay his morning visit and at the time was on his way back to the Eternal Palace, riding in a hand-drawn cart and nearing the Warm Hall. By this time there were eunuchs from the Yellow Gate of the inner palace manning the doors of all the gates. After the king had entered, the gate was closed so that the king's followers from Ch'ang-i could not enter. "What are you doing?" demanded the king, whereupon Ho Kuang knelt down before him and said, "The empress dowager has issued a command that your followers from Ch'ang-i are not to be admitted."

"You might go about it more slowly!" said the king. "There's no need to startle a person like this!"

Ho Kuang had the king's followers from Ch'ang-i driven completely out of the palace and assembled outside the Golden Horse

Gate. Then the general of carriage and cavalry Chang An-shih, leading the horsemen of the Feather and Forest Guard, seized and bound them, over two hundred persons, and had them taken off to the commandant of justice and the prison for persons under imperial indictment. Ho Kuang ordered the palace attendants and courtiers who had formerly been attached to Emperor Chao to keep watch on the king, warning them to guard the king carefully. "If in the confusion he should be killed or should commit suicide, I would be guilty of betraying the empire and would be branded as a regicide!" he said.

The king still did not realize that he was about to be deposed, but said to those about him, "What crime are my old followers and attendants guilty of that the general in chief should have them all arrested?" After a while, a command came from the empress dowager summoning the king. When he heard the summons, he began to grow uneasy and said, "What crime am I guilty of that I should be summoned?"

The empress dowager was wearing a pearl-sewn coat and splendid robes, and was seated within military style curtains of state, with several hundred attendants about her, all bearing weapons. The warriors of the Rendezvous Gate were drawn up in file outside of the hall, bearing lances and guarding the steps. The various officials in the order of their rank ascended the hall and then the king of Ch'angi-i was summoned and ordered to bow down before the empress dowager and listen to her command. Ho Kuang and the other officials presented to the empress dowager a memorial concerning the king, jointly signed by them all. The chief of palace writers read the memorial aloud:

"The chancellor Yang Ch'ang, the grand marshal general in chief Ho Kuang, the general of carriage and cavalry Chang An-shih, the general who crosses the Liao, Fan Ming-yu, the general of the vanguard Han Tseng, the general of the rear Chao Ch'ung-kuo, the imperial secretary Ts'ai Yi, the marquis of I-ch'un Wang T'an, the marquis of Tang-t'u Wei Sheng, the marquis of Sui-t'ao Chao Ch'ang-lo, the marquis of Tu T'u-ch'i-t'ang,[14] the master of carriage Tu Yen-nien, the master of ritual Su Ch'ang, the minister of agriculture T'ien Yen-nien, the director of the imperial clan Liu Te,

---

[14] A non-Chinese. In the original only the personal names of the persons are recorded, along with their titles and the words "your servant." To aid identification I have supplied the surnames where commentators have succeeded in ascertaining them, though some of the surnames cannot be determined.

the privy treasurer Shih Lo-ch'eng, the commandant of justice Li
Kuang, the chief of the capital police Li Yen-shou, the director of
foreign vassals Wei Hsien, the left prefect of the capital T'ien
Kuang-ming, the right prefect of the capital Chou Te, the privy
treasurer of the Palace of Lasting Trust Chia, the director of dependent states Su Wu, the chief commandant of the capital area
Chao Kuang-han, the subordinate commander in charge of convicts P'i-ping, the various officers, doctors of learning, and counselors to the keeper of the palace gate Wang Ch'ien, Sung Chi,
Ping Chi, Tz'u, Kuan, Sheng, Liang, Ch'ang-hsin, Hsia-hou Sheng,
and the palace counselors Te and Chao Ang, risking death, address
Her Majesty the empress dowager.

"Your servant Ch'ang and the others, bowing their heads and
preparing for the death penalty, opine that the Son of Heaven is
able to protect and sustain the ancestral temples and bring unity
to all within the four seas solely because he bases his conduct upon
mercy and filial piety, ritual and propriety, and a just apportion-
ment of rewards and punishments. Emperor Chao the Filial departed from the world at an early age, leaving no heir. Your servant
Ch'ang and the others debated the matter and, since ritual tells us
that one who is chosen to succeed a man becomes in effect that
man's son, we concluded that the king of Ch'ang-i should be made
heir.[15] We dispatched the director of the imperial clan, the director of foreign vassals, and the counselor to the keeper of the palace
gate to bear the imperial credentials and summon the king of
Ch'ang-i to take charge of the funeral. But though he donned the
unhemmed mourning garments, there was no grief or sorrow in his
heart. He disregarded ritual and propriety, during the journey failing to eat simple fare.[16] He ordered his attendants to seize women,
load them into the clothes cart, and have them brought to his room
at the post station.

"After he arrived in the capital for his audience with the empress
dowager and had been made imperial heir, he constantly sent men
in secret to buy fowl and pork for his meals. When he came before
the coffin of the deceased emperor and received the *hsin* and *hsing*
seals, he returned to his place, took them out of their boxes, and

[15] That is, though the successor may be a nephew or even more distant re-
lation, when he is appointed heir he becomes qualified to perform mourning
rites and sacrifices and fulfill the other duties of an actual son.
[16] Simple fare probably means meals free of meat and wine, though one
theory is that it means uncooked food.

then failed to have the boxes sealed again.[17] He sent off his attendants one after another bearing the imperial credentials and had them summon his attendants, grooms, and government slaves from Ch'ang-i, over two hundred persons, and bring them to the palace, where he would romp and play with them in the inner quarters. In order to accomplish this, he went in person to the place where the seals and credentials are kept and took out as many as sixteen credential staffs, and when he performed his ritual lamentations in the morning and evening, he had his attendants take turns standing by with the credential staffs.[18]

"He drew up a letter which said: 'I, the emperor, address my attendant of the inner palace Chün-ch'ing. I have ordered the keeper of the imperial treasury Kao-ch'ang to present you with a thousand catties of gold with which you may procure yourself ten wives.'

"While the coffin of the deceased emperor was still lying in state in the front hall, he had musical instruments brought from the Music Bureau and summoned musicians from Ch'ang-i to strike the drum, sing songs, and offer entertainments, and when he had returned to the front hall from the interment ceremony, he had the bells and chiming stones sounded. He also summoned musicians from the altar of the Great Unity and the ancestral temples and had them brought to the covered road at Lake Mou-shou in the Shang-lin Park, where they played, sang, and danced for him, presenting various types of music for his enjoyment. He had the Ch'ang-an Kitchen supply the animals for three *t'ai-lao* sacrifices, offering them in a room along the covered road, and when the offerings were over, he joined with his attendants in drinking and eating.[19] He called out the carriage of state, had carriages with tiger skin awnings and carriages with *luan* bird flags to go before him, and galloped off to the Northern Palace and the Cassia Palace to watch swinebaiting and tiger fights. He called for the pony cart used by the empress dowager and had one of his female slaves ride on the pony's back, amusing himself in the women's quarters.

[17] There were three imperial seals; one the emperor kept hanging from a cord at his waist; the other two, the *hsin* and *hsing* seals, were kept in sealed boxes.

[18] Presumably so he could send them off immediately if he thought of anything he wanted.

[19] The *t'ai-lao* sacrifice consisted of an ox, a sheep, and a pig. If the king had such elaborate sacrifices performed in a room off the covered road in the Shang-lin Park (the road was completely enclosed so that those who used it could not be seen), there was presumably something improper about them.

He had illicit relations with Meng and other palace women who belonged to Emperor Chao the Filial, and told the supervisor of the women's quarters that if word of it leaked out, he would have the supervisor cut in two at the waist."

"Stop!" cried the empress dowager. "Could any subject or son behave in such a shameful and disorderly fashion?"

The king moved off his mat and prostrated himself. The chief of palace writers then resumed the reading of the memorial:

"He took away the seal cords of the kings, marquises, and two thousand picul officials, as well as the black cords and yellow cords of the lesser officials, and handed them out to his palace attendants and freed slaves from Ch'ang-i. He changed the color of the yak tails on the credential staffs from yellow to red. He had gold, cash, swords, jade vessels, and colored silks brought from the imperial treasury and handed them out as presents to those who joined in his amusements. He drank far into the night with his attendants and government slaves until he was completely senseless from wine. He commanded the imperial butler to have ordinary meals prepared for him, and when the supervisor of food pointed out that he was still in mourning and could not have ordinary meals, he sent another command to the imperial butler to hurry up with the meals and not to send them by way of the supervisor of food. The imperial butler did not dare comply, whereupon he began sending his own followers out to buy fowl and pork, commanding the gate keeper to let them back into the palace whenever they went out. Without telling anyone, he held a banquet of the most formal and elaborate kind in the evening in the Warm Hall, inviting as his guest his elder sister's husband, the Ch'ang-i marquis within the Pass. Though the sacrifices in the ancestral temples of Kao-tsu and Emperor Wen had not yet begun, he sent a letter under the imperial seal instructing a messenger to bear the credentials and have three sets of *t'ai-lao* sacrifices offered at the funerary park and temple of his father King Ai of Ch'ang-i, in the announcement to the spirit referring to himself as 'your son and heir, the emperor.[20]

---

[20] A new emperor was not ritually qualified to perform sacrifices to Kao-tsu and Emperor Wen until thirty-six days after the interment of his predecessor. The king should not have sacrificed to his father before he had sacrificed to the founders of the dynasty, and as the heir and successor to Emperor Chao, he should not have referred to himself as "son and heir" when addressing the spirit of King Ai.

"It has been twenty-seven days since he received the imperial seals and in that time he has sent messengers in all directions bearing the credentials and delivering commands to the various officials and bureaus to summon such and such a man or issue such and such goods. In all there have been 1,127 such instances. The doctors of learning and counselors to the keeper of the palace gate such as Hsia-hou Sheng and others, as well as the attendant in the inner palace Fu Chia, several times came forward to reprimand him for his faults and errors, but he sent a man to berate Hsia-hou Sheng with a list of offenses and had Fu Chia bound and sent to prison. He behaves in a reckless and deluded manner, disregarding what is proper and ritually correct for an emperor and throwing into confusion the statutes and regulations of the Han. Your servant Ch'ang and the others have repeatedly offered admonitions but he does not change his ways; instead he grows worse with each day. We fear that he will endanger the altars of the soil and grain and bring unrest to the empire.

"Your servant Ch'ang and the others have conferred carefully with the erudits Pa, Ch'üan She, Te, Yü-she, Shih, and Ts'ang, and they all replied, 'Emperor Kao-tsu because of the merit he achieved in founding the dynasty was given the temple name of Great Ancestor of the Han. Emperor Wen the Filial because he was kind and benevolent, virtuous and frugal, was given the temple name of Great Patriarch. Now the present emperor has become the successor of Emperor Chao the Filial, and yet his conduct is licentious and depraved, contrary to all rule. The *Odes* says:

> Though you may say you do not know better,
> You are already old enough to hold a son in your arms! [21]

Of all the crimes punishable by the five penalties, none is more serious than lack of filial piety. King Hsiang of the Chou did not know how to serve his mother, and the *Spring and Autumn Annals* wrote of him that "The heavenly king went out of the capital and dwelt in Cheng." [22] Because he lacked filial piety, he was forced to

---

[21] Mao #256; *i.e.*, the king of Ch'ang-i, who was eighteen or nineteen at the time, is not to be excused on the grounds that he is too young to know better.

[22] King Hsiang became ruler in 651 B.C. It was his stepmother whom he "didn't know how to serve," mainly because she was doing her best to have her own son Shu-tai made king in his place. Shu-tai allied himself with the Ti tribes and marched against the Chou capital, forcing King Hsiang to flee to

leave the capital, having been cast off by the empire. The ancestral temples are of greater importance than the ruler. The present emperor has not yet received the mandate of rule in the temple of Kao-tsu. He is not fit to carry on the heavenly ordained succession, to serve the temples of Kao-tsu and Emperor Wen, and to watch over the ten thousand clans like a father. He should be deposed.

"I request that the proper officials, namely, the imperial secretary Ts'ai Yi, the director of the imperial clan Liu Te, the master of ritual Su Ch'ang, along with the grand invocator, offer a *t'ai-lao* sacrifice and make a full announcement of the matter in the temple of Kao-tsu. Your servant Ch'ang and the others, risking death, submit this report."

The empress dowager commanded that the memorial be approved. Ho Kuang instructed the king to rise, bow, and receive the command. The king said, "I have heard that if the Son of Heaven has seven ministers to reprimand him, though he himself is without the Way, he need not lose possession of the empire." [23]

But Ho Kuang replied, "The empress dowager has commanded that you be deposed—what have you to do with matters pertaining to the Son of Heaven?" He then went to the king's side, grasped his arm, and undid the seal cord from his waist, presenting the seal to the empress dowager. He helped the king down from the hall and out of the Golden Horse Gate, the other officials all following along after. The king faced west and bowed, saying, "Stupid and unworthy as I am, I am not fit to bear responsibility for the Han." Then he rose, mounted the carriage used by the ruler's attendants, and was escorted by Ho Kuang to the official residence of Ch'ang-i.

"Your Highness," said Ho Kuang, "it is your own conduct that has caused you to be cast off by Heaven. I and the others have been ineffectual and cowardly and even if we were to die we could not repay your kindness. But I felt that it was better to betray you than to risk betraying the altars of the soil and grain. I beg Your Highness to look after your health. It will be a long time before I have the privilege of attending you again." With tears in his eyes, Ho Kuang took his departure.

The officials submitted a memorial stating that in ancient times

Cheng, though he later regained the throne. It is the *Kung-yang Commentary,* Duke Hsi 24th year, that censures him for not knowing how to serve his mother.

[23] The king is quoting from the *Classic of Filial Piety.*

those who had been deposed and cast out were banished to a distant region and were not allowed to participate in affairs of government. They requested that King Liu Ho be sent to the district of Fang-ling in Han-chung, but the empress dowager commanded that he return to Ch'ang-i, where he was presented with a bath-town of two thousand households.

The king's former officials from Ch'ang-i were tried on charges of having failed to assist and guide him in the proper way, instead enticing him into evildoing. Ho Kuang had them executed, over two hundred persons in all. When they were being led to their death, their wails and cries filled the market place. "We failed to strike when it was time to strike and instead we suffer disaster!" they said.

Ho Kuang took his seat in the palace and assembled the chancellor and other officials to deliberate on who should be appointed successor to the throne. The king of Kuang-ling had long ago been eliminated from consideration, and since King Tz'u of Yen had revolted and been sentenced to death, his son was not considered a candidate. The only member of the imperial family who was closely related to any of the rulers was the grandson of the heir apparent Li, Emperor Wu's son by Empress Wei, who was known as the imperial great-grandson. He was living among the common people and enjoyed the approbation of all. Ho Kuang thereupon joined with the chancellor Yang Ch'ang and the others in submitting a memorial which read:

"Ritual tells us that because in human relationships it is proper to draw close to those who are closely related to one, therefore one pays special honor to the ancestors; and because one desires to honor the ancestors, one pays greatest respect to the direct line of descent. But when there is no heir in the direct line, one may select a worthy person from among the sons and grandsons of the collateral lines to act as heir. Liu Ping-i is the great-grandson of Emperor Wu the Filial, and in Emperor Wu's time an order was given that he be raised in the women's quarters of the palace. He is now eighteen years old and has received instruction in the *Odes*, the *Analects*, and the *Classic of Filial Piety*. His conduct is temperate and restrained and he is kind and benevolent to others. He is suited to become the heir of Emperor Chao the Filial, to carry on the service of the ancestral temples of Kao-tsu and Emperor Wen, and to watch over the ten thousand clans like a father. Risking death, we make this report."

The empress dowager ordered that the memorial be approved. Ho Kuang then dispatched the director of the imperial clan Liu Te to go to the home of the imperial great-grandson in the Shang-kuan Ward, have him bathe and wash his hair, and present him with robes from the imperial treasury. The master of carriage went in a light hunting chariot to fetch him and he was taken to the office of the director of the imperial clan for fasting and purification, after which he entered the Eternal Palace, appeared before the empress dowager, and was enfeoffed as marquis of Yang-wu.[24] When that had been done, Ho Kuang bestowed on him the seal and seal cord of the emperor and presented him in the ancestral temple of Kao-tsu. He is posthumously known as Emperor Hsüan the Filial.

The following year (73 B.C.) an edict was handed down saying, "To praise virtue and reward merit has been regarded as correct practice in both past and present. The grand marshal general in chief Ho Kuang has guarded the palace with loyalty and rectitude, proclaiming the emperor's virtue, making clear his mercy, observing propriety, clinging to what is correct, and thereby insuring the safety of the ancestral temples. Let Ho-pei and Tung-wu-yang be added to his fief, increasing it by seventeen thousand households, so that, along with those he has previously been receiving revenue from, he will have a total of twenty thousand households."

Ho Kuang had on various occasions received rewards and gifts amounting to seven thousand catties of gold and sixty million cash, as well as thirty thousand rolls of various kinds of silk, 170 male and female slaves, two thousand horses, and a house and grounds of the finest kind.

From the time of Emperor Chao, Ho Kuang's son Ho Yü and his elder brother's grandson Ho Yün had both served as generals of palace attendants, and Ho Yün's younger brother Ho Shan was chief commandant in charge of the imperial carriage and an attendant in the inner palace, having charge of the soldiers of the Hu and Yüeh tribes. The husbands of Ho Kuang's two daughters were colonels of the guard in the western and eastern palaces respectively, and the husbands of his nieces and his grandsons of other surnames were all qualified to attend the spring and autumn sessions of the court, being clerks, counselors, colonels of the cavalry, or stewards of the palace. The allies and relatives of the Ho family

[24] Because it would have been unseemly for him to move directly from the rank of commoner to that of Son of Heaven.

formed a great network whose roots were firmly planted in the court.

From the *hou-yüan* era on (88–87 B.C.), Ho Kuang had had complete charge of all affairs of government. When the new emperor came to the throne, Ho Kuang tried to turn over control to him, but the emperor modestly declined to accept. As a result, all matters were reported to and cleared with Ho Kuang, and only then were they memorialized to the Son of Heaven. Ho Kuang was received in audience each morning, the emperor setting aside personal feelings, assuming a grave demeanor, and treating Ho Kuang with extreme courtesy and deference.

Ho Kuang managed affairs of government for a total of twenty years. In the spring of the second year of *ti-chieh* (68 B.C.) he fell gravely ill. The emperor went in person to Ho Kuang's house to inquire how he was, shedding tears for him. Ho Kuang submitted a letter apologizing for this imposition upon the ruler's kindness and saying, "I beg that three thousand households be detached from the towns in my fief and assigned to the chief commandant in charge of the imperial carriage Ho Shan, my elder brother's grandson, so that he may be enfeoffed as a marquis and permitted to carry on the sacrifices to my elder brother, the general of swift cavalry Ho Ch'ü-ping." [25] The request was approved and referred to the chancellor and the imperial secretary for action. On the same day, Ho Kuang's son Ho Yü was appointed general of the right.

Ho Kuang passed away, and the emperor and empress dowager came in person to perform lamentations beside his corpse. The palace counselor Jen Hsüan, along with five secretaries of the censorate, was presented with the imperial credentials and ordered to take charge of the funeral, while officials of the middle two thousand picul class prepared the tents to be erected on the grave mound. The emperor provided gifts of gold, cash, silk fabrics, a hundred embroidered coverlets, fifty boxes of clothing, jade discs, various kinds of pearls, a shroud made of pieces of jade sewn together, an inner coffin of catalpa wood, an outer coffin of camphor wood, a coffin cover made of the yellow core of cypress, fifteen coffins of fir wood for the outer burial chamber, and a "warm bright"

[25] Ho Ch'ü-ping's eldest son Ho Shan (written with a different character from the Ho Shan mentioned in the text) had succeeded to his father's title, but he died in 110 B.C., leaving no heir, and the fief was abolished. Ho Kuang is asking that it be reestablished.

supplied by the Eastern Garden Office, all the same as those used in the burial of an emperor.[26]

The coffin containing Ho Kuang's body was placed in a windowed carriage with a yellow top and plumes on the left side. Soldiers from the strong bowmen and light carriage battalions and the divisions of the northern garrison were drawn up in ranks along the road to Mou-ling to act as an escort to the burial.[27] Ho Kuang was given the posthumous title of Hsüan-ch'eng, the "Marquis of Broad Completion." The soldiers from the three provinces of Ho-nan, Ho-tung, and Ho-nei were called out to dig the grave and fill in the earth. A sacrificial hall was built on the top of the grave mound and a funerary park and village of three hundred households were set up, with officials appointed to guard and maintain the grave according to the customary laws.

After Ho Kuang had been interred, his elder brother's grandson Ho Shan was made marquis of Lo-p'ing and, as chief commandant in charge of the imperial carriage, was given the supervision of matters pertaining to the office of palace writers. The emperor, recalling Ho Kuang's merits and virtues, handed down the following edict:

"The grand marshal general in chief, the marquis of Po-lu, guarded the palace and person of Emperor Wu the Filial for over thirty years, and for over ten years he assisted Emperor Chao the Filial. When a situation of great difficulty arose, he personally chose a course that was proper, leading the three highest officials, the nine high ministers, and the counselors in devising a plan that would insure the continuance of the dynasty for ten thousand generations and guarantee the safety of the altars of the soil and grain. The multitudes of the empire because of him enjoy prosperity and peace. I am filled with the greatest admiration for the wealth and splendor of his merit and virtue. Let his descendants in ages to come be exempted from taxes and *corvée* labor. His title and lands shall all pass down to his heirs without diminution so that for gen-

[26] The fifteen coffins were probably for servants and waiting women who had committed suicide in order to follow their lord in death. A "warm bright" is said to be a square lacquer box with a mirror in the bottom which was hung above the corpse and was later sealed and buried with it. The Eastern Garden was a division of the privy treasury that handled articles used in funerals.

[27] Mou-ling, in the outskirts of Ch'ang-an, was the site of Emperor Wu's mausoleum; Ho Kuang was buried to the east of Emperor Wu.

eration after generation there shall be no one to rival them, for truly his merit ranks with that of Prime Minister Hsiao." [28]

In the summer of the following year, when Hsü Kuang-han, the maternal grandfather of the heir apparent, was enfeoffed as marquis of P'ing-en, the emperor once more handed down an edict saying, "The Marquis of Broad Completion Ho Kuang guarded the palace with loyalty and rectitude, laboring diligently for the safety of the state. In rewarding men of goodness, it is proper that the reward extend to their descendants. Therefore let the general of palace attendants Ho Yün, the grandson of Ho Kuang's elder brother, be enfeoffed as marquis of Kuan-yang."

Ho Yü had succeeded to his father's title of marquis of Po-lu, and Ho Kuang's widow Hsien now set about altering the grave which Ho Kuang had designed for himself, making it much larger and grander. She had three entrance gates constructed, with a "spirit road" leading up to one of them; the other two connected with the Chao-lin Hall to the north and the Ch'eng-en Hall to the south. She had the sacrificial hall elaborately decorated and built a covered road for hand-drawn carriages connecting it with the women's quarters of the grave keeper's house, where she had Ho Kuang's ladies in waiting, female slaves, and concubines confined with orders to tend the grave. She also enlarged her own house and grounds, building carriages and a hand-drawn cart decorated with paintings, embroidered cushions, and arm rests; it was gilded on the outside and had wheels wrapped in leather stuffed with floss. She would then have her attendants and female slaves, dressed in silks of five colors, pull her in the cart, amusing herself by going here and there within the grounds of her estate.

When Ho Kuang was alive he had shown great favoritism toward his overseer of slaves Feng Tzu-tu, consulting him whenever he made plans. When Ho Kuang died and Hsien was left a widow, she took Feng Tzu-tu for her lover. Ho Yü and Ho Shan also enlarged and improved their houses and often galloped off to hunt at the Tower of Peaceful Joy in the Shang-lin Park. Several times, when Ho Yü was supposed to attend the spring and autumn audiences at court, he pleaded illness and instead slipped out of the capital and went off with a number of his guests and attendants to spread nets and hunt in the Yellow Mountain Gardens, sending

[28] Hsiao Ho (d. 193 B.C.), the great statesman who aided Kao-tsu in founding the Han.

one of his servants to present his calling card at court. There was
no one, however, who dared censure him for such breaches of etiquette. Ho Kuang's widow Hsien and her daughters for their part
were day and night to be found coming and going in the Palace of
Lasting Trust without the slightest regard for the hour or the rules
governing such visits.[29]

From the time when he was living among the common people,
Emperor Hsüan had heard of the great honor and influence which
the Ho family had for so long enjoyed at court, and he secretly disapproved of it. After Ho Kuang passed away, the emperor began
personally tending to affairs of the court and government, with the
imperial secretary Wei Hsiang assisting him in the inner palace.
Ho Kuang's widow Ho Hsien said to Ho Yü, Ho Yün, and Ho
Shan, "You are not working hard enough to maintain the position
handed down to you by the general in chief! Now the imperial secretary is waiting on the emperor in the inner palace.[30] If someone
should once start speaking out against you, how do you think you
could save yourselves?"

Later, the slaves of the Ho and Wei families got into a street
brawl over who had the right of way and the Ho family slaves entered the office of the imperial secretary Wei Hsiang and threatened to kick open the gate to the secretary's quarters. One of the
secretary's assistants had to knock his head on the ground and
apologize before they would go away. Someone reported the incident to the Ho family, and for the first time Ho Hsien and the others began to worry.

As it happened, the imperial secretary Wei Hsiang was at this
time made chancellor and often had the opportunity to see the emperor when the latter was at leisure and discuss various matters
with him. The marquis of P'ing-en Hsü Kuang-han, the attendant
in the inner palace Chin An-shang, and others were allowed to go
in and out of the office of palace writers without special permission. At this time Ho Shan was still in charge of the office of palace
writers as he had been in the past, but the emperor gave orders
that the officials and common people were to be allowed to submit

[29] The Palace of Lasting Trust was occupied by the empress dowager, the
daughter of Shang-kuan An and Ho Kuang's eldest daughter.

[30] Wei Hsiang was an old enemy of the Ho family. While Ho Kuang was
alive, no one unfriendly to the Ho family was permitted access to the emperor, but Ho Kuang's heirs had been unable to continue exercising such
power.

sealed memorials directly to the throne without first clearing them with the office of palace writers. He also permitted the various ministers to come directly to him with their business rather than go through an intermediary. With this the members of the Ho family were filled with foreboding.

When Emperor Hsüan first came to the throne, he set up as his empress the daughter of the Hsü family whom he had married when he was living in obscurity. Ho Hsien, however, being very fond of her youngest daughter Ch'eng-chün and hoping to secure a position of honor for her, secretly had the doctor in charge of childbirth, a woman named Ch'un-yü Yen, administer poisoned medicine to Empress Hsü, from which she died. Ho Hsien then persuaded her husband Ho Kuang to have Ch'eng-chün enrolled among the ladies of the palace and in time she was made empress in the place of the deceased daughter of the Hsü family. (A discussion will be found in the "Biographies of the Families Related to the Emperors by Marriage.")

At the time of the sudden demise of Empress Hsü, the law officials arrested all the palace doctors. Ch'un-yü Yen was indicted on charges of immoral and unprincipled conduct when in attendance on the sick empress and was turned over to the prison officials, who confronted her with a list of questions and pressed her severely. Ho Hsien, fearing that the plot would come to light, confessed to Ho Kuang exactly what she had done. He was horrified and was about to report the matter himself, but he hesitated and could not bring himself to act. Just then, the law officials submitted a report on their findings, and Ho Kuang, through whose hands it passed, added a notation, as though by the emperor, saying that Ch'un-yü Yen was not to be prosecuted further.

After Ho Kuang had passed away, word of the affair gradually began to leak out and for the first time the emperor heard of it, though he did not know whether to believe it or not. Meanwhile he transferred Fan Ming-yu, the husband of Ho Kuang's second daughter, who held the titles of general who crosses the Liao and marquis of P'ing-ling and who was a colonel of the guard in the Eternal Palace, and had him made keeper of the palace gate instead. Jen Sheng, the husband of Ho Kuang's third daughter, who held the titles of official in charge, general of palace attendants, and superintendent of the Feather and Forest Guard, was sent out of the capital to take the post of governor of An-ting. After a few months, the emperor dispatched Chang Shuo, the husband of Ho

Kuang's elder sister, who held the titles of steward of the palace and counselor to the keeper of the palace gate, to the post of governor of the province of Shu, and made the general of palace attendants Wang Han, the husband of one of Ho Kuang's granddaughters, the governor of Wu-wei. He also shifted Teng Kuang-han, the husband of Ho Kuang's oldest daughter, who had been colonel of the guard in the Palace of Lasting Joy, to the post of privy treasurer of the Palace of Lasting Trust. Then he appointed Ho Yü as grand marshal, but gave him only a small cap and no seal or seal cord. At the same time, he relieved him of the garrison troops and officials that had been under his command as general of the right, leaving him with only the title and office of grand marshal, the same one which Ho Kuang had held. He also relieved Fan Ming-yu of the seal and seal cord that had been given him when he was made general who crosses the Liao. Chao P'ing, the husband of another of Ho Kuang's daughters, was chief commandant of regular and supplementary cavalry and a counselor to the keeper of the palace gate and had garrison troops under his command, but he was relieved of the seal and seal cord of chief commandant of regular cavalry. The cavalrymen of the Hu and Yüeh tribes, the Feather and Forest Guard, and the garrison troops that had been under the command of the colonels of the guard of the two palaces, were all removed from the command of members of the Ho family and assigned instead to sons and brothers of the Hsü and Shih families, whom the emperor confided in and trusted.[31]

After Ho Yü had been made grand marshal he remained at home, pleading illness. When his former chief clerk Jen Hsüan went to inquire how he was, Ho Yü said, "I don't have any illness! But if it hadn't been for my father the general in chief, the emperor would never have gotten to where he is! And now the ground is hardly dry on the general's grave mound before he's treating our whole family with coldness and instead relying on the Hsü and Shih families. He even took my seal and seal cord away from me —it's more than I'll ever understand!"

Jen Hsüan could see that Ho Yü was extremely bitter and resentful and so he said, "How could one hope to return to the days of the general in chief? He wielded authority over the entire nation and held within his hands the power of life and death. The com-

---

[31] Hsü was the family of his deceased empress, Shih the family of his paternal grandmother.

mandants of justice Li Ch'ung and Wang P'ing, the left prefect of
the capital Chia Sheng-hu, and the privy treasurer Hsü Jen, the
husband of chancellor Chü Ch'ien-ch'iu's daughter, were all accused of opposing the general in chief's will and were sent to
prison to die. On the other hand Shih Lo-ch'eng, the son of a very
low class family, managed to win favor with the general in chief
and thereby rose to become one of the nine high ministers and to
be enfeoffed as a marquis. At that time everyone from the hundred
officials on down spent all his time courting favor with Feng Tzu-
tu, Wang Tzu-fang, and the other slaves of the general in chief and
acted as though the chancellor didn't even exist. But everybody
gets his turn sometime. Now the Hsü and Shih families are flesh
and blood relations of the emperor and it's only right that they
should enjoy honor. I know it probably makes you angry and bitter, but if I may venture to say so, I think that's the wrong attitude."

Ho Yü listened in silence, but after a few days he got up and
began to tend to the duties of his office.

Ho Hsien and the other members of her family, Yü, Shan, and
Yün, could see that they were being shorn of their power day by
day, and they frequently gathered to wail and vent their anger. Ho
Shan said, "At present the chancellor Wei Hsiang is handling affairs and the emperor trusts him. He has completely changed the
laws and regulations that were made in the time of the general in
chief and is handing out public lands and revenues to the poor,
doing his best to expose the failures and shortcomings of the general in chief. In addition, many of the Confucian scholars are the
sons of indigent families who have come from distant regions and
are living lives of hunger and cold, and they love to put forth absurd theories and wild assertions without caring who they may offend or insult. The general in chief always regarded them as enemies, but nowadays the emperor seems to love talking to the
Confucian scholars. People have been told that they can submit
sealed letters stating their opinions and many of them have spoken
out concerning our family. One letter was submitted that said, 'In
the time of the general in chief, the ruler was weak and his minister strong; power was wielded in a dictatorial and arbitrary manner. Now his sons and grandsons are in charge of affairs and his
brothers grow increasingly arrogant and willful. We fear for the
safety of the ancestral temples! The disasters and unusual occurrences that have been so frequent in recent times are all due to

this state of affairs.' [32] These are harsh words indeed. I used to put such letters aside and not allow them to be submitted to the throne, but the senders became more clever, sealing the entire letter and having the chief of palace writers come out of the inner palace so they could put the letter directly into his hands without clearing it with the office of palace writers. The emperor is becoming more and more distrustful of me."

Ho Hsien said, "The chancellor has several times spoken out about our family, but surely he is not without some fault of his own, is he?"

"The chancellor is an honest and upright man," said Ho Shan. "How could we ever find anything to accuse him of? On the other hand, many of our own brothers and brothers-in-law are lacking in discretion. In addition, I hear that among the common people there is a great clamor to the effect that the Ho family poisoned and killed Empress Hsü! How could such a story have started?"

Ho Hsien, fearing that a crisis was at hand, finally told Shan, Yün, and Yü the whole truth of the matter. They were dumfounded and said, "Why didn't you tell us this earlier! This is is why the emperor has been relieving your sons-in-law of their posts and sending them off into the provinces. This is a serious offense and the punishment will not be light! What can we do?" It was at this point that they first began to plot treason.

Sometime earlier, a man named Shih Hsia who was a retainer to Ho Kuang's son-in-law Chao P'ing and an expert in astrological matters said to Chao P'ing, "Mars has taken up a position among the Imperial Stars. The Imperial Stars correspond to the master of carriage or the chief commandant in charge of the imperial carriage. If these men are not expelled, death· will result!" [33] Chao P'ing as a result became uneasy in his mind about Ho Shan and the others.

A man named Chang She, who was on close terms with Ho Yün's father-in-law Li Ching, observing that Ho Yün's family was in a state of great agitation, said to Li Ching, "At present the chan-

---

[32] Earthquakes, floods, drought, and the appearance of a comet and a solar eclipse are reported for this period. Such occurrences were believed to be caused by evil and misrule in the upper circles of government.

[33] In Chinese astrology, Mars is the indicator of rebellion, sickness, famine, war, etc. The various constellations are believed to correspond to the emperor and his court. The Imperial Stars (four stars in Scorpio) indicate matters or persons related to the imperial carriage. It will be recalled that Ho Shan was at this time chief commandant in charge of the imperial carriage.

cellor Wei Hsiang and the marquis of P'ing-en Hsü Kuang-han are in charge of affairs. It would be best to get the widow of the general in chief to speak to the empress dowager and first have these two men done away with. Then it will be within the empress dowager's power to do whatever she likes with the emperor." [34]

A commoner of Ch'ang-an named Chang Chang reported to the authorities that there was a plot afoot and the matter was turned over to the commandant of justice for investigation.[35] The chief of the capital police arrested Chang She, Shih Hsia, and others, but later a command came from the emperor that there were to be no more arrests. Ho Shan and the rest were more terrified than ever, saying to one another, "The emperor out of deference to the empress dowager has not pressed the investigation to the end, but he has already seen enough to know there is evil in the making. And on top of that there is the matter of Empress Hsü's murder. Even if His Majesty should wish to be kind and forgiving, it is unlikely that those about him would consent to such a course. Sooner or later, the affair will come to light, and when it does our whole family will be wiped out. It is best to move at once!" They then ordered the daughters of Ho Kuang to return to their various homes and report to their husbands what had happened. All said, "There's no escaping now!"

Just at this time, Ho Yün's father-in-law Li Ching was tried on charges of carrying on improper dealings with various marquises and kings, and the investigation in time implicated the Ho family. The emperor issued a command saying that it was not proper for Ho Yün and Ho Shan to be quartered in the palace as members of the guard and they were accordingly relieved of their posts and sent to their homes. The daughters of Ho Kuang failed to treat the empress dowager with the proper degree of respect, while Feng Tzu-tu, the Ho family's overseer of slaves, had several times broken the law, and the emperor berated the Ho family over these matters until Ho Shan and Ho Yün were thoroughly terrified.

Ho Kuang's widow Ho Hsien dreamed that the well in the Ho mansion overflowed till the water ran out into the courtyard, and that the kitchen stove was sitting up in a tree. Another time she

[34] It will be recalled that the empress dowager was a granddaughter of Ho Kuang and was on close terms with Ho Kuang's widow.

[35] According to a passage added to *Shih chi* 20 by Ch'u Shao-sun, Chang Chang, a minor official who had lost his position, was spending the night in the stables of the Ho mansion when he overheard the grooms discussing the Ho family's plans for revolt.

dreamed that her husband the general in chief said to her, "Do you know they're going to arrest your son? As fast as they can they're sending out the order to arrest him!" The number of rats in the Ho mansion suddenly increased and they went around bumping into people and marking up the ground with their tails. Owls several times were heard hooting in the trees in front of the main hall and the gate of the mansion fell down by itself. The middle gate of Ho Yün's house in the Shang-kuan Ward also fell down. The people at the end of the lane all saw a man standing on the roof of Ho Yün's house, pulling off the tiles and throwing them down to the ground, but when they went to look closer, they found to their amazement that he had disappeared. Ho Yü also dreamed he heard a loud clamor of carriages and cavalry coming to arrest him. The entire family was filled with fear and foreboding by these events.

Ho Shan said, "The chancellor Wei Hsiang, acting on his own authority, has eliminated the sacrifices of lambs, rabbits, and frogs in the ancestral temples—we can use that as a charge against him!" [36] Then he plotted to have the empress dowager arrange a banquet for the emperor's maternal grandmother, Lady Po-p'ing, and invite the chancellor, the marquis of P'ing-en, and the others of their group. Fan Ming-yü and Teng Kuang-han, acting on the command of the empress dowager, would then lead them out of the palace and cut them down. After that, the emperor would be deposed and Ho Yü set up in his place.

The outline of the plot was more or less settled but there had been no time to put it into effect when Ho Yün was appointed governor of Hsüan-t'u and the palace counselor Jen Hsüan was made governor of Tai. In addition, Ho Shan was accused of disclosing the contents of secret documents. Ho Hsien submitted a letter to the throne on his behalf, offering her mansion west of the city walls and a thousand horses as ransom to release Ho Shan from punishment, but the emperor merely returned word that he had received the letter and noted its contents. It was at this point that the whole plot came to light.

Ho Yün, Ho Shan, and Fan Ming-yü committed suicide and Ho Hsien, Ho Yü, Teng Kuang-han, and the others were arrested. Ho Yü was cut in two at the waist and Ho Hsien and the various

[36] According to an old law of the Han, anyone who arbitrarily made any changes in the buildings or rituals of the ancestral temples could be put to death and his body exposed in the market place.

daughters and cousins of the Ho family were all executed and their bodies exposed in the market place. Only the empress dowager was spared, being removed from her position and sent to live in the Palace of the Bright Terrace. Several thousand families were accused of being in league with the Ho family and were wiped out.

The emperor then handed down an edict saying: "Some time earlier, the clerk of the eastern weaving rooms Chang She, acting through Li Ching, a wealthy man of the province of Wei, contacted the marquis of Kuan-yang Ho Yün and plotted with him to commit treason. Out of deference to the memory of the general in chief Ho Kuang, I suppressed knowledge of the plot and did not publicize it, hoping that the persons involved would reform of their own volition. But now the grand marshal Ho Yü, marquis of Po-lu, along with his mother Ho Hsien, the lady of the marquis of Broad Completion, her husband's grandnephews Ho Yü, marquis of Kuan-yang, and Ho Shan, marquis of Lo-p'ing, and the husbands of her daughters, have plotted to commit major treason, deluding and leading astray the common people. With the aid of the holy spirits of the ancestors, the plot was discovered in time and all those involved have been punished for their guilt. I am greatly grieved by this affair and decree that all those officials who were deluded and led astray by the members of the Ho family, providing it was only during the period previous to the day *ping-shen* of the seventh month when the plot came to light, be pardoned and cleared of all guilt.

"The commoner Chang Chang was the first to report the plot, giving word of it to Tung Chung of the Rendezvous Gate. Tung Chung reported it to the clerk of the left Yang Yün, who in turn reported it to the attendant in the inner palace Chin An-shang. Yang Yün was summoned and gave an account of the matter, after which Chang Chang submitted a letter to the throne reporting the details. The attendants in the inner palace Shih Kao and Chin An-shang drew up a plan of action, advising that the members of the Ho family be barred from entering the inner palace, and thus the plot was foiled. All of these persons have won equal merit. Let Chang Chang be enfeoffed as marquis of Po-ch'eng, Tung Chung as marquis of Kao-ch'ang, Yang Yün as marquis of P'ing-t'ung, Chin An-shang as marquis of Tu-ch'eng, and Shih Kao as marquis of Lo-ling."

Earlier, when the Ho family was living in extravagance and luxury, a man named Master Hsü of Mou-ling said, "The Ho family is certain to be destroyed. He who indulges in extravagance will become rebellious, he who becomes rebellious will invariably despise his superiors, and he who despises his superiors will pursue the way of treason. When one rises to a position above others, he is bound to be hated by the mass of men. The Ho family has held the reins of power for a long time now and the people who hate it are many—in fact, the whole empire hates it. If in addition it pursues the way of treason, how can it help but be destroyed!" He then submitted a memorial saying, "The Ho family flourishes to excess. Your Majesty has already shown love and favor to its members—now is the time to curb and restrain them."

Three times he submitted letters to this effect, but the emperor merely returned word that he had received them and noted their contents. Later, when the Ho family was wiped out and those who had informed on it were all enfeoffed, someone submitted a letter to the throne on Master Hsü's behalf which read:

"Your servant has heard the following story. There was once a guest who went to visit the master of a certain house. When he saw that the kitchen stove had a straight flue and that the firewood was piled beside the stove, he told the master of the house that it would be best to have a bent flue installed and to move the firewood farther away. If not, he said, there was danger of a fire breaking out. The master of the house was silent and made no reply. Later a fire did in fact break out suddenly in the house. The people of the neighborhood joined in helping to fight it, and they finally succeeded in putting it out. The master of the house then killed an ox and set out wine, thanking his neighbors for what they had done. Those who had actually received burns from the fire were put in the place of honor, and the remainder were seated in accordance with how great their contribution to the fire fighting had been, but the man who had given the advice about the bent flue was not even invited. Someone said to the master of the house, 'If you had listened to that man's advice, you would have been spared the expense of the ox and wine and would never have been troubled by fire. Now you have arranged the guests according to their contribution, but is it right that the man who advised a bent flue and better stashed firewood should get no share of the bounty at all while those with scorched polls and seared brows are treated as guests of honor?' The master of the house then realized his error and had the man invited.

"Now Hsü Fu of Mou-ling several times submitted letters warning that the Ho family was about to rebel and advising that steps be taken to forestall such an occurrence. If Hsü Fu's words had been heeded, then the state would have been spared the expense of handing out territory and titles to the informers, and the members of the Ho family would not have had to suffer the fate of being put to death as traitors and rebels. The past cannot be changed, but I hope Your Majesty will give some thought to the fact that Hsü Fu alone has received no reward for his contribution and will show appreciation for the man with the flue and firewood plan by placing him above those who burned their heads in the affair."

The emperor accordingly presented Hsü Fu with ten rolls of silk and later made him a palace attendant.

When Emperor Hsüan first came to the throne and went to pay his respects in the temple of Kao-tsu, the general in chief rode by his side in the carriage. As a result, the emperor felt great awe and fear in his heart; it was as though he had a sharp thorn sticking in his back. Later the general of carriage and cavalry Chang An-shih took Ho Kuang's place in the carriage, whereupon the emperor felt his body grow relaxed and comfortable and he had a sense of great security and friendliness. Long afterwards, when Ho Kuang had died and his family had all been put to death, people often used to say to one another, "A minister whose might overawes the ruler should not be tolerated. The first sign of the impending downfall of the Ho family was when Ho Kuang rode with the emperor."

In the time of Emperor Ch'eng, a hundred households were established to guard Ho Kuang's grave, with officials and soldiers to tend it and offer sacrifices. In the second year of *yüan-shih* (A.D. 2), Ho Yang, the great-grandson of Ho Kuang's cousin, was enfeoffed as marquis of Po-lu with the revenue from a thousand households.

CHIN MI-TI

Chin Mi-ti, whose polite name was Weng-shu, had originally been the heir apparent of the Hsiung-nu Hsiu-t'u king.[37] During the *yüan-shou* era of Emperor Wu's reign (122–118 B.C.), the general of swift cavalry Ho Ch'ü-ping led his troops in an attack on the Hsiung-nu territory of the right, cutting off many barbarian heads

---

[37] The Hsiu-t'u and Hun-yeh kings were leaders of the Hsiung-nu tribes living in the territory of the right, the western region of the Hsiung-nu realm. They were under the command of the *Shan-yü*, the chief of all the Hsiung-nu.

and seizing the golden man of Heaven which was worshiped by the Hsiu-t'u king. That summer (121 B.C.), the general of swift cavalry once more proceeded west past Chü-yen and attacked the region of the Ch'i-lien Mountains, capturing and killing many of the enemy.

The *Shan-yü* thereupon grew angry at the Hun-yeh and Hsiu-t'u kings who lived in the western region because they had allowed the Han to inflict such losses on them, and he summoned the two kings, intending to put them to death. The kings, terrified, plotted together to surrender to the Han. The Hsiu-t'u king later regretted this decision, but the Hun-yeh king murdered him and, combining his forces with his own, surrendered. The Han enfeoffed the Hun-yeh king as a marquis. Because Chin Mi-ti's father had not surrendered but had been killed, he, his mother the consort of the late king, and his younger brother Lun all became government slaves. Chin Mi-ti was assigned as a keeper of the horses of the Yellow Gate. He was fourteen at the time.

After a considerable time had passed, the emperor one day decided to hold a banquet and review his horses. The ladies of the palace were grouped about him in large numbers as Chin Mi-ti and the other grooms, thirty or forty men in all, led their horses past the hall where the emperor was sitting. None of the other grooms failed to steal a glance at the women; Mi-ti alone did not dare to look up when his turn came to pass in review. He was eight feet two inches in height and had a very stern face and manner, and in addition his horses were sleek and well cared for. The emperor, impressed, asked him who he was and he replied with the full story of his origin. The emperor, judging him to be a man of unusual worth, on the same day ordered him to bathe, wash his hair, and put on a robe and cap, and appointed him superintendent of horses. In time he advanced to the posts of attendant in the inner palace, commandant of the imperial horses, and counselor to the keeper of the palace gate.

After Chin Mi-ti had become a favorite of the emperor he was never guilty of error or oversight. The emperor loved and trusted him greatly, presenting him with a thousand catties of gold on several occasions. Abroad he rode by the emperor's side, within the palace he was constantly in attendance. Many of the emperor's relatives and other persons in high position were secretly resentful, saying, "His Majesty by some quirk of circumstance gets himself a barbarian boy and what does he do but treat him with honor and respect!" When the emperor heard of their remarks, he only treated Chin Mi-ti more generously than ever.

Chin Mi-ti's mother had trained her two sons very carefully so that their behavior was without reproach. When the emperor was told of this, he expressed his admiration for her, and after she died of illness, he commanded that a portrait of her be painted in the Palace of Sweet Springs with the label, "Consort of the Hsiu-t'u King." Whenever Chih Mi-ti came into the presence of the portrait, he would always bow, face the portrait, and shed tears before proceeding on his way.

Chin Mi-ti's two sons enjoyed great favor with the emperor, who made them his playthings and kept them constantly by his side. Once one of the boys grabbed the emperor around the neck from behind. Chin Mi-ti, who was standing before the emperor, saw him and glared angrily, whereupon the boy ran away, screaming, "Father's mad at me!" The emperor reproached Mi-ti, saying, "What do you mean getting angry at my boy!" Later, however, when the boy grew up, he behaved with great indiscretion and used to go out into the palace gardens and amuse himself with the emperor's ladies in waiting. Chin Mi-ti happened to catch him at this and, disgusted by his licentious and unruly ways, finally put him to death. He was Mi-ti's eldest son. When the emperor heard of this, he was enraged, but Mi-ti bowed his head, apologized, and explained why he had killed the boy. The emperor, deeply grieved, wept for the dead boy, but in his heart he respected Mi-ti.

The archery captain of the inner palace attendants Ma Ho-lo had originally been very friendly with Chiang Ch'ung and later, when Chiang Ch'ung brought about the downfall of Emperor Wu's son by Empress Wei, the heir apparent Li, Ma Ho-lo's younger brother Ma T'ung was made a marquis in recognition of the part he took in the fight to defeat the heir apparent and his supporters. In time, however, the emperor came to realize that the heir apparent had been the victim of injustice and he had all of Chiang Ch'ung's family and associates put to death. Ma Ho-lo and his brother began to fear that they too would become involved and so they set about plotting treason. Chin Mi-ti saw that they were up to something unusual and, growing suspicious, secretly kept watch on their doings and accompanied them whenever they came and went in the palace. Ho-lo and his brother for their part realized what was in Chin Mi-ti's mind and for a long time were accordingly unable to put their plot into action.

At this time (88 B.C.) the emperor was visiting the Forest Glow Palace at Sweet Springs, and Chin Mi-ti, who was slightly ill, was sleeping in a small waiting room next to the emperor's bedchamber. Ma Ho-lo and his brother T'ung, along with their youngest brother An-ch'eng, forged an order allowing them to leave the palace at night, waylaid and murdered one of the imperial envoys, and used his credentials to call out the troops. The next morning at dawn, before the emperor had risen, Ho-lo managed without difficulty to get back into the palace. Chin Mi-ti had gotten up to go to the toilet, but feeling suddenly uneasy in his mind, he entered the emperor's chambers and sat down beside the door to the inner bedroom. Before long, Ho-lo crept in from the eastern verandah, a dagger concealed in his sleeve. When he saw Mi-ti, he turned pale and made a dash toward the bedroom door, hoping to get at the emperor, but he stumbled over a large and elaborately decorated zither and fell to the floor. Mi-ti managed to fling his arms around him, at the same time shouting to the guards, "Ma Ho-lo has revolted!" The emperor leaped out of bed in astonishment and his attendants drew their swords, preparing to strike at Ho-lo, but the emperor, fearing that they would wound Mi-ti, ordered them not to attack. Mi-ti grabbed Ho-lo by the throat and dragged him out of the hall, and he was seized and bound. Pressed by the law officials, Ho-lo and the others all admitted their guilt, and as a result of the affair Mi-ti became famous for his loyalty and devotion.

Chin Mi-ti served at the emperor's side for over thirty years but he never questioned the emperor's authority by so much as a defiant glance. The emperor presented him with one of the palace ladies in waiting whose period of service had ended but he never dared to become intimate with her. The emperor wanted him to enter his daughter among the ladies of the palace but he would not consent. From these examples one can see how devoted and circumspect he was. The emperor regarded him as a truly rare and unusual man.

When the emperor fell ill, he asked Ho Kuang to assist his youthful successor. Ho Kuang deferred in favor of Chin Mi-ti, but Mi-ti said, "I am a foreigner. Moreover, if I were to accept the task, it would cause the Hsiung-nu to look upon the Han with disrespect." As a result he ended by acting as Ho Kuang's assistant. Ho Kuang gave his daughter as a bride to Mi-ti's son and heir, Chin Shang.

Earlier, Emperor Wu had left a testamentary edict saying that Chin Mi-ti was to be enfeoffed as marquis of Tu because of the merit he achieved in capturing Ma Ho-lo, but because Emperor Chao was still a boy, Mi-ti declined to accept the title. After assisting in affairs of government for over a year, he was stricken with illness and exhaustion. The general in chief Ho Kuang requested the emperor to enfeoff him, and he was presented with the seal and seal cord as he lay in bed. The following day he passed away. The emperor presented the articles required for his funeral and land for his grave, and his body was attended by war chariots and armored warriors drawn up in ranks along the road to Mou-ling. He was given the posthumous title of Ching, the "Respectful Marquis."

Chin Mi-ti's two sons Shang and Chien both became attendants in the inner palace. They were roughly the same age as Emperor Chao and were always at his side, waking or sleeping. Chin Shang was appointed chief commandant in charge of the imperial carriage and Chin Chien was made commandant of the imperial horses. Later, Chin Shang succeeded to his father's title of marquis and hence came to have two seal cords at his waist. The emperor said to general Ho Kuang, "The Chin brothers shouldn't be allowed to have two seal cords, should they?"

Ho Kuang replied, "Shang has succeeded his father as marquis, that's all."

The emperor laughed and said, "It's up to me and you to decide who gets to be a marquis, isn't it?" But Ho Kuang replied, "According to the rule laid down by your father, the late emperor, only those who have won some merit may be enfeoffed as marquises!" At the time, Emperor Chao and the Chin brothers were still boys of eight or nine.

When Emperor Hsüan came to the throne, he appointed Chin Shang as master of carriage. When the first signs that the Ho family was plotting against the throne came to light, Chin Shang submitted a letter to the throne renouncing his wife.[38] In the end the emperor took pity on him and, when the other persons related to the Ho family were being tried and put to death, Chin Shang alone was spared.

In the time of Emperor Yüan he was made keeper of the palace gate. He passed away, leaving no son, and the fief was abolished. During the *yüan-shih* era (A.D. 1–5), when fiefs that had gone out of existence were being reestablished, Chin Chien's grandson Chin

[38] So he would not be held responsible for crimes committed by his wife's relatives of the Ho family.

Tang was made marquis of Tu in order to carry on the line of Chin Mi-ti.

Earlier, Chin Mi-ti's younger brother Lun, who had surrendered to the Han at the same time as Mi-ti and whose polite name was Shao-ch'ing, had been made an attendant of the Yellow Gate, but he died early. Chin Mi-ti's two sons enjoyed high positions, but with the following generation the family fortunes waned. Chin Lun's descendants, on the other hand, in time gained great affluence and distinction. His son Chin An-shang was the first to achieve eminence and to be enfeoffed as a marquis.[39]

In appraisal we say: From the time he bound up his hair and entered manhood Ho Kuang served within the palace. Beginning as an attendant by the palace stairs and door, he was steadfast in his attention to duty and his worth in time became apparent to the ruler. Charged with the care of the infant emperor and entrusted with the fate of the house of Han, he took his place in the temples and halls of state, guarded the young ruler, foiled the evil ambitions of the king of Yen, and overthrew the Shang-kuan family, exercising the power vested in him, curbing the enemies of the state, and thereby manifesting the utmost loyalty. When he faced the question of whether to depose the king of Ch'ang-i or not, he followed the course of justice and refused to be swayed. In all, he brought rectitude to the nation, insured the safety of the altars of the soil and grain, protected Emperor Chao, and placed Emperor Hsüan on the throne to succeed him. As a mentor and guardian, he is unsurpassed even by the Duke of Chou and Yi Yin of ancient times.

But Ho Kuang lacked learning and over-all strategy and was blind to fundamental principles. He shielded his wife's nefarious designs, had his daughter made empress, and drowned himself in an ever-swelling sea of desires, thus hastening the day when disaster would strike. Barely three years after his death his entire family was wiped out, a sad fate indeed! In ancient times Ho Shu, the younger brother of King Wu of the Chou, was enfeoffed in the territory of Chin. Chin corresponds to the region of Ho-tung, Ho Huang's birthplace, and I wonder if Ho Kuang could have been a descendant of Ho Shu.

[39] I have omitted at this point a long dry account of the various posts and honors held by Chin An-shang and his numerous descendants.

Chin Mi-ti was a barbarian, the son of a vanquished nation, who came to the Han court as a prisoner in bonds. But his devotion to duty and respectful demeanor won recognition from the ruler and his loyalty and trustworthiness became manifest to all. His meritorious deeds are recorded among the stars and his fief was handed down to his heirs, who were known throughout the realm for their loyalty and filial piety and who for seven generations served within the palace. How splendid an achievement!

Chin Mi-ti's father the Hsiu-t'u king made an image of a man out of gold and used it in the worship of the Heavenly Lord, and for this reason when Mi-ti came to the Han court he was given the surname Chin, meaning gold.

Ch'üan Pu-i, Shu Kuang, Yü Ting-kuo, Hsüeh Kuang-te, P'ing Tang, and P'eng Hsüan

CH'ÜAN PU-I WAS ADMIRABLE AND ALERT; faced with sudden crisis, he knew what steps to take. He refused Ho Kuang's marriage proposal and pursued his duties with a sense of modesty. Shu Kuang knew how to live out his life to the end, scattering gold for the delight of the elders. Yü Ting-kuo's good fortune was due to the benevolence shown by his father. Hsüeh Kuang-te, P'ing Tang, and P'eng Hsüan had a nearly perfect sense of reticence and shame. So I have transmitted the Biographies of Ch'üan Pu-i, Shu Kuang, Yü Ting-kuo, Hsüeh Kuang-te, P'ing Tang, and P'eng Hsüan.

CH'ÜAN PU-I

Ch'üan Pu-i, whose polite name was Man-ch'ien, was a native of Po-hai. He studied the *Spring and Autumn Annals* and was recognized by his province as a man of learning. In all his comings and goings he invariably abided by the dictates of ritual, and his name was known throughout the provinces.

In the late years of Emperor Wu's reign many thieves and bandits appeared in the provinces and feudal states. Pao Sheng-chih, acting as a directly appointed envoy of the emperor, donned embroidered robes, took his ax of authority in hand, and set out to pursue and seize the criminals, inspecting the provinces and feudal states east as far as the sea and using military procedures to punish those who failed to obey the law. All the surrounding regions trembled at his might.

Pao Sheng-chih had earlier heard of Ch'üan Pu-i's reputation as a man of worth, and when he reached Po-hai, he dispatched one of his clerks to invite Ch'üan Pu-i to call on him. Ch'üan Pu-i put on his "cap for advancing worthies," [1] buckled on a sword with elaborately carved hilt, fastened circular and semi-circular jade discs at his belt, donned a flowing robe and wide girdle, and, dressed in this highly formal manner, presented himself at Pao Sheng-chih's gate. The gate keeper tried to force him to remove his sword, but Ch'üan Pu-i replied, "The sword is the gentleman's weapon of defense, the means by which he guards his person—it cannot be laid aside! If it is impossible to admit me as I am, I beg permission to retire."

The clerks reported this to Pao Sheng-chih, who ordered them to open the small door at the side of the gate and invite Ch'üan Pu-i to enter. Looking at Ch'üan Pu-i from a distance, however, he perceived that he had a stern and lofty bearing and was dressed in splendid attire, and he therefore scrambled into his shoes and hastened forward to greet him, leading him up into the hall and guiding him to a seat.

Ch'üan Pu-i, placing his hands on the floor and bowing politely, said, "Though I live at the faraway border of the sea, I have long heard the awesome name of Pao Kung-tzu [2]—and now I am able to meet and speak to you face to face! It has always been my feeling that if an official is too unbending he risks the danger of sudden downfall, while if he is too easygoing he becomes ineffectual. Act forcefully, but temper your acts with kindness—then you may achieve merit, spread your name abroad, and enjoy the blessings of Heaven to the end of your days."

Pao Sheng-chih, recognizing that Ch'üan Pu-i was no ordinary man, listened with respect to this admonition and treated him with utmost courtesy. The conversation then turned to various administrative matters of the time. Pao Sheng-chih's gatekeepers and attendants, all of them distinguished officials selected from the various provinces, were listening by his side, and all were unfailingly astounded by the answers that Ch'üan Pu-i gave. The interview lasted until evening, when Ch'üan Pu-i took his leave and went

[1] A high-crowned cap worn by Confucians and civil officials.
[2] Pao Sheng-chih's polite name.

home. Pao Sheng-chih later submitted a memorial recommending him to the throne and he was summoned to the office of public carriage and appointed provincial director of Ch'ing-chou.

After some time, Emperor Wu passed away and Emperor Chao came to the throne. Liu Tse, the grandson of King Hsiao of Ch'i, joined with men of powerful family in other provinces and kingdoms to plot revolt. As a first step he planned to kill Ch'üan Pu-i, the provincial director of Ch'ing-chou, but the latter learned of the affair and arrested the conspirators. All those involved were brought to justice.

Ch'üan Pu-i was selected to become prefect of the capital and was awarded a gift of a million cash. The officials and people of the capital respected him for his seriousness and integrity. Whenever he would return home after a tour through the districts of the capital for the purpose of reviewing criminal cases, his mother would immediately ask, "Did you reverse or lighten any sentences? How many men did you save from the death penalty?" If he had reversed or lightened the sentence in a number of cases, then his mother would laugh merrily, eat her dinner, and chat with him. But at other times, if he reported that he had been unable to save anyone, she would grow sullen and refuse to eat the food put before her.[3] As a consequence, Ch'üan Pu-i in exercising his official duties was stern but never heartless.

In the fifth year of the *shih-yüan* era (82 B.C.), a man riding in a cart drawn by yellow calves with a yellow pennant at its side, and wearing a single yellow cloak and yellow cap, appeared at the north gate of the imperial palace, claiming that he was crown prince Li, the son of Emperor Wu by Empress Wei.[4] The chief of public carriage reported the matter to the emperor, who sent down an order for the high ministers, generals, and officials of the two thousand picul class to go in a group and confirm the man's identity. Meanwhile, thirty or forty thousand officials and citizens of Ch'ang-an crowded around to watch; the general of the right called out his soldiers and stationed them in front of the gate so as to be prepared for any emergency. The chancellor, the imperial secretary, and the two thousand picul officials all arrived on the

---

[3] In an age when filial piety demanded that a son do everything possible to keep his parents in good health and humor, such behavior on the part of Ch'üan's mother could not be lightly overlooked.

[4] Who had led an abortive revolt against the government in 91 B.C., fled the capital, and later committed suicide.

spot but none dared to speak up. The prefect of the capital Ch'üan Pu-i, arriving late, shouted to his attendants to seize and arrest the young man.

"We don't know whether he is the real prince or not," someone objected. "Wouldn't it be well to proceed more slowly?"

Ch'üan Pu-i replied, "Why are you gentlemen worried about the crown prince? In ancient times crown prince K'uai K'uei broke the law and was forced to flee from the state, and when his son Ch'e later blocked his way and refused to let him reenter the capital, the *Spring and Autumn Annals* gave its approval.[5] Crown prince Li committed an offense against his father, the former emperor, and then fled instead of facing death. Now if he dares to show himself, he should be treated as a criminal!" Ch'üan Pu-i thereupon had the man sent to the prison for offenders who are under imperial indictment. The emperor and the general in chief Ho Kuang, when they heard of his action, expressed their approval, saying, "In appointing high ministers and major officials, it pays to use those who have mastered the lessons of the Classics and understand basic principles!"

As a result of this incident, Ch'üan Pu-i won considerable fame and reputation at court, and those in office all admitted that they were no match for him. The general in chief Ho Kuang wanted to give him one of his daughters as a wife, but Ch'üan Pu-i steadfastly refused, insisting he was unworthy of the honor. After some time, he retired from office because of illness, but though he spent the remainder of his days in retirement at his home, the people of the capital did not forget him. Later, when Chao Kuang-han became prefect of the capital, he said, "In matters pertaining to the prevention of crime and the wiping out of evil, I carry considerable weight among the officials and common people, but when it comes to court matters, I'm a long way from equaling Ch'üan Pu-i!"

Meanwhile, the commandant of justice had been conducting an investigation to determine the identity of the man who had ap-

---

[5] K'uai K'uei, heir apparent of Duke Ling of Wei, angered his father by plotting to kill the duke's consort and was forced to flee the state. On the death of Duke Ling, K'uai K'uei's son Ch'e was appointed successor to the title. K'uai K'uei attempted to reenter the capital but was blocked by the forces loyal to his son. The *Spring and Autumn Annals,* supposed to have been edited by Confucius, records the event under Duke Ai 2d year (493 B.C.) and according to tradition indicates Confucius' approval of Ch'e's action.

peared at the palace gate, and in time discovered the details of his nefarious plot. A native of Hsia-yang, his family name was Ch'eng and his personal name Fang-sui; he lived in the district of Hu and made his living as a diviner. One of those who came to consult him was a retainer of the late crown prince Li, and this man remarked to Ch'eng Fang-sui that he bore a striking resemblance to the prince in both face and figure. Fang-sui secretly schemed to turn his words to profit and, hoping to obtain riches and honor, presented himself at the palace gate, falsely claiming that he was the crown prince. The commandant of justice also sent out a summons for the arrest of Chang Tsung-lu and others who had been associates of Fang-sui in his home town. Fang-sui was accused of malicious falsehood and unprincipled behavior and was cut in two at the waist in the eastern market. Another account states that his family name was Chang and his personal name Yen-nien.

SHU KUANG AND SHU SHOU

Shu Kuang, whose polite name was Chung-weng, was a native of Lan-ling in Tung-hai. As a youth he was fond of study and was an expert on the *Spring and Autumn Annals.* He lived at home and gave instruction, students coming from great distances to study with him. Later he was chosen to become an erudit and palace counselor.

In the third year of *ti-chieh* (67 B.C.), when the heir apparent to Emperor Hsüan was designated, Ping Chi was chosen to act as grand tutor and Shu Kuang as lesser tutor. After a few months, Ping Chi was transferred to the post of imperial secretary and Shu Kuang was made grand tutor in his place.

Shu Shou, whose polite name was Kung-tzu, was the son of Shu Kuang's elder brother; he was selected as a man of worth and goodness and appointed overseer of the heir apparent's household. Shu Shou paid the strictest attention to ritual and good manners and was alert and well-spoken. When Emperor Hsüan visited the heir apparent's palace, Shu Shou greeted him and responded to his inquiries, and when wine had been set out and the feasting had begun, he offered a toast to the emperor's health. His words and behavior were marked by poise and elegance and the emperor was exceedingly pleased with him. After a while, Shu Shou was appointed lesser tutor to the heir apparent.

The maternal grandfather of the heir apparent, the specially appointed marquis of P'ing-en Hsü Kuang-han, observing that the heir apparent was still young, urged that his younger brother the general of palace attendants Hsü Shun be assigned to supervise and look after the household of the heir apparent. When the emperor questioned Shu Kuang about the matter, he replied, "The heir apparent is the future hope of the nation and the ruler's aide. His teachers and friends should be chosen from among the finest and most outstanding men of the empire—it is not right that he associate only with his maternal relatives of the Hsü family. Moreover, he has his own grand tutor and lesser tutor and all the posts in his household are already filled. If on top of this Hsü Shun should be appointed to supervise the heir apparent's household, it would appear a rather narrow-sighted move, certainly not one calculated to enhance the prince's reputation for virtue in the world!"[6]

The emperor thought highly of his words, and when he reported them to the chancellor Wei Hsiang, the latter doffed his hat in a gesture of apology and said, "I'm afraid I and the others could never have answered so wisely." As a result of this, Shu Kuang came to be looked upon with great admiration and respect; he often received rewards and gifts from the emperor. Whenever the heir apparent would appear at court, his tutors would accompany him into the presence of the emperor, the grand tutor Shu Kuang preceding him, the lesser tutor Shu Shou following behind, uncle and nephew both serving as his mentors. The men of the court looked upon this as the height of distinction.

By the time Shu Kuang had held his post for five years, the heir apparent was twelve years of age and could recite the *Analects* and *Classic of Filial Piety*. Shu Kuang then said to his nephew, "I have heard that he who knows what is enough will not suffer disgrace and he who knows when to stop will not encounter peril.[7] When deeds have been accomplished, one should retire—that is the Way of Heaven! Now we have advanced in public service to the two thousand picul rank and have won fame as officials. If we do not withdraw now, I'm afraid we may regret it later. How would it do for the two of us, uncle and nephew, to follow each other out of the Pass, return home to our old village, and there live out the years that remain to us—wouldn't that be best?"

[6] *I.e.*, the prince would appear to be showing too great favoritism to his maternal relatives.

[7] Shu Kuang is quoting Lao Tzu, *Tao-te-ching* 44.

Shu Shou bowed his head and replied, "I leave it to you, uncle."

On the very same day both uncle and nephew reported that they were suffering from illness. When the customary three months waiting period had passed, they were granted a leave of absence, but Shu Kuang, pleading that his illness was critical, submitted a memorial asking that he be released from government service. In view of the fact that he was old and in precarious health, the emperor agreed to release both him and his nephew, in addition presenting them with a gift of twenty catties of gold. The heir apparent for his part presented them with fifty catties. The high ministers and officials, along with the Shus' old friends and neighbors, rigged curtains and prepared a farewell feast for them outside the gate on the road leading to the Eastern Capital. Several hundred carriages filled with people came to see them off as they said goodby and started on their way. Those who saw them passing along the road all exclaimed, "What fine gentlemen these two are!" and some sighed and shed a tear for them.

After Shu Kuang had returned home, he would each day order his family to prepare wine and food, and would invite his relatives, old friends, and their guests to join him in making merry. From time to time he would ask his family how much of the gold was left and then would send them scurrying off to sell some more of it and buy provisions. After a year or so of this, Shu Kuang's sons and grandsons took one of Shu Kuang's cousins aside, an elderly man whom Shu Kuang loved and trusted, and said to him, "We had hoped while the old gentleman is still alive to lay the foundations for something of a family fortune, but with all this drinking and eating every day the money is almost all used up. Perhaps you could speak to him, as though it were your own idea, and urge him to buy some land and houses."

The old cousin accordingly waited until a time when Shu Kuang was at leisure and then approached him with this suggestion. Shu Kuang replied, "Am I some kind of old fool, that you think I don't give any thought to my sons and grandsons? But if you stop to consider, they have the fields and cottages that have been in the family all along, and if they work hard, there's plenty there to provide food and clothing and allow them to live the same as other ordinary folk. Now if I were to increase their holdings and create a surplus of riches, I would only be encouraging my sons and grandsons to become careless and lazy. A worthy man with much wealth finds his high ideals tarnished; a fool with much wealth finds his faults magnified. Moreover, riches incite the envy of the common crowd. Since I have in the past failed to instruct my sons and grandsons properly and instill in them high moral principles, I certainly do not want to add to their faults and make them the target of envy. This gold, after all, was given by our holy sovereign to provide for his old minister. Therefore I enjoy it with my neighbors and relatives, so that we may all share in the bounty. If I finish out my days in this manner, is there any great harm?"

Shu Kuang's relatives good-naturedly expressed their agreement, and he and his nephew lived to a ripe old age.

YÜ TING-KUO

Yü Ting-kuo, whose polite name was Man-ch'ien, was a native of T'an in Tung-hai. His father Lord Yü had been district prison official and a judge of criminal cases for the province and was very fair in his administration of justice. Whenever a case was brought before the officials, if Lord Yü handed down the decision, none of the parties had any cause for resentment. While he was still living a shrine was erected to him in the province called the Shrine of Lord Yü.[8]

In Tung-hai there was a young wife noted for her filial conduct whose husband died early and left her without any children. She continued to look after her mother-in-law with great diligence, and though the latter urged her to remarry, she steadfastly refused. The mother-in-law said to a neighbor, "The young wife does her best to take good care of me but I pity her, having no children and being obliged to stay with me. I am old—I don't know why I should go on being such a burden to the young." Shortly afterwards, the mother-in-law hanged herself.

The daughter of the mother-in-law reported to the officials that the young wife had murdered her mother and the officials accordingly arrested the wife. The wife insisted that she had not killed her mother-in-law, but the officials pressed their investigation until the wife finally gave a false confession, whereupon the case was turned over to the provincial office. Lord Yü considered that, since the wife had already taken care of her mother-in-law for over ten years and was well known for her filial conduct, she would cer-

---

[8] After eminent and worthy men died, shrines were often erected to them in the places where they had lived or worked, but this is said to be the earliest case in which a shrine was erected to a man while he was still alive.

tainly not commit such a murder, but the governor refused to listen to him. When Lord Yü saw that he could not persuade the governor of her innocence, he gathered up the documents pertaining to the case, performed ritual lamentations in the provincial office, and resigned his post on grounds of illness. In the end, the governor sentenced the young wife to death.

For three years following, the province was afflicted with drought. When a new governor arrived to replace the former one, he conducted divinations in an effort to determine the cause of the drought. Lord Yü said, "The filial wife should not have been condemned to death, but the former governor insisted upon carrying out the sentence. I wonder if this may not be where the blame lies."

The new governor thereupon slaughtered an ox and offered it as a sacrifice at the grave of the young wife, at the same time setting up a marker beside her grave. Immediately the skies sent down rain and the harvest for the year was bountiful. Because of this the people of the province looked on Lord Yü with great respect and veneration.[9]

When Yü Ting-kuo was young he studied law under his father, and after his father's death he in like manner became a prison official and judge of criminal cases for the province. He was appointed a clerk under the commandant of justice and was thereafter selected to serve under the middle aide to the imperial secretary. His duty was to investigate persons charged with treason and he won high praise for his ability. He was appointed as one of the secretaries of the censorate, and from there advanced to the post of middle aide to the imperial secretary.

Just at that time, Emperor Chao passed away and the king of Ch'ang-i was summoned to take the throne. He behaved in a wild and disorderly manner, however, and Yü Ting-kuo submitted a letter to the throne censuring him. He was shortly afterwards deposed and Emperor Hsüan set up in his place. The general in chief Ho Kuang, who was in charge of the office of palace writers, then compiled a list of the various officials who had reprimanded the king of Ch'ang-i and submitted it to the throne, asking that all those on the list be given special promotion. As a result, Yü Ting-kuo was made counselor to the keeper of the palace gate and was

[9] This is the earliest example I know of the theme, so popular in later Chinese literature, of a victim of unjust punishment whose ghost causes mischief until the injustice is exposed and righted.

put in charge of the office of palace writers, being entrusted with a position of grave responsibility. After a few years he was shifted to the post of director of waterworks, and later was granted special promotion to that of commandant of justice.

Yü Ting-kuo then sent for a teacher and began instruction in the *Spring and Autumn Annals*, he himself holding the copy of the text, facing north and waiting on his teacher in accordance with the ritual demanded of a disciple.[10] As a man, he was modest and unassuming, and he showed the highest respect for scholars of classical learning. Though they might be men of the humblest station who were obliged to go about on foot, if they came to visit Yü Ting-kuo, he treated them all with the courtesy due to an equal. He was the very model of kindness and deference, and men of learning all praised him for it.

In judging cases and administering the law, Yü Ting-kuo strove to protect the helpless commoner, the widow and the widower. If the case was a doubtful one, he would apply the lightest possible sentence, and he pursued his duties with thoroughness and circumspection. The men of the court praised him, saying, "When Chang Shih-chih was commandant of justice, there were in fact no people in the empire who suffered injustice; but now that Yü Ting-kuo is commandant of justice, people assume as a matter of course that there will be no injustice." [11]

Yü Ting-kuo was a great consumer of wine and could drink several piculs without losing control of himself. During the winter months when he was busy disposing of criminal cases, the more he drank the more clear-headed and perceptive he became.[12]

After serving as commandant of justice for eighteen years, he was transferred to the post of imperial secretary, and during the *kan-lu* era (53–50 B.C.) he replaced Huang Pa as chancellor and was enfeoffed as marquis of Hsi-p'ing. Three years later, Emperor

[10] The *Spring and Autumn Annals*, which was supposed to embody Confucius' "praise-and-blame" judgments of the men of history, was regarded with particular importance by those concerned with legal matters; hence Yü Ting-kuo's attention to it when he became commandant of justice.

[11] Chang Shih-chih was commandant of justice under Emperor Wen (r. 179–157 B.C.) and was noted for his fairness in administering the law.

[12] According to the Five Elements system of thought, it was improper to administer punishment in the spring, the time for new life and growth, and therefore there was always a rush to finish disposing of criminal cases before the end of winter. One picul in liquid measure was equal to about 20 quarts; one can only suppose that Han wine was very low in alcoholic content.

Hsüan passed away and Emperor Yüan came to the throne. Because Yü Ting-kuo had been in office for a long time, the new emperor treated him with gravity and respect. At this time Ch'en Wan-nien was imperial secretary, and he and Yü Ting-kuo managed to serve side by side for eight years without once becoming involved in a clash of opinion. Later, Kung Yü replaced Ch'en Wan-nien as imperial secretary, and he often had occasion to differ with Yü Ting-kuo, but because the latter was well versed in the handling of government affairs, the emperor customarily gave his approval to Yü Ting-kuo's views.

The new emperor had just begun his reign, and east of the Han-ku Pass natural disasters had afflicted the region for a number of years in a row, sending a stream of refugees flowing west through the Pass into the capital region. Those who offered opinions on such matters laid the blame for this state of affairs on the high ministers. Several times when court day came around,[13] the emperor summoned the chancellor and the imperial secretary to a private interview, and when they had entered his presence, handed them an imperial order berating them item by item for deficiencies in their performance of duty. One such order read:

"Evil officials, fearful that they will be blamed for criminal activity in their area, cast wild aspersions on harmless persons, causing those who are innocent to suffer death. Often when thieves and bandits appear, the officials make no haste to pursue them, but instead arrest those who were the victims of their plunder, so that in time people become afraid to report damage and the evil grows more widespread than ever. Many of the people have suffered injustice but the provinces do nothing to rectify their cases and hence there is a constant stream of them from distant regions presenting petitions at the palace gate. The process of selecting the two thousand picul officials has not been carried out judiciously and as a consequence there are many men in office who are not competent to fulfill their duties. The people's farms are visited by disaster and yet the officials are unwilling to grant them exemptions from taxes, instead pressing them for payment until they are more distraught and heavily burdened than ever. The people streaming in from east of the Pass are starving, cold, and worn out by disease. I have already issued orders to the officials to transport supplies for their relief, emptying the granaries, opening up the store houses, attempting to alleviate their distress and provide

[13] The court assembled once every five days.

clothing for those who are suffering from the cold, but by spring I am afraid the supplies will be exhausted. Now as chancellor and imperial secretary, what measures would you propose to remedy this grave situation? I want you to set forth your ideas in detail and tell me exactly what fault I have committed!" [14]

Yü Ting-kuo thereupon submitted a letter to the throne apologizing for having failed in his duty.

In the first year of the *yung-kuang* era (43 B.C.), frost fell in the spring, the summer was cold, and the sun shone gray and lusterless. The emperor once more issued an order berating the chancellor and imperial secretary on a number of counts, saying, "Palace attendants returning from the east tell me that the people are in such desperate straits that father and son turn their backs on one another. Are the officials under your jurisdiction hiding the truth and failing to report it to you? Or are those who come from the east exaggerating the true state of affairs? Why should there be such discrepancies? I want to know the truth! It is too soon to predict what kind of harvest we will have this year, but if there should be floods or droughts, the damage will be far from slight. You, the high officials, are supposed to be able to take steps to prevent future disasters and to remedy those which have already occurred, are you not? I want each of you to give a sincere reply, without fear of saying anything that will offend me!"

Yü Ting-kuo, thoroughly alarmed, thereupon submitted a letter to the throne heaping blame on himself, returning the seals of his marquisate, and begging that he be released from public service.

The emperor replied as follows: "In your relations with me you have never dared to be careless or remiss. I am aware that a countless number of matters are entrusted to your direction, and only a sage can be wholly free of error. Our present age has inherited the abuses of the Chou and Ch'in dynasties and its customs have fallen into sad decline. The people pay scant heed to ritual and right, and the yin and yang are not in harmony. But when portents and disasters appear, they do not arise from a single cause alone. The sage may attempt to classify such occurrences by analogy but even he does not venture to assign them to a single cause, and therefore how much less should we who are not sages! Day and night I ponder the reasons why they should arise, but I have not yet been able to fathom them fully. The Classic says, 'If there is blame in any of

---

[14] In customary Chinese fashion, the emperor accepts personal blame for the evils and misfortunes that befall his people.

the people of the ten thousand quarters, there must be blame in me, the ruler.' [15] Now although you occupy a high office, how could you alone be held responsible? I hope that you will be diligent in examining the provincial governors and administrators and the prime ministers of the feudal states, making sure that if there are any who are unfit for office, they are not allowed to tyrannize over the people for long. Continue as long as you are able to hold firm to the reins of good rule, strive for the utmost astuteness and perspicacity, force yourself to eat well, and guard your health!"

Yü Ting-kuo, pleading that his condition was critical, begged to be allowed to retire, whereupon the emperor awarded him a comfortable carriage, a team of four horses, and sixty catties of gold. After he left office, he retired to his home and lived for several years. He was over seventy when he passed away, and was assigned the posthumous title of An, the "Tranquil Marquis."

His son Yü Yung succeeded to the title. In his youth he was addicted to wine and was guilty of many indiscretions, but when he was about thirty he finally reformed his ways and began to be more careful in his conduct. Because of his father's career in public service, he was made attendant in the inner palace, general of palace attendants, and commander of the Ch'ang-shui garrison. When Yü Ting-kuo died, he observed the mourning period in exact accordance with ritual and gained a name for filial conduct. Having succeeded to his father's title and become a member of the nobility, he was made keeper of the palace gate in charge of supplementary cavalry and later advanced as high as the post of imperial secretary. He was married to the Kuan-t'ao princess, Liu Shih. Liu Shih was the eldest daughter of Emperor Hsüan and the aunt of Emperor Ch'eng; she was a woman of worth and high conduct and therefore Yü Yung was chosen to be her mate. The emperor was on the point of promoting Yü Yung to the post of chancellor when the latter passed away. His son T'ien succeeded him, but he was a person of shallow character and wholly undistinguished in conduct.

Earlier, when Yü Ting-kuo's father was still alive, the gate to the neighborhood where he and his family lived fell into disrepair. When the elders of the community gathered together to rebuild it, Yü Ting-kuo's father said, "Make it tall enough to admit a team of four horses and a high topped carriage. In deciding criminal cases

[15] The sentence is now found in *Analects* XX, 1, but a passage in the *Conversations from the States, Chou yü* 1, indicates that it was probably originally part of the "Oath of T'ang," a section of the *Book of Documents*.

I have done many unknown kindnesses and I've never inflicted injustice upon anyone—my sons and grandsons are bound to come up in the world!" As it turned out, Yü Tung-kuo became chancellor, his son Yü Yung became imperial secretary, and the marquisate they received passed down from generation to generation.

HSÜEH KUANG-TE

Hsüeh Kuang-te, whose polite name was Ch'ang-ch'ing, was a native of Hsiang in P'ei. He gave instruction in the Lu version of the *Book of Odes* to Hsi Sheng and Hsi She of the state of Ch'u and they treated him as their teacher. When Hsiao Wang-chih became imperial secretary, he selected Hsüeh Kuang-te to be one of his subordinates. From time to time he consulted with Hsüeh Kuang-te and, being much impressed with his ability, recommended him as a man versed in the Classics and distinguished in conduct who was worthy of a post at court. He was appointed an erudit and took part in the discussions in the Stone Conduit Hall.[16] He was promoted to the post of admonisher and later replaced Kung Yü, first as privy treasurer of the Palace of Lasting Trust and later as imperial secretary.

Hsüeh Kuang-te was a warm and courteous man, noted for his poise and refinement, but when he was promoted to imperial secretary, one of the three highest posts in the government, he did not hesitate to speak out boldly in reprimand. In the first week of his new appointment (43 B.C.), Emperor Yüan visited the Palace of Sweet Springs, performed the suburban sacrifice at the Altar of the Great Unity, and when the rituals were completed, remained in the countryside in order to hunt. Hsüeh Kuang-te thereupon submitted a letter to the throne which read:

"I have heard that east of the Pass there is dire distress and the people are leaving their homes and taking to the road, yet Your Majesty day after day strikes the bells of the fallen Ch'in dynasty and listens to the lascivious music of the states of Cheng and Wei. Truly I find it a cause for lament! Now your officers and soldiers are exposed to the dew of the field and your attendant officials are weary and exhausted. I beg you to hasten your return to the capital and join with the common people in sharing their sorrows and joys—then will the empire be blessed indeed!"

[16] A gathering of scholars convened by Emperor Hsüan in 51 B.C. for the purpose of discussing varying interpretations of the Confucian Classics.

The emperor returned to the capital on the very same day.

In the autumn of the same year the emperor went to offer sacrifices in the ancestral temples. He left the city by the Pien Gate, intending to cross the Wei River by cabined boat, but Hsüeh Kuang-te stationed himself beside the carriage in which the emperor was riding, removed his cap, bowed his head, and said, "It would be well to go by way of the bridge."

"Put on your cap, sir!" the emperor commanded, but Hsüeh Kuang-te replied, "If Your Majesty refuses to listen to me, I will cut my throat and spatter blood all over the carriage wheels so that it will be impossible for Your Majesty to enter the ancestral temples!" [17]

The emperor was very put out, but the counselor to the keeper of the palace gate Chang Meng, who was riding in the vanguard, came forward and said, "I have heard that if the ruler is a sage, his ministers will speak frankly. To travel by boat is dangerous, to go by the bridge is safe. A sage ruler does not embark on a course of danger—it would be well to heed the words of the imperial secretary!"

The emperor said, "When one is trying to persuade others, he should go about it the way you have, should he not?" He then proceeded by way of the bridge.

A month or so later, because the harvests were poor and many of the people had taken to vagrancy, Hsüeh Kuang-te joined with the chancellor Yü Ting-kuo and the grand marshal general of carriage and cavalry Shih Kao in requesting release from government service. All were presented by the emperor with comfortable carriages, teams of four horses, and sixty catties of gold apiece. Hsüeh Kuang-te served a total of ten months as imperial secretary before being relieved of office. After his dismissal, he returned east to his home in P'ei. The governor met him at the border of the province and the people of P'ei took pride in his achievements. He hung up the comfortable carriage for safe keeping so that it could be handed down to his sons and grandsons. [18]

---

[17] Because of ritual pollution.

[18] I have omitted at this point the biographies of P'ing Tang and P'eng Hsüan, two men who, like the others treated in this chapter, attained office because of their knowledge of the Classics and, when they felt the time had come to do so, obtained release from public service and retired to their homes to live out their lives in peace.

In appraisal we say: Ch'üan Pu-i was called to government service because of his learning and carried out his duties without a misstep. He performed deeds of great renown and his story is worthy to be told from beginning to end. Shu Kuang knew when to stop and what is enough, thus avoiding the snares of disgrace and danger—he deserves to rank next in place. Yü Ting-kuo and his father took pity on the helpless and were astute in judging criminal cases; they were men who were well fitted for their tasks. Hsüeh Kuang-te cherished his comfortable carriage and the honor it represented, P'ing Tang held back out of a sense of shame, and P'eng Hsüan stopped because he saw danger ahead—they differed from those men who grab at a thing for fear of losing it!

HAN SHU 74: THE BIOGRAPHIES OF
Wei Hsiang and Ping Chi

WEI HSIANG, THE MARQUIS OF KAO-P'ING, a model of models, knowing that the sovereign alone has the right to exercise majesty, strove to banish evil and harm, aiding the Son of Heaven. Ping Chi, the marquis of Po-yang, refused to boast, though his merit was ample and far-reaching; Heaven brought to light his faithfulness and blessing flowed to his heirs and descendants. So I have transmitted the Biographies of Wei Hsiang and Ping Chi.

WEI HSIANG

Wei Hsiang's polite name was Jo-weng; he was born in Ting-t'ao in Chi-yin and later moved to P'ing-ling. In his youth he studied the *Book of Changes* and became a clerk in the provincial government. He was chosen as a man of worth and goodness and, having received a high mark for his answers to the questions posed on the government examination, was appointed magistrate of Mou-ling.

Some time later, one of the private retainers of the imperial secretary Sang Hung-yang, claiming that he was a clerk of the censorate in the imperial secretary's office, demanded to be put up at the official lodging house in Mou-ling. Moreover, because the assistant to the magistrate of Mou-ling was somewhat late in appearing at the lodge to pay his respects, the retainer became enraged and had the assistant put in bonds. Wei Hsiang, suspecting that something irregular was afoot, ordered the retainer arrested and, after conducting an investigation and exposing him as an impostor, had him put to death and his corpse exposed in the market place. After this, Mou-ling was a model of good order.

Wei Hsiang was later transferred to the post of governor of Honan. He put a stop to evil and lawlessness and the powerful and influential families of the area feared and obeyed him.

Just at that time, the chancellor Chü Ch'ien-ch'iu died (77 B.C.). Earlier, Chü Ch'ien-ch'iu's son had been appointed chief of the military arsenal in Lo-yang, in the province of which Wei Hsiang was governor. Now that his father was dead, he began to fear that, with Wei Hsiang's reputation for strict rule in the province, he would be accused of some fault; he therefore resigned his post and left the area. Wei Hsiang sent some of his clerks to pursue the man and invite him back, but he refused to return to his post. Wei Hsiang, much disturbed, said to himself, "When the general in chief Ho Kuang hears that the chief of the arsenal has left his post, he is bound to think that I am trying to profit by his father's death and refusing to treat the son with proper respect. If I stir up the powerful people of the day and give them occasion to criticize me, I'm sure to face trouble!"

Meanwhile, the chief of the arsenal proceeded west until he reached Ch'ang-an and thereafter, as Wei Hsiang had feared, the general in chief Ho Kuang began to berate Wei Hsiang over the matter, saying, "In these critical times when the ruler is still young and has newly ascended the throne, I have appointed the younger brother of the late chancellor as colonel of the Han-ku Pass, since the pass is the key to the defense of the metropolitan area, and have appointed the chancellor's son as chief of the military arsenal, since it is the assembly point for the finest troops of the empire. Now you are acting as governor of Ho-nan, and yet you fail to give careful consideration to the over-all welfare of the nation. Instead, because you see that the chancellor is no longer around to protest, you hound his son out of office—a very mean and shallow act indeed!"

Later someone accused Wei Hsiang of having persecuted and put to death an innocent man and the case was handed over to the authorities for investigation. At this time there were two or three thousand soldiers from the province of Ho-nan who were fulfilling a term of service as guards at the various administrative offices in the capital; they gathered en masse to block the general in chief's path and speak to him, requesting that their period of service in the capital be extended for a year so as to atone for the crime charged against their governor. In addition, over ten thousand men of Ho-nan, both old and young, gathered at the Han-ku Pass and begged to be allowed to proceed to the capital so that they could submit petitions to the throne on Wei Hsiang's behalf, a fact which the officials guarding the pass duly reported.

The general in chief, however, could not forget the matter of the chief of the arsenal and eventually had Wei Hsiang sent to prison for prosecution by the commandant of justice. Wei Hsiang was held prisoner for a long time, passing the winter in jail, but was released when a general amnesty was declared. He was summoned back to office by imperial command, this time to become acting magistrate of Mou-ling. Later he was promoted to provincial director of Yang-chou.

At this time a review was held of the various provincial governors and prime ministers of the feudal states, and many of them were demoted or removed from office. Wei Hsiang was on close terms with Ping Chi, who at this time was a counselor to the keeper of the palace gate; the latter sent Wei Hsiang a letter saying, "The court is already well aware of your record as a model administrator and is about to appoint you to an important post. Meanwhile I hope you will be somewhat cautious in your handling of affairs. Proceed with circumspection and keep your talents hidden from sight!"

Wei Hsiang, acknowledging the wisdom of such advice, ceased to be as stern and exacting as he had been, and after two years in the post of provincial director, he was summoned to the court to become an admonisher. Later he was sent to the provinces once more to become governor of Ho-nan. After several years, Emperor Hsüan came to the throne and Wei Hsiang was recalled to the capital, appointed minister of agriculture, and later promoted to imperial secretary.

Four years later, the general in chief Ho Kuang passed away (68 B.C.). In memory of the great services which he had performed, the emperor appointed his son Ho Yü general of the right, and enfeoffed Ho Shan, the grandson of his elder brother, as marquis of Lo-p'ing and gave him supervision over the office of palace writers. Wei Hsiang, enlisting the aid of Hsü Kuang-han, the marquis of P'ing-en, submitted a sealed memorial to the throne which read:

"The *Spring and Autumn Annals* condemns hereditary office for ministers, criticizing the state of Sung for allowing a ministerial family to hold sway for three generations in a row and censuring the dictatorial power of the Chi-sun family of Lu, since danger and disorder to the state resulted in both cases.[1] From the *hou-yüan* era on (88–87 B.C.),[2] fortune deserted the imperial household and government proceeded instead from the hands of its high minister. Now Ho Kuang has died but his son has been made general of the right and the grandson of his elder brother wields crucial authority in the inner councils of state. The sons of the Ho family and the husbands of its daughters occupy positions of power and have troops under their command, while Ho Kuang's widow Hsien and her daughters have managed to put their names on the list of those who are permitted to visit the empress dowager at the Palace of Lasting Trust and at times are even to be found going in and out of the palace late at night. I fear that such favoritism and affluence, such flagrant and unruly behavior will eventually reach the point where it cannot be checked. It would be best to strip the family of its power and block its secret schemes so that the foundations of the state may be made firm for ten thousand ages to come and the descendants of a meritorious minister may be spared the consequences of their own folly."

In addition, it had been the custom up to this time when submitting a letter to the throne to prepare two sealed copies, one of them marked "duplicate." The person who had charge of the office of palace writers would first open the seal on the duplicate copy, and if he did not approve of the contents of the letter, would put both copies aside and not allow the matter to come before the emperor. Wei Hsiang, once more acting through Hsü Kuang-han, asked that the system of submitting duplicate copies be abolished in order to foil any attempts at concealment. Emperor Hsüan approved this suggestion and also appointed Wei Hsiang to the position of steward, allowing him to come and go in the inner palace. In all matters, the emperor listened to his advice.

It was at this time that the emperor first learned that the Ho family had contrived the murder of Empress Hsü. He relieved the three marquises of the Ho family, Yü, Yün, and Shan, of their duties and sent them to their homes, at the same time transferring all their relatives and followers to posts outside the capital. At this

---

[1] The dukes of Sung for three generations married daughters of a ministerial family, a situation censured by the *Kung-yang Commentary* on the *Spring and Autumn Annals,* Duke Hsi 25th year. The Chi-sun family became so powerful that at one point they drove the duke of Lu into exile.

[2] The last years of Emperor Wu's reign.

time Wei Hsien, who had been serving as chancellor, retired on grounds of old age and poor health, and was replaced by Wei Hsiang, who was enfeoffed as marquis of Kao-p'ing with the revenue from a town of eight hundred households.

The members of the Ho family, enraged at Wei Hsiang and fearful of him as well, plotted to forge an imperial order from the empress dowager, summon Wei Hsiang, and cut him down, after which they would depose the emperor. The plot came to light, however, and they were all put to death. Emperor Hsüan then for the first time took personal command of the affairs of government, devoting all his energy to the achievement of orderly rule, carefully selecting men for official posts and making certain that the title they held was in conformity with their actual performance. Wei Hsiang supervised the various offices of government and performed his duties in a way that pleased the emperor greatly.

During the *yüan-k'ang* era (65–62 B.C.) the Hsiung-nu sent some of their armed men to attack the Han garrison and farm in Chü-shih, but were unable to force a surrender.[3] The emperor consulted with the general of the rear Chao Ch'ung-kuo and others, hoping to take advantage of the apparent weakness of the Hsiung-nu by sending a force of men to attack the western portion of their territory and intimidating them from making further trouble for the region west of China. Wei Hsiang, however, submitted a letter to the throne opposing such a plan of action and saying:

"I have heard that military action which is designed to rectify disorder and punish violence is called a campaign of righteousness; such a campaign is the mark of a true king. Action which arises unavoidably when an enemy launches an attack against one's own forces is called a campaign of response; such a campaign will be victorious. An action which arises from petty wrangling and spite, from ire and vexation that can no longer be restrained, is called a campaign of anger, and such a campaign will end in failure. An action which has as its object the exploitation of someone else's lands or treasures is called a campaign of greed and it will face defeat. An action in which one party, relying upon the superior size of its territory and boasting of the large number of its people, sets out to overawe its enemy by a show of force is called a campaign

---

[3] Chü-shih was a small state in the region of Turfan in present day Sinkiang Province.

of arrogance, and it is doomed to annihilation. These five categories are not merely something contrived by men but have their basis in the Way of Heaven.

"In recent times the Hsiung-nu have consistently manifested a spirit of good will, immediately returning to China any subjects of the Han who happened to fall into their hands and refraining from violations of the border. Although there has been a scuffle with the garrison troops in Chü-shih, it is scarcely important enough even to merit notice. And yet now I hear that the various generals are planning to call out troops and move into Hsiung-nu territory. Ignorant as I am, I am at a loss to know *what* name to assign to a campaign such as this!

"The border regions these days are beset by poverty and want, father and son sharing their pelts of lamb and dog, eating the seeds of grasses and herbs, ever fearful that there will not be enough to sustain life. It would be hard in such a time to launch a military campaign. They say that war is always followed by a year of dearth—this is because the anguished and suffering spirits of the people bring injury to the harmony of the yin and yang. Thus, although the troops that march forth may win victory, there is bound to be sorrow and suffering in its wake, and this suffering, I fear, will bring about unusual occurrences such as natural calamities and disasters.[4]

"These days there are many men serving as governors of provinces or prime ministers of feudal states who are not fitted for their jobs; the customs and folkways of the empire have grown frivolous and corrupt, and flood and drought visit us without respite. According to the statistics for the past year, there was a total of two hundred and twenty cases of sons or younger brothers who murdered their fathers or elder brothers, or wives who murdered their husbands. If I may say so, this is an 'unusual occurrence' of far from petty proportions![5] Yet those who attend Your Majesty fail to worry about this and instead propose to call out troops to repay some trifling grudge against a far-off tribe of barbarians. This is perhaps what Confucius meant when he said, 'I suspect that the

[4] Human emotions and deeds literally disrupt the harmony of the natural order and cause spells of unusual weather or other disasters.

[5] The murders are particularly ominous because they are carried out by persons of subordinate status against their social superiors, indicating a dangerous breakdown in the hierarchical order of society.

threat to the Chi-sun family lies not in Chuan-yü but within its own screens and walls.'[6] I hope that Your Majesty will consult with the marquis of P'ing-ch'ang Wang Wu-ku, the marquis of Lo-ch'ang Wang Wu, the marquis of P'ing-en Hsü Kuang-han, and other knowledgeable persons in careful deliberation before reaching a final decision."

The emperor heeded his advice and abandoned plans for an expedition against the Hsiung-nu.

Wei Hsiang was an expert in the *Book of Changes* and expounded the text just as he had learned it from his teacher. He was very fond of looking over old regulations and precedents of the Han court and reading memorials that had been submitted in the past in times of crisis. He firmly believed that, although past and present might differ in form and procedure, what was wanted at the moment was a firm adherence to the precedents of the past. From time to time he drew up accounts of the measures adopted by the government since the founding of the Han to meet various contingencies, as well as making abstracts from the words of such eminent statesmen as Chia Yi, Ch'ao Ts'o, and Tung Chung-shu, and submitted them to the throne with the request that they be put into practice, offering this explanation:

"I have heard that when an enlightened sovereign reigns above and worthy ministers act as his assistants below, then the ruler will enjoy safety and contentment and the people peace and harmony. I have graciously been permitted to occupy a post, and yet I have not succeeded in upholding the enlightened laws of the dynasty, spreading abroad its teachings, bringing order to the four directions, and proclaiming the holy virtue of its ruler. Many of the people have turned their backs on the basic pursuits of agriculture and hastened after the secondary concerns of trade, until now there are those who wear the look of hunger and poverty, a cause of concern to Your Majesty. Truly my blame is such that I deserve ten thousand deaths. Being shallow and deficient in knowledge and ability, I have failed to comprehend the basic principles of the nation or to perceive what measures are appropriate for the times. I think constantly of the people, yet do not know how to proceed.

"In my humble observation, the former emperors in the wealth of their sacred virtue, their benevolence and mercy, labored and

[6] *Analects* XVI, 1. The Chi-sun, a very powerful ministerial family of the state of Lu, was preparing to attack the tiny state of Chuan-yü, which it claimed was a threat to its power.

strove for the sake of the empire, turning their thoughts to the humble folk below them and worrying lest they suffer the calamities of flood and drought. Because the people were poor and in distress, the rulers opened the storehouses and granaries to relieve their want and hunger. They dispatched the admonishers and erudits to travel about the empire observing the customs and folkways, selecting men of worth and goodness, and redressing cases of injustice in the courts, an endless stream of such officials pouring forth from the capital. They reduced expenditures, lightened taxes, and eased the restrictions against the use of the resources of the hills, lakes, and ponds; they prohibited grain to be fed to horses, to be used in the manufacture of wine, or to be hoarded in excessive quantities. Thus they adopted all measures possible to ease the distressed, to sustain the weary, and to bring comfort and relief to the masses and benefit the common people. I cannot describe every detail of the measures they took, but I venture to risk death by presenting a list of twenty-three examples of actions taken in previous times and the edicts and memorials pertaining to them.

"It is my considered opinion that the rule of a true king must have its foundation in agriculture, giving careful attention to the accumulation and storing of goods, calculating intake and restricting outlay so as to be prepared for dearth and disaster. If there is less than enough grain in storage to sustain the nation for six years, this already deserves to be called a state of crisis. In the second year of the *yüan-ting* era (115 B.C.), the provinces of P'ing-yüan, Po-hai, T'ai-shan, and Tung-chün were afflicted with widespread disaster and the people starved and fell dead by the roadside. The fault lay with the two thousand picul officials, who had taken no precautions to deal with such an emergency. Fortunately an enlightened edict came down from the sovereign providing relief and the region was granted a new lease on life.

"The harvest this year has been a poor one and grain prices are climbing wildly. Even now in the autumn when crops are being gathered in, there are those who suffer want; when the lean months of spring come, I fear the situation will worsen until it is beyond remedy. The Western Ch'iang tribes have not yet been pacified and the armies have marched abroad. If war should come to add its burden, my heart turns cold to think what may happen! Preparations should be made as soon as possible to cope with the emergency. My only hope is that Your Majesty will condescend to take thought for the masses, adopting as a model the splendid virtue of the former emperors and bringing solace to all within the four seas."

The emperor heeded Wei Hsiang's suggestions and put them into practice. In addition, Wei Hsiang several times submitted memorials dealing with matters pertaining to the *Changes* and the yin and yang, as well as the Bright Hall and the "Monthly Commandments," speaking as follows: [7]

"Though I have graciously been permitted to become an official in the government, I have failed to perform my duties properly and have been unable to proclaim and spread abroad the teachings of the ruler. The yin and yang have not been brought into harmony and there is no end to natural disaster and calamity, a situation for which I and the other ministers are to blame.

"The *Book of Changes,* as I have been taught, states: 'Heaven and earth move according to a fixed order; therefore the sun and moon do not mistake their courses and the four seasons never fail to arrive in proper succession. The sage king moves according to a fixed order; therefore his punishments and fines are just and his people submissive.' [8]

"If there is any change or dislocation in heaven and earth, it must come about through the yin and yang. The sun determines the division between the yin and the yang,[9] and when it duly reaches the solstice in winter and summer then the winds of the eight seasons arrive in proper order and the ten thousand things are able to fulfill their respective natures, each attending to its constant duties and never interfering with its neighbor.

"The god of the east is T'ai-hao who rides on the trigram *chen* or Arousing, holds a pair of compasses, and presides over spring. The god of the south is the Fire Emperor who rides on the trigram *li* or Clinging, holds a pair of scales, and presides over summer. The god of the west is Shao-hao who rides on the trigram *tui* or Joyous, holds a T square, and presides over autumn. The god of the north is Chuan-hsü who rides on the trigram *k'an* or Abysmal, holds a

[7] The *ming-t'ang* or Bright Hall, supposedly modeled on the audience hall of the rulers of high antiquity, was a building in which the emperor performed various ceremonial acts symbolic of his cosmic authority. The "Monthly Commandments" were texts describing the ritual and governmental acts appropriate to the ruler in each month of the year, especially the section of the *Book of Rites* by that name.

[8] *Book of Changes,* the *t'uan* comment on the hexagram *yü* or Enthusiasm.

[9] The yang represents the power of the sun and the day, the yin that of the moon and night.

scale weight, and presides over winter. The god of the center is the Yellow Emperor who rides on the trigrams *k'un* or Receptive and *ken* or Keeping Still, holds a measuring line, and presides over the period pertaining to the element earth. Thus each of the Five Emperors has a particular season over which he presides.[10]

"The trigram of the east cannot be used as a basis for governing the west, nor can the trigram of the south be used in governing the north. If in the spring one tries to apply the measures appropriate to the trigram *tui* famine will arise; if in the autumn one applies the measures appropriate to *chen* the blossoms will burst forth; if in winter one applies the measures appropriate to *li* the vitality of the earth, which ought to be closed off at this period, will leak out; and if in summer one applies the measures appropriate to *k'an* then hail will fall.

"The enlightened king is diligent in paying honor to Heaven and careful in his nourishing of the people. Therefore he sets up the office of astronomer [11] in order to observe the four seasons and assign the people tasks appropriate to each. If the ruler's activities are based upon the Way and follow the natural order of the yin and yang, then sun and moon will shine brightly, wind and rain will arrive in season, and the periods of heat and cold will be balanced and in harmony. When these three conditions have been achieved, then natural disasters and calamities will not arise, the five grains will ripen, silk and hemp abound, grass and trees flourish, and birds and beasts multiply; the people will be free from sickness and premature death and there will be a surplus of food and clothing. When that happens, the ruler will be honored and the people merry, superior and inferior will bear no grudge against one another, the teachings of government will not be disobeyed, and men will be ready to listen to the dictates of humility and proper conduct.

"But if wind and rain do not arrive in season then farming and

[10] The passage is a typical example of Han cosmological thought, combining the Five Elements theory with the system of the *Changes* and various mythical figures. In the Five Elements theory, spring corresponds to the element wood, summer to fire, autumn to metal, and winter to water; for the element earth a special period had to be created between the end of summer and the beginning of autumn. The deities of the directions were often regarded as actual rulers of high antiquity and are referred to as the Five Emperors.

[11] Literally Hsi Ho, the names of two men said to have been charged with the supervision of matters pertaining to the heavenly bodies and the calendar in the time of the sage ruler Emperor Yao.

sericulture will suffer, and when farming and sericulture suffer, the people will face hunger and cold. When hunger and cold beset a man, he loses his sense of honesty and shame, and this is how theft and villainy arise. In my humble opinion, the yin and yang constitute the very foundation of the king's activities and govern the fate of all living beings. The worthies and sages from ancient times have invariably acted with the yin and yang in mind.

"The actions of the Son of Heaven should take Heaven and earth as their sole pattern and be carried out in the light of the practices of the former sages. Among the edicts handed down by Emperor Kao-tsu, the eighth, dealing with the vestments of the Son of Heaven, reads as follows:

" 'The grand master of guests Hsiang Chang received an imperial command in the Palace of Lasting Joy saying, "Let the various officials discuss what vestments it is proper for the Son of Heaven to wear so that he may bring peace and good government to the world." The prime minister Hsiao Ho and the imperial secretary Chou Ch'ang dutifully consulted with the general of the army Wang Ling, the grand tutor to the heir apparent Shu-sun T'ung, and others and reported: "In spring, summer, autumn, and winter the vestments of the Son of Heaven should be patterned upon the proportions of heaven and earth and should be in harmony with man who dwells in between these two. Thus if all those from the Son of Heaven, the kings and marquises, and the other land-holding lords down to the members of the populace are willing to abide by the pattern of heaven and earth and follow the succession of the four seasons in ordering their states and families, then they will be spared misfortune and calamity and will enjoy many long years of life. This is the basic ritual principle to be observed in attending the ancestral temples and bringing peace to the world, and we ask that it be duly followed. The middle master of guests Chao Yao should be appointed to supervise the affairs pertaining to spring, Li Shun to supervise those of summer, Ni T'ang to supervise those of autumn, and Kung Yü to supervise those of winter, each of the four men having charge of one season." The grand master of guests Hsiang Chang submitted the proposal to the throne and the emperor gave his approval.'

"In the reign of Emperor Wen the Filial, the government performed acts of charity and kindness toward the empire in the second month, handing out gifts to those who had behaved in a filial or brotherly fashion or had worked hard in the fields, as well as to soldiers who had seen long service in the army, and performing sacrifices to those who had died, though such acts were not entirely appropriate to the season.[12] The imperial secretary Ch'ao Ts'o, who was at the time acting as overseer of the heir apparent's household, submitted a memorial calling attention to the situation.

"Your servant Hsiang humbly observes that Your Majesty is extremely generous in bounty and kindness, and yet the calamities and dislocations of the weather do not cease. I venture to ask if it could be because the imperial edicts and commands are not being issued in the appropriate season. I urge Your Majesty to select four men who are versed in the Classics and have a thorough understanding of the yin and yang so that one may be assigned to each season. As the seasons arrive, each man in turn shall describe clearly the duties appropriate to the time. In this way harmony will be brought to the yin and yang and the empire will enjoy great blessing."

Wei Hsiang often suggested measures that he felt were expedient for the government to take, and the emperor listened to his suggestions and put them into action.

Wei Hsiang gave instructions to the clerks and secretaries in his office that when they had been abroad investigating affairs in the provinces and feudal states or when they had returned to the capital after vacationing in their old homes, they should immediately report to him any unusual happenings that had occurred in the four quarters of the empire. In this way he sometimes learned of rebels or bandits, unusual spells of wind or rain, or other natural disasters that the provincial officials had neglected to report, and in such cases he would immediately submit a memorial informing the throne.

At this time Ping Chi was acting as imperial secretary and he and Wei Hsiang worked in accord to assist the government. The emperor treated them both with great respect. Wei Hsiang was by nature stern and inflexible, quite different from the rather easygoing Ping Chi.

After fulfilling the duties of chancellor for nine years, Wei Hsiang passed away in the third year of the *shen-chüeh* era (59 B.C.). He was given the posthumous title of Hsien, the "Model Marquis." His son Wei Hung succeeded to the marquisate but

---

[12] Though spring is the proper time for acts of charity, these measures should probably have been taken in the first rather than the second month of spring.

during the *kan-lu* era (53–50 B.C.) was accused of a crime and was reduced to the rank of marquis within the Pass.

PING CHI

Ping Chi, whose polite name was Shao-ch'ing, was a native of the state of Lu. He studied the laws and ordinances and became a prison official in Lu. Accumulating a record for meritorious service, he gradually moved up until he reached the post of superintendent of the right under the commandant of justice, but he was accused of an offense, removed from office, and sent back to Lu, where he once more served in the regional government.

Towards the end of Emperor Wu's reign the so-called black magic affair arose. Because of his previous experience as superintendent under the commandant of justice, Ping Chi was summoned to the capital and ordered by the emperor to conduct an investigation of the affair in the prison attached to the Chün-ti, the lodge for official visitors from the provinces. At this time Emperor Wu's great-grandson, the future Emperor Hsüan, was only a few months old, but because his grandfather, the heir apparent Li, was among those accused in the affair, the baby was imprisoned along with the others of the family. Ping Chi was filled with pity when he saw him, and knowing in his heart that the heir apparent was not guilty of the charges brought against him, he did all he could to comfort and protect the innocent child, who was known as the imperial great-grandson. To this end he selected several women prisoners of reliable conduct and generous disposition and ordered them to nurse and take care of the child, assigning them to a room that was quiet and dry.

The investigation of the black magic affair dragged on for several years without reaching a conclusion. In the second year of *hou-yüan* (87 B.C.) Emperor Wu fell ill and spent most of his time going back and forth between the Long Willows and Five Oaks palaces in the suburbs. A man who was skilled at reading signs in the sky announced that he could see configurations indicating the presence of a Son of Heaven in the prisons of Ch'ang-an. The emperor thereupon dispatched messengers to the prisons attached to the various ministries in the capital, instructing them to submit lists of the inmates and, regardless of whether the charges against them were serious or light, to have all of them put to death. The master of guests in the inner palace Kuo Jang, being one of those dispatched by the emperor, arrived at night at the Chün-ti jail, but Ping Chi shut the gate and refused to let him in, saying, "The imperial great-grandson is imprisoned here! It is not right to put any innocent man to death, and certainly not an actual great-grandson of the emperor!" Kuo Jang waited outside the gate until dawn but, failing to gain admittance, finally returned and reported to the emperor, at the same time drawing up an indictment against Ping Chi. Emperor Wu, however, put the indictment aside, saying, "Heaven wants it this way!" and he issued an amnesty to the empire. Because of Ping Chi's efforts alone, the prisoners in the Chün-ti jail were saved from execution, and his act of mercy in time brought blessing to the entire area within the four seas.

The imperial great-grandson was sickly and several times it seemed as though he would not survive. Ping Chi frequently had to order the women who were acting as his wet nurses to send for a doctor and administer medicine. He treated the child with great tenderness and paid for its food and clothing out of his own private funds.

Later he was made master of the commissary under the general of carriage and cavalry and from there was promoted to the post of chief clerk to the general in chief Ho Kuang, who regarded him very highly. He was transferred to service in the palace, where he became a counselor to the keeper of the palace gate and a steward of the palace.

When Emperor Chao passed away without leaving an heir, Ho Kuang sent Ping Chi to summon Liu Ho, the king of Ch'ang-i, to come to the capital and take the throne, but Liu Ho was shortly afterwards deposed because of his scandalous and disorderly conduct. Ho Kuang then joined with the general of carriage and cavalry Chang An-shih and the other great ministers in discussing who should be appointed emperor. They had reached no decision when Ping Chi submitted a memorandum to Ho Kuang which read:

"As general in chief you served Emperor Wu the Filial, were charged with the protection of his child heir, and entrusted with the fate of the empire. Emperor Chao the Filial passed away at an early age, leaving no heir, and all within the four seas were filled with anxiety and fear, longing quickly to receive word of who should succeed to the position of ruler. When the day for the imperial funeral came around, it became necessary for ritual purposes to appoint someone to act as successor, but the one who was chosen proved not to be the man for the position and was accordingly deposed. There is no one in the empire who does not acknowledge the correctness of the action taken at that time.

"Now, however, the fate of the altars of the soil and grain, of the ancestral temples, and indeed of all living beings hangs upon the choice about to be made by you. I have listened to the common people and taken care to find out what they are saying, and, if I may speak boldly, there does not seem to be anyone among the marquises and other titled members of the imperial family who enjoys any degree of reputation with the populace. There is, however, the great-grandson of Emperor Wu named Liu Ping-i who, in accordance with instructions left by Emperor Wu at his death, was raised in the home of his grandmother's relatives and later in the women's quarters of the palace.[13] In former times I was attached to the Chün-ti prison and had occasion to see him when he was a little child. Now he is eighteen or nineteen and has acquired a thorough knowledge of the teachings of the Classics. He is a person of admirable ability, stable in conduct and mild in manner. I hope you will inquire carefully into his qualifications, consult the arts of divination, and if possible give him the recognition and eminence which he deserves. He may be assigned first to service in the palace of the empress dowager and then, when the world has come to fully know and appreciate him, the final step in the great plan can be taken and the whole empire enjoy the blessings thereof."

Ho Kuang read through the proposal and in the end decided to set up the imperial great-grandson as ruler. He then dispatched the director of the imperial clan Liu Te to go with Ping Chi to fetch him and escort him to the women's quarters of the palace.

When the new emperor came to the throne, he enfeoffed Ping Chi with the title of marquis within the Pass.[14] Ping Chi was by nature very warm and generous and never boasted of his good deeds. When the imperial great-grandson was unexpectedly raised to the position of highest honor, Ping Chi never made the slightest reference to the acts of kindness he had performed in the past, and

[13] Liu Ping-i's father, mother, and paternal grandmother Shih were all put to death at the time of the black magic affair, but Liu Ping-i was raised by his relatives of the Shih family and later was taken into the palace. His name Ping-i means "Illness Surmounted" and was no doubt given him to help him overcome the sickly constitution mentioned above.

[14] The lowest grade among the marquises and a rather paltry reward for someone of Ping Chi's importance.

for this reason no one in the court realized how great Ping Chi's merit had been.

In the third year of *ti-chieh* (67 B.C.) when the heir apparent of Emperor Hsüan was officially designated, Ping Chi was appointed as his grand tutor, and a few months later he was transferred to the post of imperial secretary. After the members of the Ho family were wiped out and the emperor in person began to administer the affairs of government, Ping Chi was also given charge of the office of palace writers.

At this time a woman named Tse who was a maid in the women's quarters of the palace, enlisting the help of the man who had been her husband before she entered service in the palace, submitted a letter to the throne claiming that in the past she had performed meritorious service as nursemaid to the emperor. The matter was referred to the supervisor of the women's quarters, who called in the maid for cross-examination. She insisted that the former imperial envoy Ping Chi was acquainted with the facts of the case and could confirm her story, whereupon the supervisor escorted her to the office of the imperial secretary and brought her into Ping Chi's presence. Ping Chi, recognizing her, said, "You were reprimanded for failing to look after the imperial great-grandson with proper care and were dismissed from your post with a beating—what kind of meritorious service did you ever perform! The only ones who were really good to him were Hu Tsu of Wei-ch'eng and Kuo Cheng-ch'ing of Huai-yang."

To clarify the matter, he thereupon submitted a memorial describing the great pains which Hu Tsu and her companion had taken in looking after the emperor. The emperor commanded Ping Chi to conduct a search for Hu Tsu and Kuo Cheng-ch'ing. It was found that they had both died sometime earlier, but their sons and grandsons were all presented with generous rewards. The emperor also commanded that the maid Tse be pardoned for her offense, released from service, and made a commoner with a gift of a hundred thousand cash. The emperor called her into his presence and questioned her, and for the first time learned of the great service which Ping Chi had performed in the past. He was filled with admiration for Ping Chi, particularly in view of the fact that the latter had never mentioned the matter, and issued a command to the chancellor saying: "In the past when I was living in humble and obscure circumstances, the imperial secretary Ping Chi treated me with great kindness and solicitude. Laudable indeed is his virtue, and as the *Book of Odes* says, 'No virtue but shall have its reward!' [15] Therefore let Ping Chi be enfeoffed as marquis of Po-yang with a town of 1,300 households."

When the time came for the enfeoffment ceremony, Ping Chi fell gravely ill. The emperor, anxious that the ceremony be carried out while Ping Chi was alive and afraid that he was too weak to rise from his bed to accept the seals of enfeoffment, was about to send a man to tie the seal cords to the sash of Ping Chi's robe and perform the ceremony in this fashion, but the grand tutor to the heir apparent Hsia-hou Sheng said, "He is not going to die. I have heard that when one performs virtuous deeds in secret, he is bound to enjoy happiness later, even to the time of his sons and grandsons. Now Ping Chi is very ill, but since he has not yet received his reward, I know it's not the kind of illness that will prove fatal."

As it turned out, Ping Chi did in fact recover. He then submitted a letter to the throne adamantly declining to accept the marquisate and arguing that it was improper for him to receive a reward merely because of some empty claim to virtue. The emperor replied, "I did not enfeoff you on the basis of any 'empty claim.' If you send me a letter returning the seals of the marquisate, all you do is make more glaring my lack of virtue. Now that the empire is relatively untroubled, I hope you will gather your spirits together, forget your worries, take the medicines the doctor prescribes, and concentrate on regaining your health."

Five years later, Ping Chi replaced Wei Hsiang in the post of chancellor. Ping Chi had originally started out as a petty clerk in charge of legal and penal affairs but later he studied the *Book of Odes* and the ritual texts and mastered their principles. When he took over the duties of chancellor, he endeavored to be as tolerant and liberal as possible and liked to do things in a courteous and self-effacing manner. If any of the clerks and secretaries in his office committed an offense he would not formally discharge the man but would merely send him off on a "long vacation," and would refrain from conducting any investigation into the matter. One of his guests once said to him, "My lord, you are chancellor of the Han, and yet when evil officials work for their own private gain, you do nothing to reprimand or punish them!"

Ping Chi replied, "I hold one of the three highest offices in the nation—if I were to gain a name for investigating the conduct of the officials under me, I would personally consider it a disgrace!"

[15] Mao #256.

The men who replaced Ping Chi in the office of chancellor in later times all took his words as a precedent, and from Ping Chi's day on it became the custom not to investigate the conduct of the officials in the three highest ministries.[16]

With regard to the clerks, secretaries, and other officials under him, Ping Chi did his best to gloss over their faults and make known their good points. He had a carriage driver who was very fond of wine and would often slip away and go off drinking. Once when the driver was attending Ping Chi on an outing he got so drunk that he vomited on the cushions of Ping Chi's carriage. The clerk in charge of personnel wanted to have the man discharged, but Ping Chi said, "If the man is to be dismissed just because of some slip he made when he had had too much to drink, then I'm afraid he will never be able to hold down a position anywhere! You will just have to forgive him—after all, all he did was soil the cushions of the chancellor's carriage." In the end he refused to dismiss the man.

As it happened, this carriage driver came originally from the border provinces and was thoroughly familiar with the system used by the frontier officials in sending dispatches and warnings to the capital. Once when he was out on the road he happened to see a post-horse rider carrying a red and white satchel and, realizing that the man was bearing a dispatch from the border provinces, he followed him to the office of public carriage, where the dispatch was to be delivered; there he sounded the man out and learned that the barbarians had invaded the provinces of Yün-chung and Tai. He hurried back to the chancellor's office, requested an interview with Ping Chi, and reported what he had learned, adding, "I'm afraid that in the border provinces where the barbarian invasions have taken place, the senior officials are in some cases too old or sickly to take up arms and ride a horse. It might be well to make a preliminary check into the matter."

Ping Chi, approving of this suggestion, ordered the clerk in charge of such matters to examine the files on the senior officials in the border provinces and make a detailed report on each man. Before the report had been completed, a command came from the emperor summoning the chancellor and the imperial secretary into his presence, where he informed them of the barbarian invasion and asked about the officials in the provinces that were affected.

[16] The offices of the chancellor, grand marshal, and imperial secretary. Presumably the officials in these ministries were on a kind of honor system.

Ping Chi gave very thorough answers, but the imperial secretary, having been caught off guard, was unable to supply any detailed information, and was scolded as a consequence. Ping Chi, on the other hand, was looked upon as a man who was truly concerned about the safety of the border and who paid close attention to the duties of his office—all because of the help of his carriage driver. When it was over, Ping Chi sighed and said, "No man is truly useless—each one has something he is good for! If the chancellor had not first heard the words of a carriage driver, how would he ever have been praised for his diligence and care?" As a result of this incident, Ping Chi's clerks and secretaries came to regard him even more highly than before.

Once when Ping Chi was passing through the streets of the capital he came upon a group of street cleaners [17] brawling with a mob of citizens. The dead and injured lay sprawled about the road, but Ping Chi passed by without inquiring what was happening, much to the surprise of his clerks and attendants. When Ping Chi had gone a little farther, he met a man driving an ox; the ox was panting and its tongue was hanging out. Ping Chi stopped his carriage and sent one of his riders to ask how many miles the man had driven the ox. The clerks concluded that the chancellor had lost all sense of when it was appropriate to ask questions and when it was not, and one of them ventured to criticize him to his face, but Ping Chi replied, "If the citizens are brawling and inflicting injury on one another, it is the duty of the magistrate of Ch'ang-an and the prefect of the capital to put a stop to it and make arrests. All I have to do is to review their records at the end of the year, decide whether they have done a proper job or not, and recommend to the emperor that they be rewarded or punished. The chancellor does not interfere in such petty matters himself, and it is certainly not proper for him to stop along the road and ask questions. On the other hand, we are now in the season of spring, a time when the yang has not yet reached its full power, and the weather should not be particularly hot. But if an ox after walking only a short distance is already panting from the heat, then it must mean that there is some dislocation in the weather and the seasons, and I am afraid that harm and injury will result. The three highest ministers are charged with the task of harmonizing the yin and yang

---

[17] Men whose duty was to see that the streets were clean and clear when the emperor or a religious procession was due to pass by.

and therefore it is my duty to worry about such things—that was why I stopped to make inquiries." Ping Chi's clerks admitted the wisdom of this answer, realizing that it was based on a comprehension of the true basic principles underlying the matter.

In the spring of the third year of *wu-feng* (55 B.C.) Ping Chi fell gravely ill and the emperor came in person to inquire how he was, saying, "If that which I hesitate to mention should come about, who would be suitable to replace you as chancellor?"

Ping Chi declined to answer, saying, "The conduct and ability of his ministers is well known to an enlightened ruler—I am not competent to reply to such a question."

When the emperor insisted upon an answer, Ping Chi bowed his head and said, "Tu Yen-nien, the governor of Hsi-ho, is versed in matters pertaining to the laws and regulations and understands the precedents that govern the nation. He held a position among the nine high officials for over ten years and now he is serving in the provinces; as an administrator he is able and well spoken of. The commandant of justice Yü Ting-kuo administers the law with fairness and exactitude so that no one in the empire complains of injustice. The master of carriage Ch'en Wan-nien has served his stepmother with true filial piety and shown complete honesty and sincerity in his conduct. These three men are all superior to me in ability—it remains only for Your Majesty to decide among them."

The emperor, having found Ping Chi's opinions to be reliable in the past, agreed to follow this advice. After Ping Chi passed away, he transferred the imperial secretary Huang Pa to the post of chancellor and summoned the governor of Hsi-ho Tu Yen-nien to the capital to become imperial secretary. Tu Yen-nien was well along in years, however, and declined the office on grounds of illness, asking that he be released from government service. The emperor therefore appointed the commandant of justice Yü Ting-kuo to the post of imperial secretary and later, when Huang Pa passed away, moved him up to the post of chancellor, appointing the master of carriage Ch'en Wan-nien to replace him as imperial secretary. All three men won praise for the manner in which they exercised their duties and the emperor admired Ping Chi's judgment in having recommended them.

When Ping Chi passed away, he was given the posthumous title of Ting, the "Steadfast Marquis." His son Ping Hsien succeeded to the marquisate but during the *kan-lu* period (53–50 B.C.) was accused of a fault and was reduced to the rank of marquis within the

Pass. In public office he rose as high as the post of colonel of the guard and master of carriage.

Earlier, when Ping Hsien was young and serving as a clerk in charge of handling memorials, he had occasion to attend the emperor at a sacrifice in the ancestral temple of Kao-tsu, but he waited until the evening before the ceremony, when the articles to be used were being examined, and then sent a messenger to fetch the robes to be worn at the sacrifice. His father, the chancellor Ping Chi, was furious and said to his wife, "The ancestral temples should be treated with the highest reverence, and yet Hsien is as careless and lacking in respect as this—it will be he who will lose the title of marquis I have acquired!" Ping Chi's wife had to intercede for the boy before the matter was finally closed.

Ping Chi's second son Ping Yü served as director of waterworks, and his youngest son Ping Kao became commander of the gate for the northern garrison.

In the time of Emperor Yüan (48–33 B.C.) a man of Ch'ang-an named Tsun, a soldier who had previously held a rank among the lesser nobility, submitted a letter to the throne saying:

"When I was young I served as a petty official in the Chün-ti, the lodge for official visitors from the provinces, and had occasion to catch a glimpse of Emperor Hsüan the Filial, then known as the imperial great-grandson, who was in the Chün-ti prison. At that time the envoy Ping Chi was in charge of the prison, and seeing the imperial great-grandson held captive in spite of his innocence, he was moved in his heart and wept tears of pity and compassion. He then selected a woman named Hu Tsu to nurse and look after the child, and twice each day he would take me along with him to pay respects in the courtyard outside the room where the baby was sleeping. Later the command came from the emperor to list the inmates of the prison, but Ping Chi stoutly resisted it and refused to let any harm come to the child, although he knew that in doing so he was risking the most severe punishments of the law.

"Later, after a general amnesty had been issued, Ping Chi remarked to Shui-ju, one of the officials in charge of the Chün-ti lodge, that it was improper for the imperial great-grandson to be quartered in such a place, and he asked Shui-ju to convey a letter from him to the prefect of the capital. At the same time he sent Hu Tsu to escort the imperial great-grandson to the prefect's residence, but the prefect refused to accept responsibility for them and they were obliged to return.

"In time Hu Tsu's term of penal servitude came to an end and she was about to leave, but the imperial great-grandson was so attached to her that Ping Chi paid her a wage out of his own pocket and persuaded her to stay at the lodge for a while longer. Meanwhile he employed Kuo Cheng-ch'ing to assist Hu Tsu for several months in looking after the boy, and only then did he discharge Hu Tsu and send her on her way.

"Later the keeper of stores for the women's quarters informed Ping Chi that he had received no authorization from the emperor to issue food to the imperial great-grandson. Ping Chi accordingly had to set aside monthly rations of food out of his own allotment of grain and meat. If he himself happened to be sick, he would invariably send me morning and evening to inquire of the imperial great-grandson's health, to examine his mat and bedding to make certain they were dry, and to observe Hu Tsu and Kuo Cheng-ch'ing and not allow them to go wandering off and leave the child alone either day or night. From time to time, he would send over sweets and delicacies from his own table. In this way he protected and kept alive the soul of the sacred child and nourished his holy body until it grew to maturity. The merit and virtue he displayed are beyond estimation. At that time he could not have foreseen that the child would one day inherit the empire, so it was not the hope of reward that motivated him, but rather the innate benevolence and kindness that welled up within his heart. Even Chieh Chih-t'ui, who severed his own flesh to save the life of his lord, cannot compare to Ping Chi! [18]

"In the time of Emperor Hsüan I submitted a letter describing the above circumstances and the emperor referred it to Ping Chi. But Ping Chi in his modesty was unwilling to boast of his own accomplishments and instead suppressed my words and gave all the credit to Hu Tsu and Kuo Cheng-ch'ing. As a result, they both received rewards of land, houses, gifts, and money, and Ping Chi was enfeoffed as marquis of Po-yang. I did nothing that would allow me to be compared to Hu Tsu and Kuo Cheng-ch'ing, but I am an old man living in poverty and I may die at any moment; I am afraid that if I do not speak out now, I may cause merit to go unrecognized. Now Ping Chi's son Ping Hsien has been convicted of

---

[18] When Duke Wen of Chin (d. 628 B.C.) was wandering in exile and about to die of hunger, his retainer Chieh Chih-t'ui cut a piece of flesh from his own thigh and gave it to his lord to eat.

some petty offense, deprived of his title, and reduced to the rank of marquis within the Pass. Ignorant though I am, it seems only proper to restore his fief and title to him as a reward for his father's merit and virtue."

Previous to this, Ping Hsien had held the post of master of carriage for over ten years, but he had connived with the officials under him to acquire all kinds of illegal gains, accumulating over ten million cash by underhanded means. The subordinate commander in charge of convicts, a man named Ch'ang, investigated the matter and brought charges against Ping Hsien, accusing him of the most serious kind of wrongdoing and requesting that he be arrested, but the emperor replied, "The late chancellor Ping Chi at one time performed acts of great kindness—I cannot bear to see his line cut off." Ping Hsien was accordingly relieved of his post and his fief was reduced by four hundred households, but later he once more held office, this time as subordinate commander of the city gate. When Ping Hsien died, his son Ping Ch'ang succeeded to the title of marquis within the Pass.

In the time of Emperor Ch'eng (32–7 B.C.), efforts were made to reestablish the fiefs of meritorious ministers that had been discontinued. Because Ping Chi's kindness had been of such importance to the dynasty, an imperial edict was issued to the imperial secretary in the first year of *hung-chia* (20 B.C.), saying: "I have heard that to reward merit and virtue and provide for the continuance of lines that are in danger of dying out is the way to show respect for the ancestral temples and attract sages and men of worth to one's court. The late marquis of Po-yang Ping Chi was enfeoffed because of the great kindness and merit he showed in the past, but the sacrifices that accompanied his fief have now been discontinued, a fact which grieves me deeply. That the recognition of goodness should extend to the sons and grandsons of the doer is a principle accepted in ages both past and present. Therefore let Ping Chi's grandson, the general of palace attendants and marquis within the Pass Ping Ch'ang, be enfeoffed as marquis of Po-yang so that he may act as successor to the line and carry on the sacrifices to Ping Chi."

Thus, after a lapse of thirty-two years, the fief was restored; it passed down to Ping Ch'ang's son and grandson, but in the time of Wang Mang was finally abolished.

In appraisal we say: When men of antiquity fixed the names of things, they invariably chose a name that would be symbolic of the thing itself, sometimes looking to the objects around them for a suitable term, sometimes looking to the parts of their own body. Therefore the Classics speak of the ruler as the "head," and his ministers as "arms and legs." Such terms make clear that the two are part of one body, and that each must have the other before there can be completion. Hence it has been regarded as a constant rule of past and present, a natural state of affairs, that ruler and minister should assist one another.

Turning to recent centuries to examine the prime ministers of our own Han, we find that in the time of Kao-tsu, the founder of the dynasty, Hsiao Ho and Ts'ao Ts'an were the most outstanding; and in the revival under Emperor Hsüan the Filial, Ping Chi and Wei Hsiang won highest praise.[19] At that time promotions and demotions were carried out in proper fashion and all official duties tended to with exactitude; the high ministers were in most cases men well fitted for their posts and all the people within the four seas devoted themselves to the practice of ritual and courtesy. Observing the actions of these men, we see that it was not in vain that they were called the arms and legs of the ruler!

[19] Pan Ku uses the term *chung-hsing*, "revival" or "restoration" to refer to the fact that Emperor Hsüan brought peace, prosperity, and stability to the empire after the excesses of Emperor Wu's rule and the brief reign of the ineffectual Emperor Chao.

HAN SHU 78: THE BIOGRAPHY OF
Hsiao Wang-chih

HSIAO WANG-CHIH WAS A MAN OF DIGNITY AND COMPOSURE, but his interview with Ho Kuang did not lead to promotion; only in the time of Emperor Hsüan was he finally advanced, and as tutor to Emperor Yüan assisted in affairs of state. But he failed to plan and take sufficient forethought and was finally undone by Shih Hsien and Hsü Chang. So I have transmitted the Biography of Hsiao Wang-chih.

Hsiao Wang-chih, whose polite name was Ch'ang-ch'ien, was born in Lan-ling in Tung-hai but later moved to Tu-ling. His family had for generations been farmers but Wang-chih showed a great fondness for learning and specialized in the Ch'i version of the *Book of Odes*, studying under Shih Ts'ang, a man of the same district, for almost ten years. He was summoned to the capital to continue his studies under the master of ritual. In addition he studied with the erudit Po Ch'i, who was also a disciple of Shih Ts'ang, and received instruction from Hsia-hou Sheng in questions relating to the *Analects* and the rituals of mourning. The Confucian scholars of the capital all spoke highly of him.

At this time the general in chief Ho Kuang was handling affairs of government. His chief clerk Ping Chi recommended Wang Chung-weng, Hsiao Wang-chih, and several other Confucian scholars, and all were summoned to court. Some time earlier the general of the left Shang-kuan Chieh had plotted with Princess Kai to assassinate Ho Kuang, and though Ho Kuang had had Shang-kuan Chieh and the other conspirators put to death, from that time on he took special precautions to protect himself in his comings and goings. When any officials or private citizens came to him for an interview, he would have them stripped and searched for knives or other concealed weapons and then brought into his presence flanked by guards on either side. Hsiao Wang-chih, however, refused to submit to such treatment but marched out of the audience chamber, declaring, "I have no desire for an interview!" The guards tried to drag him back, and when Ho Kuang heard the ensuing clamor, he ordered the guards to take their hands off him, after which Wang-chih was willing to come forward for the interview. He said to Ho Kuang, "Because of your merit and virtue, general, you have been chosen to assist the young ruler, and are working to spread the great teachings of government abroad and bring about a state of harmony and peace. This is the reason that the gentlemen of the empire stretch their necks and stand on tiptoe, vying with one another in volunteering their services to assist in this lofty and enlightened undertaking. But now when gentlemen are to be granted an interview with you, they are first stripped, searched, and escorted under guard. I fear this is not the way it was done when the Duke of Chou acted as regent for King Ch'eng, spitting out food if he was in the midst of a meal, binding up his hair if he was in the midst of washing it, and hurrying to grant an interview even to the poorest dweller in a grass-thatched hut!"

As a result of this incident, Hsiao Wang-chih alone was not taken into service. Wang Chung-weng and the others of the group, however, were all made clerks in the staff of the general in chief, and in the course of three years Wang Chung-weng advanced to the posts of counselor to the keeper of the palace gate and steward of the palace.

Meanwhile, Hsiao Wang-chih, his answer to the examination questions posed by the emperor having been given the highest grade, was made a palace attendant and was assigned as keeper of the east gate of the Small Garden. Whenever Wang Chung-weng went in or out of the gate, he was accompanied by a slave attendant who jumped down from the carriage, hurried to the gate, and called out for it to be opened for a personage who enjoyed great favor with the ruler. On one such occasion, Wang Chung-weng turned to Hsiao Wang-chih and said, "You refused to be like everybody else, so now you end up tending a gate!"

"Each person does what he thinks is right," replied Hsiao Wang-chih.

Several years later, Hsiao Wang-chih's younger brother was convicted of a crime and it was judged that Wang-chih, as elder
brother of an offender, was unfit to be a member of the palace
guard; he was accordingly dismissed and returned to his home,
where he became a provincial official. Later, the imperial secretary
Wei Hsiang selected him to become one of his subordinate officials
and, perceiving that he was a man of integrity, had him made a
clerk in charge of rites under the grand messenger.

At this time the general in chief Ho Kuang had passed away but
his son Ho Yü was acting as grand marshal, his elder brother's
grandson Ho Shan was in charge of the office of palace writers,
and his other relatives all served in the palace and were members
of the guard. In the summer of the third year of *ti-chieh* (67 B.C.)
hail fell on the capital. Hsiao Wang-chih thereupon submitted a
memorial asking that he be granted an audience with the emperor
when the latter was at leisure so that he might explain in person
the meaning of such unusual occurrences. Emperor Hsüan when he
was living among the common people had heard of Wang-chih's
name, and he exclaimed, "This must be Master Hsiao of Tung-hai!"
He then referred the matter to the privy treasurer Sung Chi, instructing him to find out what it was that Wang-chih had to say
and to assure him that he should speak out without fear of giving
offense.

Hsiao Wang-chih replied to these inquiries by saying: "According to the *Spring and Autumn Annals,* there was a violent hail-
storm in the third year of Duke Chao of Lu (539 B.C.). At that time
the Chi-sun family of Lu had complete control of the government,
and eventually they drove Duke Chao from the state. If the ruler
of Lu had been careful to observe the portents sent by Heaven, he
would not have met with this sad fate. Now Your Majesty in the
holiness of your virtue has ascended the throne, turning all your
thoughts to rule, seeking men of worth, recapturing the spirit of
the sage rulers Yao and Shun of old. In spite of this, however, no
felicitous portents appear, but instead the yin and yang manifest
these signs of disharmony—this is brought about because the high
ministers are exercising the power of government, and because one
clan has arrogated all authority to itself alone. If the limbs are too
large they do injury to the trunk of the tree; if private families
flourish to excess they endanger the ruling house. An enlightened
ruler should exercise control of the ten thousand matters in person,
selecting members of his own surname and promoting men of

worth and talent to be his confidants, and consulting with them on government policy. When the high officials and great ministers appear in court and submit their reports, one should make certain that each man speaks only on those matters within the jurisdiction of his particular post and then judge him on the basis of his ability and the results he achieves. If this is done, then all affairs will be well tended to, the public interest will be advanced, evil and wrongdoing will find their path blocked, and there will be an end to the exercise of private authority."

When this reply of Hsiao Wang-chih's was conveyed to the emperor, he honored Wang-chih by appointing him a master of guests.

At this time Emperor Hsüan had newly come to the throne and he was anxious to promote men of worth and good character. Many memorials were submitted to him proposing various measures that would be of benefit to the government, and all such proposals he would immediately turn over to Hsiao Wang-chih for examination. Those which seemed of greatest merit Hsiao Wang-chih would direct to the chancellor or imperial secretary with a request for action; those of only mediocre interest were turned over to the officials of the middle two thousand picul class or their authors were given a trial position in the government, and at the end of a year an inquiry was made to determine how well the proposal or the person had fared; those of least interest were returned with the information that they had been read and the contents duly noted, and sometimes the author was advised to leave the capital and return to his home. The matters which Wang-chih brought to the emperor's attention all met with the latter's approval and he was promoted step by step from the post of admonisher to that of director of rectitude under the chancellor, advancing three times within one year until he had reached the two thousand picul level. Not long afterwards, the members of the Ho family were found to be plotting treason and were all wiped out, and Hsiao Wang-chih was gradually entrusted with even greater responsibility than before.

At this time a number of men who were versed in government affairs were chosen from among the erudits and admonishers to fill posts that had come vacant as governors of provinces or prime ministers of the feudal states. Hsiao Wang-chih was among these, having been appointed governor of P'ing-yüan. But Wang-chih's thoughts were centered constantly about the court and he was not at all happy serving as the governor of a distant province. He therefore submitted a memorial saying: "Your Majesty, taking pity on the common people and fearful that your virtuous teachings will not be thoroughly disseminated, has dispatched all the admonishers from the capital and sent them abroad to fill posts as provincial officials, but such action may be called 'worrying about the branches and forgetting the root.' If the court is without audacious ministers it will never learn of its errors; if the state is without men of vision it will never hear words of wisdom. I beg Your Majesty to select men who are versed in the principles of the Classics, who cherish the old and understand the new, men of subtle understanding who are skilled at laying plans, and appoint them ministers of the court so that you may consult with them on matters of government. Then when the feudal lords hear of it, they will know that the state is willing to listen to admonition and is deeply concerned about the problems of government, determined that it shall be guilty of no lack or oversight. If this course is pursued with diligence, an age of peace and prosperity such as prevailed under kings Ch'eng and K'ang of the Chou dynasty may perhaps be once more attained! What need is there to worry whether faraway provinces are well ordered or not?"

When the emperor received this communication, he recalled Hsiao Wang-chih to the capital and gave him a provisional appointment to the post of privy treasurer. In his estimation, Wang-chih, with his thorough knowledge of the Classics, gravity of bearing, and inexhaustible skill in debate, had the kind of talent that would fit him for the post of chancellor, but wishing to make a more thorough test of his administrative abilities, he assigned him to the post of left prefect of the capital area. Wang-chih, seeing that he was being removed from the post of privy treasurer in the palace to one in the government in the metropolitan area, supposed that he was being demoted because of some failure to please the emperor and decided to decline the new appointment on grounds of illness. The emperor, hearing of his intentions, instructed the attendant in the inner palace Chin An-shang, the marquis of Ch'eng-tu, to enlighten him on the matter, saying, "The ruler makes use only of those officials who have had experience in the governing of the people and have been judged on the basis of their achievements in that capacity. You were formerly appointed as governor of P'ing-yüan but held the post for only a short while; therefore you are being given another trial, this time in the administration of the metropolitan area. You have not been assigned to this position because of any unfavorable report concerning your conduct or ability." Having received this reassurance, Hsiao Wang-chih took up the duties of his new post.

This year (61 B.C.) the Western Ch'iang tribes revolted and the Han sent the general of the rear Chao Ch'ung-kuo to lead a campaign against them.[1] The prefect of the capital Chang Ch'ang submitted a letter to the throne saying: "The troops have marched abroad and the army has spent a whole summer in the field. From the provinces of Lung-hsi north and An-ting west, the officials and common people are all busy transporting supplies. As a result they have had to neglect their farming, and that in a region that never had a surplus of goods and produce to begin with. Thus even though the Ch'iang barbarians may be defeated, when spring comes the people are bound to suffer a severe shortage of food. In such distant and out-of-the-way regions there is nothing to be bought even if one has money, and the government does not have enough supplies of grain on hand to provide relief. I would like to ask that all those who are guilty of crimes (with the exception of those who have committed theft or murder, accepted bribes, or committed other unpardonable offenses) be permitted to send an appropriate amount of grain to these eight provinces as a form of reparation for their misdeeds. Every effort should be made to increase the supply of grain so that the government will be prepared to meet any emergency that may befall the people."

The emperor turned the matter over to the officials for discussion, whereupon Hsiao Wang-chih joined with the privy treasurer Li Ch'iang in submitting this appraisal:

"It is our view that the people, imbued with vitality by the breath of the yin and yang, possess hearts moved both by concerns of benevolence and righteousness and by the longing for personal profit. The teachings and example of the government will decide which of these two types of concerns is to be encouraged. Although a sage ruler such as Emperor Yao may occupy the throne, he cannot remove from the hearts of the people their longing for personal profit, but he can see to it that such longing is unable to overcome the desire for righteousness. And although an evil tyrant such as Chieh may occupy the throne, he cannot remove from the hearts of the people their desire for righteousness, but he can bring it about that the desire for righteousness is unable to overcome the longing

[1] The Western Ch'iang, often called simply the Ch'iang, were a nomadic people of proto-Tibetan stock who lived on the western border of Han China.

for personal profit. Hence the difference between a Yao and a Chieh lies in this question of righteousness as opposed to personal profit, and it is therefore necessary to exercise the greatest care in the way in which one leads the people.

"If now one decides to let the people ransom themselves from punishment by presenting a measure of grain, as this proposal suggests, then the rich man will be saved and only the poor will face death—in which case the rich and poor will be undergoing different penalties and the law will cease to have any uniformity. Moreover, it is only human nature that if a man is poor and his father or elder brother is a criminal in bonds and he hears that he can save their lives by offering a sum of wealth, then as a son and a younger brother he will not hesitate to risk death and destruction or to resort to any kind of violent and despicable act in his headlong search for wealth with which to ransom his kin. Thus in the saving of one life ten other lives will be lost. In such circumstances, the kind of purity of conduct exemplified by Po Yi cannot but be destroyed, and the lack of selfish desire for which Meng Kung-ch'o was praised cannot but be wiped out.[2] And once the teachings of the government have been turned upside down in this fashion, I fear that even with the aid of sages such as the dukes of Chou and Shao, they cannot be righted again!

"In ancient times goods were left stored among the people; if the government felt a lack, they were gathered in; if it had a surplus, they were handed out. When the *Odes* says:

> He reaches the pitiful people,
> Has compassion on these widowers and widows! [3]

it is describing how those above extend mercy to those below. And when it says:

> Let rain fall on our public fields,
> And on my private fields as well.[4]

it is describing how those below take thought for the urgent needs of those above. Now there is a military campaign on the western border and the people have been called away from their tasks. But

[2] Po Yi and Meng Kung-ch'o were men of ancient times praised by Confucius for their integrity and freedom from desires.
[3] Mao #181.　　[4] Mao #212.

even if one has to resort to a levy on households or a tax on individuals to relieve the situation, this would still be in accord with the accepted practice of antiquity and not something that the common people would consider wrong. But to set people to murdering others so that they can ransom the lives of their condemned kin— this we fear will never do!

"Your Majesty has spread virtue abroad and promulgated the teachings of government, and these teachings have converted the people to ways of goodness—even Yao and Shun could do no better. But now to open the road to selfish profit and thereby do injury to that transformation would, if we may venture to say so, pain us deeply!"

The emperor once more referred the matter to the officials for discussion, and the chancellor and the imperial secretary questioned Chang Ch'ang about the objections which had been raised to his proposal. He replied: "The remarks of the privy treasurer and the left prefect of the capital represent merely the position held by very ordinary persons on the matter. The former ruler Emperor Wu conducted campaigns against the barbarians of the four directions and kept his troops in the field for over thirty years and yet, without imposing any additional taxes upon the common people, he was able to supply the needs of the army. Now the Ch'iang are no more than one miserable little tribe in a corner of the empire, stirring up mischief in the mountain valleys. All the Han has to do is to allow criminals to present goods in exchange for commutation of their penalties and then get on with the task of punishing these barbarians—that would certainly be looked upon as a far more sagacious policy than causing trouble and concern to innocent people by imposing a lot of irresponsible taxes and levies. Moreover, those who are guilty of truly heinous crimes such as theft or murder, men who are loathed and despised by the common people, will not be allowed to participate in the plan. But where a person attempts to shield an offending relative or an official knowingly allows a criminal to evade punishment, there is a feeling that the present system of punishing the relative or official in the same way as the offender himself is unjust, and in the past it has been proposed that such acts be treated more leniently.[5] If

[5] A person in a lower position within the family who attempted to shield his superior (*e.g.*, a son shielding his father, a wife her husband, etc.) was guilty of the crime called *shou-ni* and was punished as severely as the person he attempted to shield. An official who knowingly failed to bring an offender to

now the perpetrators of such acts are allowed to pay a ransom this will obviously be to everyone's advantage. How could it possibly bring confusion to the moral teachings of the government? The 'Code of Marquis Lü' in its treatment of punishments says that small faults should be forgiven and minor crimes ransomed, listing the amounts of gold appropriate in various cases.[6] Thus we know that this practice has been in use for a long time. Why should it lead to an outbreak of crime? I have worn the black robes of an official for over twenty years and I have often heard of men ransoming themselves from punishment but I have never heard of its bringing about an increase in thieves and bandits.

"Personally I feel great pity for the area of Liang-chou, beset as it is by invaders. Even now in autumn, the time of plenty, its people suffer from want and hunger and lie sick and dying by the roadside. By the time spring comes, how great will their distress be! If one does not quickly devise some plan to bring relief, but merely criticizes proposals because they differ from the way things are done in normal times, I am afraid he will face grave consequences afterwards. Ordinary men can be trusted to keep things going in normal times, but they cannot be called upon in times of emergency. I have been fortunate enough to be ranked among the high officials of the government and I feel it is my duty to assist the offices of the chancellor and the imperial secretary in so far as I can—therefore I have not dared to stint in my efforts, worthless as they may be."

Hsiao Wang-chih and Li Ch'iang replied to this as follows: "The former ruler, Emperor Wu, being the very embodiment of virtue and having good and worthy men to serve under him, fashioned regulations and handed down laws which may serve as a model for all time. He knew that the border regions are perpetually troubled by want, and therefore in the first section of the 'Ordinances Pertaining to Currency and Cloth' it is stated: 'The provinces on the border have several times suffered the ravages of war and been afflicted by hunger and cold, so that the young die before they can live out the years Heaven gave them and father and son are driven

---

justice was guilty of the crime called *chien-chih* and was punished as severely as the offender. Both laws originated during the years of Emperor Wu's reign and were regarded by many as excessively severe; the former was particularly offensive to Confucian ideals of family loyalty.

[6] The "Code of Marquis Lü" or *Lü hsing* is a section of the *Book of Documents* dealing with penal matters.

apart; therefore let the rest of the empire join in supplying provisions to assist them.' This of course refers to a situation in which the army is suddenly called out into the field.

"We have heard that once, in the fourth year of the *t'ien-han* period (97 B.C.), an ordinance was issued permitting persons condemned to the death penalty to pay a sum of 500,000 cash in exchange for which the penalty would be lightened by one degree. At that time the persons of power 'and means among the officials and commoners solicited, extorted, borrowed, and in some cases even stole in order to obtain the funds for their ransom. After that, evil and malefaction became rampant, bands of robbers rose up on all sides, going so far as to attack walled cities and murder the governors of provinces; they filled the mountains and valleys and the law officials could not control them. Then an enlightened edict came from the ruler ordering his special envoys in their brocade robes to call out the troops and strike down the offenders. Over half were wiped out, and only then did the outbreak of evil subside and come to an end. Ignorant though we are, it seems to us that this is the disorder that results when one allows men who are condemned to death to ransom themselves from punishment, and therefore we say that it is not an expedient measure to take."

At this time the chancellor Wei Hsiang and the imperial secretary Ping Chi were of the opinion that the Ch'iang would very soon be crushed and that the wants of the border provinces could be supplied by the transportation of goods, and so in the end they did not attempt to put Chang Ch'ang's proposal into effect. Hsiao Wang-chih served as left prefect of the capital for three years, winning praise from the residents of the metropolitan area, after which he was shifted to the post of director of foreign vassals.

Sometime earlier, the *Kun-mi* or chief of the Wu-sun people, whose name was Weng-kuei-mi, had submitted a letter to the Han by way of Ch'ang Hui, the marquis of Ch'ang-lo, requesting permission to appoint as heir his son Yüan-kuei-mi, whose mother was a princess of the Han imperial family. He also asked that another Han princess be sent as a bride for his son so that the Wu-sun could be bound to the Han through further ties of marriage and could break off all relations with the Hsiung-nu.[7] The emperor com-

---

[7] The Wu-sun were a nomadic people living in the region north of the Tarim Basin. They had originally been a part of the Hsiung-nu nation but at this time were attempting to become more independent and to establish closer ties with the Chinese.

manded the high officials to deliberate on the matter. Hsiao Wang-chih expressed the opinion that, since the Wu-sun lived in such a remote and distant region, it would not be a wise policy to trust in their pleasing assurances and agree to a marriage proposal with someone ten thousand miles away.

The emperor did not listen to his opinion but in the second year of *shen-chüeh* (60 B.C.) dispatched Ch'ang Hui, the marquis of Ch'ang-lo, with orders to escort a young princess of the Han to the Wu-sun to become the bride of Yüan-kuei-mi. Before the party had crossed the border, however, word came that Weng-kuei-mi had died and that his elder brother's son K'uang-wang, disregarding the previous agreement made with the Han, had set himself up as ruler. Ch'ang Hui sent a letter from the border asking that he be allowed to leave the princess at Tun-huang Province and proceed by himself to the region of the Wu-sun, where he would protest the violation of the agreement, make certain that Yüan-kuei-mi was appointed ruler, and then return to the border to fetch the princess.

The emperor commanded the high officials to give their opinion, and Hsiao Wang-chih once more expressed disapproval. "The Wu-sun are two-faced and never abide by their promises," he said, "and it is easy enough to see what the final result will be! Once before, a princess [8] was sent to the Wu-sun and lived among them for over forty years but she was never treated with affection or favor and her presence did not bring any peace to the border regions— so we have the evidence of past events to tell us what will happen. Now if we recall the princess from the border on the grounds that Yüan-kuei-mi, the groom-to-be, did not become ruler after all, we cannot be accused of breaking our word or showing bad faith in our dealings with the foreign tribes on our four borders, and at the same time we will bring great happiness to the Middle Kingdom. But if, on the other hand, the princess goes through with the marriage, I fear we may in time be obliged to call out troops and lead an expedition as a result!"

The emperor followed his advice and recalled the princess from the border. Later, although the Wu-sun nation split into two parts, Yüan-kuei-mi was set up as Great *Kun-mi*, but the Han did not reopen the matter of his marriage.

In the third year of *shen-chüeh* (59 B.C.) Hsiao Wang-chih replaced Ping Chi as imperial secretary. During the *wu-feng* era

[8] The mother of Yüan-kuei-mi.

(57–54 B.C.) the Hsiung-nu tribes were torn by internal strife, and many people who were in a position to advise the emperor said, "The Hsiung-nu have plagued us for many years—now is the time to take advantage of their weakness and disorder to call out the troops and destroy them!" The emperor commanded the grand marshal and general of carriage and cavalry Han Tseng, the official in charge of discipline and marquis of Fu-p'ing Chang Yen-shou, the keeper of the palace gate Yang Yün, and the master of carriage Tai Ch'ang-lo to inquire of Hsiao Wang-chih what strategy he thought best.

Hsiao Wang-chih replied: "According to the *Spring and Autumn Annals,* Shih Kai of Chin led his armies in an invasion of the state of Ch'i, but when he heard that the marquis of Ch'i had died, he immediately withdrew his forces and returned home. The gentleman admired him for not attacking a state that was in mourning.[9] It would appear that his kindness was of a degree to win him the gratitude of the son who was in mourning, and his sense of honor sufficient to impress the other feudal lords. Formerly the *Shan-yü,* attracted by the culture of China, turned his face toward goodness and spoke of himself as a younger brother of the Han ruler, sending his envoys to seek peaceful and friendly relations with our court. All within the four seas rejoiced at this news and there were none of the foreign tribes who did not hear of it. But before an actual treaty could be concluded, misfortune occurred and the *Shan-yü* was murdered by one of his own subjects. Now if we should launch an attack, we would be trying to profit from disorder and to turn someone else's disaster to our own advantage. The Hsiung-nu would undoubtedly flee to some distant region, and unless we were prepared to launch a major campaign on grounds of principle, I'm afraid we would wear ourselves out without accomplishing anything. The proper action would be to send an envoy to convey condolances to the *Shan-yü's* heir and ask if we can be of any assistance in strengthening his position and helping him to surmount this disaster. When the other foreign tribes hear of this, they will esteem China for its benevolence and righteousness. And if as a result of our charitable assistance the heir is able to recover the position of *Shan-yü,* he will surely acknowledge allegiance to the Han

---

[9] The incident is recorded in the *Kung-yang Commentary,* Duke Hsiang 19th year, with the comment that Shih Kai was praised for his action. The "gentleman" is Confucius, who it was believed had expressed his praise or blame through the terminology he used in compiling the *Annals.*

and obey its wishes. This way lies the course of true virtue!"

The emperor decided to follow Hsiao Wang-chih's counsel, and later on dispatched troops to protect and assist the *Shan-yü* Hu-han-yeh in restoring peace to his nation.

At this time Keng Shou-ch'ang, the middle aide to the minister of agriculture, submitted a memorial proposing the establishment of an "ever-constant granary." [10] The emperor was pleased with the proposal but Hsiao Wang-chih criticized Keng Shou-ch'ang for it. The chancellor Ping Chi was by this time well along in years and was treated with great respect by the emperor, but Hsiao Wang-chih submitted a memorial saying: "There is want and privation among the common people, thieves and bandits have yet to be wiped out, and many of the two thousand picul officials are of inferior ability and unfit for the jobs they hold. If the three highest ministries are not occupied by the proper men, then the three luminaries of the heavens, the sun, the moon, and the stars, will as a result fail to shine brightly. Now we are in the first month of a new year and the sun and moon appear somewhat dimmed—the fault must lie with me and the others who occupy the three ministries."

The emperor concluded that Hsiao Wang-chih's intention was to belittle the chancellor and he therefore instructed the attendant in the inner palace and colonel of the guard of the Chien-chang Palace Chin An-shang, the keeper of the palace gate Yang Yün, and the middle aide to the imperial secretary Wang Chung to go as a group and question Hsiao Wang-chih on his behavior. Wang-chih removed his cap in a gesture of humility but declined to answer their questions. The emperor was displeased by such conduct.

Sometime later, P'o Yen-shou, the director of rectitude in the office of the chancellor, submitted a memorial saying: "When the attendant in the inner palace and master of guests Liang had been sent to convey an imperial command to Hsiao Wang-chih, the latter merely bowed twice, and when Liang spoke to him, he failed to rise; on the contrary, he made a point of placing his hands on the floor, remarking to his secretary, 'Liang is not very careful about his manners!' [11] Moreover, according to the practice in times past,

---

[10] A plan by which the government would buy up and store grain when it was cheap and sell it when it was expensive, thus preventing the price from fluctuating too violently. It was put into practice and proved effective.

[11] It is not clear exactly what breaches of etiquette are involved, but the supposition is that Liang failed to place his hands on the floor and bow to Hsiao, and the latter reproached him by placing his own hands on the floor

if the chancellor is taken ill, the imperial secretary immediately goes the following day to inquire of his health; and when memorials are being presented or there is a gathering of the court, it is customary for the imperial secretary to remain in a position somewhat behind the chancellor, and only if addressed by the chancellor to step forward and bow. Yet now the chancellor has been ill several times and Hsiao Wang-chih has never gone to inquire about his illness; furthermore, when there is a gathering of the court, he behaves as though he were the equal of the chancellor, and if there is a discussion and he disagrees with the chancellor, he says, 'You may be old, sir, but you're not my father!' [12]

"He knows that the imperial secretary is not permitted to order his subordinates about on any errands he pleases, and yet he often sends his secretaries off to Tu-ling, providing them with carriages and horses and instructing them to look after family business for him. He has his petty clerks dressed up in their official caps and acting as footmen to his wife's carriage, and he also sends them out to buy and sell, accumulating a private profit of 103,000 in cash this way.

"Hsiao Wang-chih, it should be noted, is a high official, versed in Classical learning, occupying a position above the nine high ministers, and looked up to by the entire court. And yet he fails to uphold the law and discipline himself, instead behaving with swaggering insolence and a total lack of humility. He deserves the same penalty as those who accept bribes and pervert the law—two hundred and fifty blows of the stick! I beg that he be arrested and brought to trial."

The emperor thereupon issued a communication to Hsiao Wang-chih which read: "The authorities have submitted a memorial stating that you have accused an imperial envoy of a breach of etiquette, treated the chancellor with discourtesy, won no plaudits for integrity, but instead behaved with arrogance and lack of humility, showing that you lack the qualifications to act as leader of the hundred officials in assisting the government. Absence of sufficient forethought has led you astray into this despicable conduct, but I cannot bear to see you subjected to punishment. I am there-

---

and bowing pointedly. In any event, Hsiao should not have made any criticism of the emperor's envoy, and there is also a suggestion that something about Hsiao's behavior when he first received the imperial command was irregular.

[12] *I.e.,* I don't have to defer to you.

fore sending the keeper of the palace gate Yang Yün with an imperial command demoting you to the post of grand tutor to the heir
apparent. When you receive the seals of this appointment, you will
surrender the seals of your previous appointment to the envoy, who
will then lead you to your new office. I trust you will strive to uphold the Way and make clear the teachings of filial piety. Let truth
and uprightness be your companion, give all your thoughts to the
avoidance of error, and do not complain about what has happened
in the past."

After Hsiao Wang-chih had been demoted, Huang Pa took his
place as imperial secretary. A few months later, Ping Chi passed
away and Huang Pa moved up to the position of chancellor. When
Huang Pa in turn passed away, he was replaced as chancellor by
Yü Ting-kuo. Thus Hsiao Wang-chih, having suffered disgrace, was
never able to reach the post of chancellor. Instead, as grand tutor
he gave instruction in the *Analects* and the rituals of mourning to
the heir apparent.

Earlier, when the Hsiung-nu *Shan-yü* Hu-han-yeh first announced that he wished to come and pay his respects at the Han
court, the emperor commanded the high ministers to discuss what
ritual should be followed. The chancellor Huang Pa and the imperial secretary Yü Ting-kuo presented this proposal: "It is the practice of the sage king to spread virtue abroad and observe the dictates of ritual, putting the interests of the capital area above those
of the other regions of the empire, and putting the interests of the
other regions of the empire above those of the barbarian tribes.
The *Odes* says:

> Obeying ritual, never overstepping,
> He looked after his people to the benefit of all.
> Great was the majesty of Hsiang-t'u;
> Even beyond the seas all was well ordered.[13]

Your Majesty's sacred virtue fills heaven and earth and its light
shines upon the four outer regions. The *Shan-yü* of the Hsiung-nu,
looking toward the ways of China and longing to share in its culture, offers his rarest treasures in tribute to the court. Such a thing
has never happened before. He should be received with the ritual

---

[13] Mao #304, one of the "Hymns of Shang." The first two lines refer to
Hsieh, the founder of the Shang royal family in the time of Emperor Shun;
Hsiang-t'u was Hsieh's grandson.

appropriate to a king or marquis, being assigned a rank just below the actual kings and marquises of the Han."

Hsiao Wang-chih, however, pointed out that the *Shan-yü* did not follow the calendar promulgated by the court of China and therefore his nation was referred to as an "independent state." "He should not be treated as a vassal of China," said Hsiao Wang-chih, "but should be assigned a rank above that of the feudal kings and marquises. If the tribes of foreign lands bow their heads and offer to declare themselves tributaries, then China should modestly decline to accept and should not treat them as vassals. In such a case one may reap the benefits of restraint, and enjoy the blessings of a 'modesty which prevails.' [14] The *Book of Documents* speaks of the 'Jung and Ti tribes of the distant wastelands,' meaning that it is very uncertain when such tribes will come to the Chinese court.[15] If in later times the heirs of the Hsiung-nu ruler should suddenly flit away like birds or scurry off like rats into their holes, failing to appear at court and present their accustomed tribute, we will not be obliged to treat them as subjects who are in revolt. This, I believe, is the best plan, allowing us to gain a reputation among the Man and Mo tribes for trustworthiness and humility and insuring a never-ending flow of blessings for ten thousand generations to come."

The emperor decided to adopt this policy, handing down an edict which said: "It has been said that the Five Emperors and the kings of the Three Dynasties in ancient times did not attempt to exercise governmental control over those regions to which their moral and cultural teachings had not extended. Now the *Shan-yü* of the Hsiung-nu, styling himself a tributary of the north, has come to pay honor to the court and its calendar, but I am unworthy of such honor, since I have been unable to extend my virtue to cover such distant regions. Therefore let him be received with the ritual appropriate to a guest. The *Shan-yü* shall be assigned a rank above that of the feudal kings and marquises, and when he announces himself at the audience he shall refer to himself as 'your servant' but need not use his personal name." [16]

[14] A reference to the explanation of the hexagram *ch'ien* or Modesty in the *Book of Changes*.

[15] No such passage is found in the present text of the *Book of Documents*.

[16] Chinese lords and officials, no matter how eminent, were obliged to refer to themselves by their personal names when addressing the emperor, but the *Shan-yü* is here excused from this duty. The pronoun *ch'en*, "your servant" or

When Emperor Hsüan fell ill and his condition gradually worsened, he selected several of the high ministers who he thought could be entrusted with the management of affairs, summoning his paternal grandmother's nephew, the attendant of the inner palace and marquis of Lo-ling Shih Kao, the grand tutor to the heir apparent Hsiao Wang-chih, and the lesser tutor Chou K'an to come to his apartments in the inner palace. There he appointed Shih Kao as grand marshal and general of carriage and cavalry, Hsiao Wang-chih as general of the vanguard and keeper of the palace gate, and Chou K'an as counselor to the keeper of the palace gate; all received testamentary edicts instructing them to assist the heir apparent in the conduct of the government and putting them in charge of the office of palace writers.

When Emperor Hsüan passed away (48 B.C.), the heir apparent succeeded to the position of highest honor and is posthumously known as Emperor Yüan the Filial. Because Hsiao Wang-chih and Chou K'an had been his tutors, they were treated with great honor and respect when he became ruler and often had occasion to meet with him in moments of leisure, discussing with him the principles of government and describing the ways appropriate to a true king. Hsiao Wang-chih recommended that Liu Keng-sheng,[17] a supplementary cavalryman and admonisher who was a member of the imperial family, an expert in the Classics, and a man of wide learning, be appointed steward of the palace, and that he, along with the attendant of the inner palace Chin Ch'ang, be charged with the task of waiting on the emperor and correcting any defects and omissions they might observe. These four men, Hsiao, Chou, Liu, and Chin, worked in close accord to further their plans and proposals, urging the emperor to return to the institutions of antiquity, hoping in this way to effect various reforms and improvements. The emperor was much impressed by their suggestions and put them into effect.

Previously, when Emperor Hsüan was alive, he had not paid much heed to the policies of Confucianism but had relied mainly on laws and regulations. The eunuchs of the office of palace writers took care of government matters and the chief of palace writers Hung Kung and his assistant Shih Hsien had long been accus-

---

"your subject," was presumably so conventionalized in usage that it would not offend the *Shan-yü*.

[17] The famous scholar and writer Liu Hsiang (77–6 B.C.), here called by the name he used in his youth, Keng-sheng.

tomed to deciding on the most secret and crucial affairs of state, being highly practiced in the handling of documents and the application of the law. In addition they worked in close cooperation with the general of carriage and cavalry Shih Kao, they in the inner palace, he in the outer, and arranged that whenever a matter came up for discussion, it was determined merely to follow the precedents of the past rather than to listen to the suggestions of Hsiao Wang-chih and the other officials. There were also times, however, when their decisions were overturned and rejected.

Hsiao Wang-chih was of the opinion that the office of palace writers was vital to the conduct of the government and should therefore be staffed with men chosen for their worth and understanding. Because Emperor Wu had spent so much of his time amusing himself in the women's quarters of the palace, it had become customary to use eunuchs, but this, he declared, was not in accordance with the practice of the state in ancient times and moreover violated the age-old principle that the ruler should not associate with men who had undergone punishment.[18] He therefore requested that the office be staffed once more with ordinary officials, and as a result a strong enmity developed between him and the eunuchs Hung Kung and Shih Hsien. Emperor Yüan, however, having just come to the throne, wished to create an impression of reticence and humility and regarded it as a serious matter to make such a drastic change; therefore for a long time no decision was made concerning Hsiao Wang-chih's proposal. Meanwhile Liu Keng-sheng was assigned to a post in the outer court as director of the imperial clan, and Hsiao Wang-chih and Chou K'an from time to time recommended eminent Confucian scholars and other men of outstanding talent who they believed would be suitable to fill posts as admonishers.

At this time a certain Cheng P'eng of K'uai-chi, secretly hoping to curry favor with Hsiao Wang-chih, submitted a memorial stating that the general of carriage and cavalry Shih Kao was sending his retainers to the various provinces and feudal kingdoms to seek illegal gains; he also mentioned certain crimes and faults commit-

---

[18] The eunuchs were in most cases men who had been condemned to suffer castration because of some offense. Emperor Wu had found it convenient to conduct much of the business of government from the women's quarters, and since no ordinary official was allowed entrance, he had perforce to employ eunuchs to handle memorials and state papers. Thus began a struggle for power between the eunuchs of the inner court and the officials of the outer.

ted by other male members of the Shih clan, and by the male members of the Hsü clan, the family of the emperor's mother. The emperor showed the memorial to Chou K'an, who summoned Cheng P'eng to the capital to await the imperial command at the Golden Horse Gate.

Cheng P'eng then addressed a letter to Hsiao Wang-chih, saying: "You, general, who embody the virtue of the dukes of Chou and Shao, possess the wholesome nature of Meng Kung-ch'o, and inspire as much awe as Chuang of Pien, have now attained the age where you may 'follow your ear' [i.e., sixty]. You occupy a post from which you can thwart all enemies of the state and you are honored with the title of general—truly the highest eminence that any man could hope to attain! Even the humble commoners in their hovels and caves all rejoice in you, saying, 'The general is our man!'

"Now I wonder if, having become a distinguished statesman like Kuan Chung and Yen Ying of old, you are content to rest on your laurels, or whether you aspire to imitate the ways of the dukes of Chou and Shao, who were so busy with state affairs that the sun set before they had time to eat a meal? If you are content to be simply a Kuan Chung or a Yen Ying, then your humble and unworthy servant will forthwith return home to the lakeside of Yen-ling, tend his fields and gardens, mind the chickens, sow the millet, and watch while his two sons grow to maturity and his own teeth fall out, and that will be the end of the matter. If, however, you have loftier aims, planning your actions and nurturing your thoughts so that you may block the dangerous path of evil and perverseness, open up the way for stable government based upon the principle of the Mean, restore the institutions that were created by the dukes of Chou and Shao, and imitate their virtue by devoting all day to the personal superintendence of government affairs, then your humble and unworthy servant hopes he may be permitted to exhaust what paltry talent he possesses, whetting and honing the point and blade of his sword so that he may offer a modicum of service!" [19]

Hsiao Wang-chih summoned Cheng P'eng to an interview and, approving of his views, treated him with consideration. Cheng P'eng from time to time would speak very favorably of Hsiao Wang-chih and at the same time belittle the carriage and cavalry

[19] The letter, in addition to being outrageously flattering in tone, is laden with literary allusions which it would be tedious to explain in full.

general Shih Kao and describe various faults and errors of the members of the Shih and Hsü families. Later Cheng P'eng fell into evil ways and Hsiao Wang-chih broke off relations and refused to have anything more to do with him.

When Cheng P'eng was assigned to await the imperial command, he found himself in the company of a man named Li Kung, a secretary under the minister of agriculture. Chou K'an recommended Li Kung to the emperor and he was made an attendant of the Yellow Gate. Cheng P'eng, being a typical southerner of the region of Ch'u, was filled with anger and resentment that he too had not received such an appointment, and decided to switch his allegiance and ingratiate himself with the Shih and Hsü families. Questioned about the charges that he had earlier made against members of these families, he replied, "Those were all things that Chou K'an and Liu Keng-sheng told me to say. I come from east of the Pass—how would I have known of such things myself?"

The attendant of the inner palace Hsü Chang thereupon spoke to the emperor and had Cheng P'eng summoned to an audience. When Cheng P'eng emerged from the audience, he announced in a loud voice, "I saw His Majesty and informed him of five minor faults and one major offense that the general of the vanguard is guilty of. The chief of palace writers was at the emperor's side—he can tell you exactly what I said!"

The general of the vanguard Hsiao Wang-chih, hearing this, proceeded to question the chief of palace writers Hung Kung and his assistant Shih Hsien. Hung Kung and Shih Hsien were afraid that if they pressed charges against Hsiao Wang-chih, he would in turn bring charges against them; they therefore decided to have some other official handle the matter and accordingly enlisted the services of Cheng P'eng and another man named Hua Lung who had also been assigned to await the imperial command. (Hua Lung had been assigned along with Chang Tzu-ch'iao and others to await the imperial command in the time of Emperor Hsüan but because of disreputable conduct had failed to advance. He tried to ally himself with Chou K'an and the others of his party, but they would have nothing to do with him, and he had therefore joined forces with Cheng P'eng.)

Hung Kung and Shih Hsien arranged for these two men, Cheng P'eng and Hua Lung, to bring charges against Hsiao Wang-chih and his associates, stating that they were attempting to drive the carriage and cavalry general Shih Kao out of office and to alienate the emperor from his relatives of the Hsü and Shih families, supplying evidence to support the charges. They waited until Hsiao Wang-chih had left the court and gone home for his day of rest and then had Cheng P'eng and Hua Lung submit the charges to the emperor. The matter was referred to Hung Kung for investigation, but when he questioned Hsiao Wang-chih, the latter replied, "Many of the emperor's relatives of the Hsü and Shih families who hold office are given to extravagant and disorderly ways. My desire was to restore order and propriety to the state—I have done nothing wrong!"

Hung Kung and Shih Hsien, however, submitted a recommendation to the emperor which read: "Hsiao Wang-chih, Chou K'an, and Liu Keng-sheng have formed a clique to further their own interests, on several occasions bringing slanderous charges against a high minister and defaming and creating estrangement between the ruler and his own kin in their desire to gather all power and authority into their own hands. As officials they are guilty of disloyalty, and they have deliberately attempted to deceive the ruler, a crime of the greatest magnitude. We request that the master of guests be instructed to summon them and turn them over to the commandant of justice."

At this time the emperor had just come to the throne and he did not realize that the phrase "instruct the master of guests to summon them and turn them over to the commandant of justice" meant that they were to be taken to prison, and he therefore approved the recommendation. Later, when he asked to have Chou K'an and Liu Keng-sheng called into his presence, he was told, "They are bound and in prison!" Astounded at this information, he said, "I thought they were only to be taken to the commandant of justice for questioning!" and he began to berate Hung Kung and Shih Hsien. The two knocked their heads on the floor in apology, after which the emperor said, "See to it that they are released from prison and restored to their positions!"

Hung Kung and Shih Hsien then instructed Shih Kao to say to the emperor, "Your Majesty has just ascended the throne and your virtue and moral teachings are still unknown to the empire, and yet you have already subjected your former tutor to an investigation and have sent him to prison along with two officials who hold positions among the nine high ministers. The only proper thing to do now is to have sentence passed on them and to relieve them of their positions."

The emperor thereupon handed down an edict to the chancellor and the imperial secretary saying: "The general of the vanguard Hsiao Wang-chih was my tutor for eight years; he has committed no other offense or error in the past, and even the offenses that he is now charged with occurred a long time ago and it is difficult to recall the facts and discover clear proof of them. Therefore his crime shall be pardoned; he shall be relieved of the seals of general of the vanguard and keeper of the palace gate and, along with Chou K'an and Liu Keng-sheng, shall be dismissed from office and made a commoner." At the same time, Cheng P'eng was made an attendant of the Yellow Gate.

After a few months, however, the emperor once more handed down an edict to the imperial secretary, saying: "A state that would flourish must honor its teachers and pay respect to its tutors.[20] The former general of the vanguard Hsiao Wang-chih was my tutor for eight years, guiding me in the study of the Classics— the services he performed were manifold indeed! Let him be presented with the title of marquis within the Pass and the revenue from a town of six hundred households; he shall be made a steward of the palace and shall be permitted to attend audiences on the first and fifteenth day of each month, being seated next to the generals."

The emperor at this time relied heavily on Hsiao Wang-chih and was about to appoint him as chancellor when Hsiao Wang-chih's son, the supplementary cavalryman and palace attendant Hsiao Chi, submitted a letter to the throne claiming that his father had formerly been unjustly accused of criminal offenses. The matter was handed over to the authorities for investigation and they referred it back to the emperor with a memorial stating: "The charges previously brought against Hsiao Wang-chih were supported by clear and incontrovertible evidence; they were no mere irresponsible slanders. Hsiao Wang-chih has now instructed his son to submit a letter to the throne, quoting from the *Odes* and claiming that he is guiltless. Such conduct is wholly unbecoming to a high official and shows a lack of respect for Your Majesty. We ask that he be placed under arrest."

Hung Kung, Shih Hsien, and the others of their group, knowing that Hsiao Wang-chih was by nature a man of high principles who could not bear to suffer insult, expressed their opinion as follows:

---

[20] The sentence is based upon a passage in *Hsün Tzu*, sec. 27.

"In former times when Hsiao Wang-chih was a general and took part in affairs of government, he attempted to drive the members of the Hsü and Shih families out of office and to arrogate to himself all the power of the court. He was fortunate enough not to be punished for his crimes but was presented with a title and fief and was once more allowed to take part in affairs of government, but he refused to acknowledge his offenses or feel any remorse over his errors, instead nursing feelings of profound anger and resentment. He instructed his son to submit a letter to the throne, attempting to lay the blame for what had happened on Your Majesty and assuming that because of his former position as tutor he would never be subjected to punishment. It would appear that unless he is made to suffer a certain amount of disgrace by being put in prison and is cured of his grumbling and fractious heart, it will be impossible for Your Majesty's sacred court to treat him with kindness and mercy!"

"But the grand tutor Hsiao is of an unbending nature," said the emperor. "How would he ever be willing to place himself in the hands of the law officials?"

"It would certainly be a serious matter to endanger a man's life," replied Shih Hsien and the others, "but the charges against Hsiao Wang-chih involve only minor offenses of speech and he is certain to realize that he has nothing really to worry about."

The emperor finally gave his approval to the proposal, whereupon Shih Hsien and the others sealed it and handed it over to the master of guests, ordering him to summon Hsiao Wang-chih and place it directly in his hands. They then sent an order to the master of ritual and had him send an urgent call to the chief of the capital police to hurry to Tu-ling with his carriages and cavalry and surround Hsiao Wang-chih's house.[21] When the emperor's envoy arrived, he summoned Hsiao Wang-chih and conveyed the emperor's command.

Hsiao Wang-chih was about to commit suicide but his wife stopped him, saying, "I cannot believe that this is what His Majesty intends!" Hsiao Wang-chih then asked the opinion of Chu Yün, a student in his household, but Chu Yün, being a man who placed honor above all else, urged him to settle the matter by his own hand. Hsiao Wang-chih then looked up to heaven with a sigh and said, "I once held the post of general and high minister but

[21] Since Tu-ling was the site of Emperor Hsüan's grave, it was under the jurisdiction of the master of ritual, but the latter, having no soldiers under his command, had to call on the chief of the capital police for military assistance.

now I am over sixty. If an old man like myself were to go to prison in an effort to prolong his life at any cost, what a miserable spectacle it would be!" Then, addressing Chu Yün by his polite name, he said, "Yu, hurry and mix me some medicine—don't make me wait for death any longer!"

In the end he drank a dose of aconite and died. When the emperor heard the news, he was shocked and, wringing his hands, said, "I suspected all along that he would never go to prison! So now they have finally killed my worthy tutor!"

The imperial butler was just then serving the noon meal, but the emperor pushed the food aside and wept so bitterly over what had happened that those about him were moved to pity. Then he sent for Shih Hsien and the others and berated them for having presented such an unwise proposal. They all removed their caps and begged forgiveness, but only after a long while were they finally permitted to withdraw.

Since Hsiao Wang-chih had been charged with crimes at the time of his death, the authorities requested that he be deprived of his title and fief, but the emperor ordered that special mercy be shown and allowed his eldest son Hsiao Chi to succeed to the title of marquis within the Pass. The emperor did not forget Hsiao Wang-chih but continued to keep him in his thoughts, and each year, when the time came around, he sent an envoy to perform sacrifices at Hsiao Wang-chih's grave. By the end of Emperor Yüan's reign, three of Hsiao Wang-chih's eight sons had attained high office, Hsiao Yü, Hsiao Hsien, and Hsiao Yu.[22]

In appraisal we say: Hsiao Wang-chih held posts as a general and a high minister and, aided by the special favor that he enjoyed as former tutor, he seemed on such friendly and intimate terms with the ruler that nothing could come between them. But later his plans to reduce the power of the Hsü and Shih families leaked out and a gulf opened between them; slander and wickedness played their part until at last he fell victim to the machinations of the vile and glib-tongued eunuchs, a pitiful end indeed! A man of dignity and stature who could be broken but not bent, he was a master of Confucian learning and possessed the ability to aid and assist the ruler, one of the true protectors of the altars of the soil and grain in recent centuries!

[22] I have omitted at this point the brief biographies of these three sons, which are mainly recitals of their various official posts and promotions.

HAN SHU 92: THE BIOGRAPHIES OF
the Wandering Knights [1]

IN FOUNDING STATES and carrying on families, there are laws and regulations. A private family must not keep stores of arms, a state must not impose the death penalty arbitrarily; and how much more so is this true in the case of ordinary individuals! If they take it upon themselves to terrorize or hand out favors, why not correct them? That is what rites and laws are for. So I have transmitted the Biographies of the Wandering Knights.

In ancient times the Son of Heaven founded the state, the feudal lords set up their families, and from the great ministers and high officials down to the common people, everyone had his own distinct station in life. Because of this the people submitted to and served their superiors, and those in low position harbored no inordinate ambitions. Confucius said, "When the Way prevails in the

[1] The word "knight" here should not be understood as designating any particular formal rank in society. It is used rather to suggest the kind of honorable and self-sacrificing conduct which characterized this group of men at their best. Such self-appointed "bosses" or protectors of others no doubt served a very useful purpose in the chaotic society of late Chou and early Han times. With the restoration of peace and stability, however, they often became a nuisance and the Han government took strict measures to suppress them. Ssu-ma Ch'ien, as mentioned in the Introduction, had written rather sympathetically of them, but Pan Ku takes a sterner view of their activities. It is difficult to determine just what, in Pan Ku's eyes, qualified a man to be called a "knight" (hsia) or "strong man" (hao), outside of a certain swaggering contempt for conventional morality, an elaborate concern for honor, and a fondness for the

world, government will not be in the hands of the high officials." [2]
The hundred officials and those in authority obeyed the laws, accepted commands, and attended to what was in their charge.
Those who managed their duties badly were punished; those who usurped someone else's office were judged guilty of a crime. Therefore, superior and inferior went along with one another and all affairs were properly ordered.

But when the house of Chou declined, "rites, music, and punitive military expeditions proceeded from the feudal lords." [3] From the time of dukes Huan and Wen and afterwards, the high officials exercised power generation after generation and the ministers of the feudal lords began to issue commands. The situation continued to deteriorate until the age of the Warring States, when some rulers joined the Vertical Alliance, some the Horizontal Alliance, when strength alone governed and the states competed for mastery. At this time there were young lords from various states such as Hsin-ling of Wei, P'ing-yüan of Chao, Meng-ch'ang of Ch'i, and Ch'un-shen of Ch'u who, relying upon their positions as nobles, vied with each other in playing the part of wandering knights. Impersonators of roosters, thieving dogs—there was no one they failed to welcome as their guest.[4] Yü Ch'ing, the prime minister of Chao, abandoned his state and renounced his lord in order to come to the aid of his hard-pressed friend Wei Ch'i. Wu-chi of Hsin-ling stole the tally of office, forged orders, killed the rightful general, and alone led the troops to relieve the siege of Chao.[5] All by their deeds won the respect of the feudal lords and spread their fame throughout the empire. Of those who gripped their arms in a ges-

---

grand gesture. Such ways apparently appealed greatly to certain elements in Han society and won for their possessors large bands of ardent followers who were often an embarrassment and the source of their undoing. The chapter is especially valuable for the glimpses it gives into the lives of the petty officials and commoners of the time.

[2] *Analects* XVI, 2.

[3] *Ibid.*

[4] Lord Meng-ch'ang had among his "guests" or retainers one who could imitate the crowing of a cock and one who could steal as cleverly as a dog. Both proved on occasion to be extremely valuable.

[5] Yü Ch'ing defied the authority of the king of Chao by harboring his friend Wei Ch'i and protecting him from the wrath of an old enemy. Wu-chi persuaded a concubine to steal the tally of office and with it called out the troops and led them to rescue the state of Chao, which was besieged by the state of Ch'in. The king of Chao's consort was Wu-chi's elder sister.

ture of determination and wandered about as counselors, we may take these "Four Strong Men," the lords of Hsin-ling, P'ing-yüan, Meng-ch'ang, and Ch'un-shen, as the most outstanding. At this time men thought it their duty to turn their backs on the public good and to die for their own clique; attending to one's office and serving one's superior had ceased to be the ideal.

Later, when the Han arose, the net of the law was widely spread and full of holes, for it had not yet been tightened and repaired. Because of this Ch'en Hsi, the prime minister of Tai, was able to gather a following of a thousand chariots, and kings Liu P'i of Wu and Liu An of Huai-nan both attracted retainers to their courts by the thousands. Men like the great ministers Tou Ying, the marquis of Wei-ch'i, and T'ien Fen, the marquis of Wu-an, who were related to the imperial family by marriage, competed with one another in the capital area, while hemp-robed commoners such as the wandering knights Chü Meng and Kuo Hsieh galloped through the lanes and byways and exercised authority in the provinces and outlying areas. Their strength humbled dukes and marquises, and the common people glorified their names and deeds, envied and looked up to them. Though they were condemned to suffer for their crimes, they died believing that they were thereby fulfilling their reputation; like Chi Lu and Ch'ou Mu, they went to their death without regret.[6]

This is what Tseng Tzu meant when he said, "The rulers have failed in their duties, and the people have for a long time gone astray."[7] If there is no enlightened monarch above who can show them what is good and what is evil and regulate them by rites and laws, then how will the people come to understand the prohibitions and return to what is correct—that is, to the correct laws of ancient times? The Five Dictators offended against the kings of the Three Dynasties; the Six States offended against the Five Dictators. The Four Strong Men in turn offended against the Six States. How much more, then, have those like Kuo Hsieh offended who, though mere commoners in rank, arrogate to themselves the authority to take human life! The guilt they incur by doing so is too great to be excused from punishment. When we observe their kindness and universal lovingness, when we see them aiding the dis-

---

[6] Chi Lu, a disciple of Confucius, died fighting to protect his lord, the ruler of Wei. Ch'ou Mu, a high official of Sung, hastened to avenge the assassination of his ruler and was killed in the attempt.

[7] *Analects* XIX, 19.

tressed, helping those in trouble, behaving in a modest and retiring fashion and not boasting of their deeds, then, to be sure, we recognize in them qualities that are far removed from the ordinary. But what a pity they could not have proceeded in accordance with the Way and virtue! Instead they allowed themselves to drift into a shabby and inferior way of life. That they brought death to themselves and destruction to their families was no mere stroke of ill fortune.

From the time of the marquises of Wei-ch'i and Wu-an and the king of Huai-nan, the Son of Heaven gnashed his teeth in anger, and Wei Ch'ing and Ho Ch'ü-ping were careful to behave correctly. Yet everywhere in the provinces and feudal kingdoms there were "strong men" and heroes, and in the capital there were the imperial in-laws, their caps and carriage covers never out of sight of each other on the streets. This is a situation common to all times, ancient and modern, and hardly worth mentioning. But in the reign of Emperor Ch'eng the guests and retainers of the Wang families were especially numerous, and Lou Hu was the leader among them. Later, in Wang Mang's time, among the various gentlemen Ch'en Tsun was the hero, and among the knights of the streets and alleys, Yüan She was the chief.

CHU CHIA

Chu Chia was a contemporary of Emperor Kao-tsu, but while most of the men of Lu were teachers of Confucianism, Chu Chia won fame as a knight. He sheltered and concealed hundreds of "strong men" in his house, thus saving them from their enemies, while the ordinary men among his followers were too numerous to mention. Yet all his life he never boasted of his abilities nor bragged of the favors he had done for others. On the contrary, his only fear was that the people he had once aided might come to see him and try to repay him. In helping men who were in need, he considered first those who were poor and humble. He and the members of his family had little money, they wore no fine clothes, their food was simple, and their carriage nothing more than an oxcart. He spent all his time hastening to the side of others who were in trouble, considering their well-being more important than his own. Once he concealed Chi Pu, who was fleeing from the anger of Emperor Kao-tsu, but later, when Chi Pu became honored at the Han court, Chu Chia never made any attempt to see him again. Among the people living east of the Pass there were none who did not stretch forth their necks, longing to become friends with Chu Chia.

T'ien Chung of Ch'u won a reputation as a knight, yet he looked up to Chu Chia as a father and considered that he himself could never equal Chu Chia's deeds.

CHÜ MENG

After T'ien Chung died, there was Chü Meng, a native of Lo-yang. The men of the old region of Chou rely mostly on commerce for their livelihood, but Chü Meng won a name by his deeds of chivalry.

When the kings of Wu and Ch'u began their revolt, Chou Ya-fu, the marquis of T'iao, was made grand commandant of the Han armies and hastened by relay carriage east to Ho-nan, where he met Chü Meng. He was delighted and said, "Wu and Ch'u have embarked on a very serious undertaking, but since they have not sought your services, I am sure they will not be able to accomplish anything!" By this he meant that, at a time when the whole empire was in turmoil, the support of Chü Meng was worth more to him than the conquest of one of the rebel kingdoms. Chü Meng's conduct was much like that of Chu Chia except that he was fond of dice and other amusements of young people. Yet when his mother died, people came from great distances to attend the funeral, their carriages numbering as many as a thousand. When Chü Meng himself died, the wealth of his family did not amount to ten catties of gold.

There was also a man of Fu-li named Wang Meng who won fame as a knight in the region between the Yangtze and Huai rivers. At this time the Hsien family of Chi-nan and Chou Fu of Ch'en were both noted for their "strong man" activities. When Emperor Ching heard of this, he sent an envoy to execute all the members of their group. After this, various members of the Po clan of Tai, as well as Han Wu-pi of Liang, Hsüeh K'uang of Yang-ti, and Han Ju of Chia, came to prominence.

KUO HSIEH

Kuo Hsieh was a native of Chih in Ho-nei. He was a grandson on his mother's side of the famous physiognomist Hsü Fu, who was skilled at reading faces. Kuo Hsieh's father was executed in the time of Emperor Wen because of his activities as a knight.

Kuo Hsieh was keen and quick-tempered; he did not drink wine. In his youth he was sullen, vindictive, and quick to anger when crossed in his will, and this led him to kill a great many people. In addition, he would take it upon himself to avenge the wrongs of his friends and conceal men who were fleeing from the law. When he was not engaged in some kind of violence, robbing or assaulting people, he was counterfeiting money or looting graves—it would be impossible to say how many times he was guilty of such actions. But he met with extraordinary luck, and no matter what difficulties he found himself in, he always managed to escape or was pardoned by a general amnesty.

When he grew older, he had a change of heart and became much more upright in his conduct, repaying hatred with kindness, giving generously and expecting little in return. In spite of this, he took more and more delight in daring and chivalrous actions. Whenever he had saved someone's life, he would never boast of his achievements. At heart he was still as ill-tempered as ever, however, and his meanness would often flare forth in a sudden angry look. The young men of the time emulated his actions and would often take it upon themselves to avenge his wrongs without telling him.

The son of Kuo Hsieh's elder sister, relying upon Hsieh's power and position, was once drinking with a man and tried to make him drink up all the wine. Though the man protested that it was more than he could manage, Hsieh's nephew threatened him and forced him to drain the cup. In anger the man stabbed and killed the nephew and then ran away.

Hsieh's sister was furious. "In my brother's own lifetime someone murders my son and gets away with it!" she exclaimed. Then she threw her son's corpse into the street and refused to bury it, hoping to shame Hsieh into action.

Kuo Hsieh sent men to discover where the murderer was hiding and the latter, fearful of the consequences, returned of his own accord and reported to Hsieh exactly what had happened. "You were quite right to kill my nephew," said Hsieh. "He was at fault!" Then he let the murderer go and, laying the blame for the incident entirely on his nephew, took the corpse away and buried it. When men heard of this, they all admired Hsieh's righteousness and flocked about him in increasing numbers.

Whenever Kuo Hsieh came or went, people were careful to get out of his way. Once, however, there was a man who, instead of moving aside, merely sat sprawled by the road and stared at

Hsieh. Hsieh sent someone to ask the man's name. Hsieh's retainers wanted to kill the man on the spot, but Hsieh told them, "If I am not respected in the village where I live, it must be that my virtue is insufficient to command respect. What fault has this man committed?" Then he sent secret instructions to the military officials of the district, saying, "This man is very important to me. Whenever his turn comes for military service, see that he is let off!"

As a result, the man was let off from military service every time his turn came, and the officials made no attempt to look for him. The man was baffled by this and asked the reason, whereupon he discovered that Hsieh had instructed that he be excused. The man then went to Hsieh and, baring his arms, humbly apologized for his former disrespect. When the young men of the district heard of this, they admired Hsieh's conduct even more.

In Lo-yang there were two men who were carrying on a feud and although ten or more of the worthy residents and "strong men" of the city tried to act as mediators between them, they refused to listen to talk of a settlement. Someone came to ask Kuo Hsieh to help in the matter and he went at night to visit the hostile families, who finally gave in and agreed to listen to Hsieh's arguments. Then he told them, "I have heard that the gentlemen of Lo-yang have attempted to act as mediators, but that you have refused to listen to any of them. Now, fortunately, you have consented to pay attention to me. However, I would certainly not want it to appear that I came here from another district and tried to steal authority from the virtuous men of your own city!" He therefore went away the same night so that people would not know of his visit, telling the feuding families, "Pay no attention to my advice for a while and wait until I have gone. Then let the 'strong men' of Lo-yang act as your mediators and do as they say!"

Kuo Hsieh was short in stature and respectful and frugal in his ways. When he went abroad, he never had horsemen attending him, and he would not venture to ride in a carriage when entering the office of his district. He would often journey to neighboring provinces or kingdoms in answer to some request for aid. In such cases, if he thought he could accomplish what had been asked of him, he would undertake to do so, but if he thought the request was impossible, he would go to pains to explain the reasons to the satisfaction of the other party, and only then would he consent to accept food and wine. As a result, people regarded him with great awe and respect and vied with each other in offering him their services. Every night ten or more carriages would arrive at his gate bearing young men of the town or "strong men" of the neighboring districts who had come begging to be allowed to take some of Hsieh's guests and retainers into their own homes.

When the order went out for the "strong men" in the provinces to be moved to the city of Mou-ling, Kuo Hsieh's family was exempted, since his wealth did not come up to the specified amount.[8] He was so well known, however, that the officials were afraid they would get into trouble if they did not order him to move. General Wei Ch'ing spoke to the emperor on his behalf, explaining that Kuo Hsieh's wealth was not sufficient to require him to move. But the emperor replied, "If this commoner has enough influence to get you to speak for him, general, he cannot be so very poor!" So in the end Kuo Hsieh's family was ordered to move, and the people who came to see him off presented him with over ten million cash as a farewell gift.

A district official named Yang, the son of one Yang Chi-chu of Chih, tried to prevent Kuo Hsieh from receiving the gift, whereupon the son of Hsieh's elder brother cut off the head of the Yang official.

After Kuo Hsieh entered the Pass, the "strong men" and persons of worth within the Pass, both those who had known him before and those who had not, soon learned of his reputation and vied with each other in making friends with him.

Meanwhile, someone in the city of Chih murdered Yang Chi-chu, the father of the official who had tried to interfere with Kuo Hsieh. The Yang family sent a letter of protest to the throne, but someone murdered the bearer of the letter of protest outside the gate of the imperial palace. When the emperor learned of this, he sent out the law officials to arrest Kuo Hsieh. Hsieh fled and, leaving his mother and other members of his family at Hsia-yang, escaped to Lin-chin.

Chi Shao-weng, who had charge of the pass at Lin-chin, had never known Kuo Hsieh and therefore allowed him to go through the pass. After having received permission to leave from Chi Shao-weng, Hsieh turned and entered the region of T'ai-yüan. Whenever

---

[8] Emperor Wu had established his mausoleum at Mou-ling, and in 127 B.C. he ordered that rich and powerful families be moved there from other parts of the empire. The purpose was to populate the town and at the same time to break the power of the big provincial families and settle them near the capital where they could be more easily watched.

Hsieh stopped anywhere in his flight, he would make his destination known to his host, so that the law officials were able to trail him without difficulty. When his trail led to Chi Shao-weng, the latter committed suicide to keep from having to give any information.

After some time, Kuo Hsieh was captured, and a thorough investigation made of all his crimes. It was found, however, that all the murders he had committed had taken place before the last amnesty.

There was a certain Confucian scholar from Chih who was sitting with the imperial envoys at Kuo Hsieh's investigation. When one of Hsieh's retainers praised Hsieh, the Confucian scholar remarked, "Kuo Hsieh does nothing but commit crimes and break the law! How can anyone call him a worthy man?" The retainer happened to overhear the remark and later killed the Confucian scholar and cut out his tongue. The law officials tried to lay the blame on Hsieh, though as a matter of fact he did not know who had committed the murder. The murderer disappeared, and in the end no one ever found out who he was.

The officials finally submitted a report to the throne stating that Hsieh was innocent of the charges brought against him, but the imperial secretary Kung-sun Hung objected, saying, "Hsieh, although a commoner, has taken the authority of the government into his own hands in his activities as a knight, killing anyone who gave him so much as a cross look. If he did not know the man who murdered the Confucian scholar, his guilt is greater than if the crime had been committed by someone he knew. He should be condemned as a treasonable and unprincipled criminal!" In the end Kuo Hsieh and all the members of his family were executed.

After this there were a great many men who acted as knights, but they were an arrogant lot and hardly worth mentioning. In the area within the Pass, there was Fan Chung-tzu of Ch'ang-an, Chao Wang-sun of Huai-li, Kao Kung-tzu of Ch'ang-ling, Kuo Weng-chung of Hsi-ho, Lu Weng-ju of T'ai-yüan, Erh Ch'ang-ch'ing of Lin-huai, and Ch'en Chün-ju of Tung-yang, but although they acted as knights, they were rather timid and retiring and had the manners of gentlemen. Others such as the Yao family of the northern region, the various members of the Tu family of the west, Ch'ou Ching of the southern region, T'o-yü Kung-tzu of the east, and Chao T'iao of Nan-yang, were no more than robbers and brigands of the lowest sort and certainly do not deserve to be treated here. To do so would only be an insult to former men such as Chu Chia.

CHÜ CHANG

Chü Chang, whose polite name was Tzu-hsia, was a native of Ch'ang-an. Ch'ang-an at this time was a great and flourishing city and each street and lane had its "strong men" and knights. Chü Chang lived in the Willow Market of the western sector and so was called "Chü Tzu-hsia of the western sector." He was supervisor of retainers to the prefect of the capital and accompanied the prefect when he visited the palace. The palace attendants, feudal lords, and men of eminence all fell over one another in their haste to greet him, but no one spoke a word to the prefect. Chü Chang was very apologetic, fearful of what the prefect's reaction might be. After this the prefect never took him along when he went to the palace.

Chü Chang was a good friend of the chief of palace writers Shih Hsien, and hence enjoyed the benefits of Shih Hsien's authority and power; the carriages of important visitors constantly crowded his gates. But at the beginning of Emperor Ch'eng's reign, Shih Hsien was convicted of having exceeded his authority and usurped power, and was dismissed from office and sent back to his old home in the provinces. Shih Hsien's wealth was very great and when he was ready to leave the capital, he set aside his furniture, household utensils, and other belongings worth several million cash, intending to give them to Chü Chang. Chü Chang, however, refused to accept them. When one of his retainers asked the reason, he sighed and said, "Though I am only a commoner, Lord Shih has always been kind to me. But now Lord Shih's family is ruined and I have no way to help him out. If I were to make off with his wealth and goods, I would be exploiting the misfortunes of the Shih family and turning them into a stroke of good luck for my own family, would I not?" Everyone agreed with his view and praised him for it.

During the *ho-p'ing* era (28–25 B.C.), Wang Ts'un became prefect of the capital. He seized and punished the "strong men" and knights, putting to death Chü Chang, as well as the arrow-maker Chang Hui, Chao Chün-tu of the Wine Market, and Chia Tzu-kuang. All were famous as "strong men" of Ch'ang-an who avenged wrongs and grudges and gave support to professional killers.

LOU HU

Lou Hu, whose polite name was Chün-ch'ing, was a man of Ch'i. His father's family for generations had been doctors and when Hu was young he joined his father to become a doctor in Ch'ang-an, coming and going in the houses of the nobles and relatives of the emperor. He could recite the classics of medicine, books of pharmacology, and works on medical practices, which ran to several hundred thousand words. Men of prominence all loved and respected him and used to say, "With your talents, Chün-ch'ing, why don't you study for public office?" Because of this, he took leave of his father, studied the Classics and commentaries, and became an official in the office of the prefect of the capital for several years, attaining great honor and fame.

At this time the Wang family was at the zenith of its power and guests and retainers filled its gates. The so-called Five Marquises, all brothers of the Wang clan, competed for fame. Retainers of the five customarily had a single household at which they were supported and were not permitted to pass back and forth from one household to another; only Lou Hu was received at the homes of all five marquises, for everywhere he had won acceptance. Among the gentlemen and great officials with whom he associated there were none who did not welcome him, while in his friendships with prominent people he was treated with special care and respect. Because of this, everyone looked up to him.

He was a short man, slight in build, and clever in argumentation. In discussions he always reasoned according to honor and justice so that his listeners all admired him. He and Ku Yung together were the chief retainers of the Five Marquises. In Ch'ang-an people would speak of "the brush and writing tablet of Ku Tzu-yün [Ku Yung] and the lips and tongue of Lou Chün-ch'ing." By this they meant that these could be trusted and used to good effect. When Lou Hu's mother died, the funeral procession reached two or three thousand carriages. In the lanes and alleys they sang a jingle that went:

> That funeral of Lou Chün-ch'ing—
> the Five Marquises staged the whole thing!

After some time, Wang T'an, the marquis of P'ing-a, recommended Lou Hu as a man of honesty and uprightness and he was given a post as an admonisher and sent out into the provinces and feudal states. Before leaving, he borrowed money and bought a great many presents of silk. When he passed through Ch'i, he sent a letter to the emperor asking for permission to visit his ancestors' graves and, taking advantage of the opportunity, he assembled his relatives and old friends and gave each one a gift of so many bolts of silk, the number of bolts depending upon how close a friend or relative he was. In one day Lou Hu handed out goods worth a hundred measures of gold. When he returned to the capital and reported on his mission, the emperor was pleased and promoted him to the post of governor of T'ien-shui. After several years he retired from office and made his home in Ch'ang-an.

At this time Wang Shang, the marquis of Ch'eng-tu, became grand marshal and general of the guard. When Wang Shang left the court one day, he decided to visit Lou Hu, but his secretary advised him, saying, "General, you are a man of the highest position. It is not proper for you to go off into the lanes and side streets like this!" Wang Shang paid no attention, however, and pushed on until he reached Lou Hu's house. The house was very small and cramped and his attendants had to stand outside by the carriages. He remained there for some time and after a while it clouded up and began to rain. The secretary then remarked to the chief clerk, "I was reluctant to argue with him too strongly about not coming, and so now we have to stand around in the rain in a back alley!" When Wang Shang returned, someone reported to him what the secretary had said. Wang Shang was very angry and had the secretary dismissed on some other pretext, seeing to it that he would be barred from holding office for the rest of his life.

Later, Lou Hu was again recommended and took office as governor of Kuang-han. In the *yüan-shih* era (A.D. 1–5), Wang Mang became Duke Who Brings Safety to the Han, holding sole authority in the government. Wang Mang's eldest son Yü, with his wife's elder brother Lü K'uan, devised a plot to take blood and smear Wang Mang's gate with it, hoping to frighten him into restoring power to the rightful government. The plot came to light, however, and Wang Mang, greatly angered, killed his son Yü. Lü K'uan managed to escape and, since his father had formerly been acquainted with Lou Hu, he journeyed to Kuang-han and visited Hu, though he did not reveal the real reason for his visit. After several days, a document arrived ordering the arrest of Lü K'uan by name, and Lou Hu accordingly had him seized. Wang Mang was delighted and summoned Lou Hu to come to the capital and take charge of the region of Ch'ien-hui-kuang. Lou Hu was enfeoffed as marquis of Hsi-hsiang and ranked among the nine high officials.

During Wang Mang's period of regency, the traitors Chao P'eng, Ho Hung, and others of their group began a rebellion in Huai-li, which soon overflowed into the territory of Ch'ien-hui-kuang. Lou Hu was tried for negligence of duty and dismissed from office, being reduced to the rank of commoner. The salary, bribes, and gifts that he had acquired through his position and title had already been spent before this, and so he retired and lived in the back alleys. By this time the Five Marquises were all dead. In their old age they had lost their power and the number of their retainers had gradually diminished.

When Wang Mang usurped the throne, he summoned Lou Hu and because of his former services enfeoffed him as a vassal squire of his old community. At the same time he appointed Wang Yi, the son of Wang Shang, the marquis of Ch'eng-tu, as minister of works, promoting him to a position of honor and importance. All Wang Yi's father's old friends treated him with extreme respect; only Lou Hu was at ease with him as he had been in former days. Wang Yi in turn treated Lou Hu as a father and did not dare to be remiss with him. At this time he invited a number of guests and personally offered Lou Hu a cup of wine, referring to himself as a "worthless son" and proposing a toast to Hu's long life. The guests, who numbered in the hundreds, all moved off their mats and bowed. Only Hu remained seated upright in the place of honor facing east and, addressing Wang Yi by his polite name, said, "Kung-tzu, why do you honor me like this?"

Formerly, Lou Hu had an old friend named Mr. Lü who, being without children, turned to Lou Hu for support. Lou Hu ate with Mr. Lü while his wife ate with Lü's elderly wife, and the couple even moved into the same house with Lou Hu. But Lou Hu's wife detested Mr. Lü, and when Hu heard of this, he wept and upbraided his wife, saying, "Mr. Lü is an old friend, and now that he is along in years and worn out, he has entrusted himself to me. It is only right that I should take care of him." In fact he looked out for Mr. Lü to the end of his days. When Lou Hu died, his son inherited his title.

CH'EN TSUN

Ch'en Tsun, whose polite name was Meng-kung, was a man of Tu-ling. His grandfather was Ch'en Sui, polite name Chang-tzu. When Emperor Hsüan was living among the common people, he and Ch'en Sui were friends and used to play *liu-po* and chess together. Sui frequently lost, but was unable to pay the future ruler what he owed. When Emperor Hsüan came to the throne, he employed Ch'en Sui and gradually advanced him to the post of governor of T'ai-yüan. At this time he sent Sui a letter bearing the imperial seal and reading: "By edict you are assigned to the post of governor of T'ai-yüan. The position is one of honor and the salary generous. This way perhaps you can pay up your gambling debts! Your wife Chün-ning was at your side when the debts were incurred and can testify to their existence." Ch'en Sui thereupon declined to accept the appointment, adding by way of explanation, "The debts were incurred before the first year of *yüan-p'ing* (74 B.C.) and hence have been canceled by the general amnesty of that year!" This is an indication of the warm and intimate way in which Sui was treated. In the time of Emperor Yüan, Sui was summoned to be prefect of the capital and later advanced to the office of commandant of justice.

Ch'en Tsun was orphaned when still a boy. He and Chang Sung, whose polite name was Po-sung, both became clerks in the office of the prefect of the capital. Chang Sung was a man of wide learning and superior understanding who was careful to conduct himself with integrity and temperance. Ch'en Tsun, on the other hand, was quite unrestrained and did just as he pleased. Yet, though their actions differed greatly, they remained close friends. By the end of the reign of Emperor Ai people were mentioning them by name as the most promising of the younger officials. Together they took positions in one of the three highest ministries of the government. The clerks of the ministry all went about in dilapidated carts with puny horses to draw them, caring nothing about stylishness, but Ch'en Tsun alone provided himself with the finest of carriages, horses, and clothes. Outside his gate, the visitors' carriages and horsemen literally fell over each other. In addition, he would go out every day and come back drunk, so that he often neglected his duties as a clerk. The chief clerk, following the customary practice, would give him a demerit for such behavior. Whenever this happened, one of the attendant clerks would rush off to the lodging house attached to the office to report this, saying, "Mr. Ch'en, sir, because of a certain affair today you have been given a demerit!" Ch'en Tsun would reply, "When I have been given a full hundred of them, then come and tell me about it!" According to the old regulations, anyone who got a hundred demerits was dismissed.

Eventually, Ch'en Tsun got a full hundred demerits and the chief clerk requested that he be dismissed. The minister of education Ma Kung, a prominent Confucian, was a patron of men of worth and held Ch'en Tsun in great esteem. He told the chief clerk, "This man is a gentleman of great capability. How can you nag at him over such a petty affair?" Then he recommended Ch'en Tsun as someone who would be able to govern one of the more troublesome districts of the capital area, and he was assigned to the post of magistrate of Yü-i in the region of Fu-feng. After some time, however, having failed to get along with the other Fu-feng officials, he retired from the office of his own accord.

When the traitors Chao P'eng, Ho Hung, and others raised their revolt in Huai-li, Ch'en Tsun was made a company commander and distinguished himself in attacks against Chao P'eng and Ho Hung. He was enfeoffed as marquis of Chia-wei and made his home in Ch'ang-an. The feudal lords, influential courtiers, and families related to the throne all honored and respected him. When local governors were about to set out for their posts or when "strong men" and heroes from the provinces and kingdoms came to the capital, they all took advantage of the opportunity to call at Ch'en Tsun's home.

Ch'en Tsun was very fond of drinking, and whenever there was a large gathering at his house and the guests filled the hall, he would immediately shut the gate, pull the linch-pins from the guests' carriages and throw them down the well so that, even though the guests might be in a hurry to leave, they could not do so. Once a circuit inspector who had to make a report to the throne went to call on Tsun, who happened at the time to be drinking. The circuit inspector, much upset at being unable to leave, waited until Tsun had become completely helpless with drink and then dashed into the inner chambers of the house and made his way to Tsun's mother, where he knocked his head on the floor and explained that he had to go to the office of palace writers to keep an appointment. Tsun's mother had him let out by the back gate so he could go on his way.

Ch'en Tsun was nearly always drunk, but at the same time his affairs did not seem to suffer from neglect. He was something over eight feet in height, with a long head, large nose, and very imposing features. He had browsed through the commentaries and chronicles sufficiently to know something about literary style, and by nature he was good at calligraphy. When he wrote letters to people, the recipients always carefully put them away as something of great value. Whatever he asked for, people could not bring themselves to deny him, only fearful that they might lag behind others in doing so. At this time there was a feudal lord with the same surname and polite name as Tsun. Every time this man went to someone's gate and announced himself as "Ch'en Mengkung," all the occupants of the house would begin to rush around in great excitement until they found out who it was. As a result, the man was nicknamed "Ch'en Who-turns-the-house-upside-down."

Wang Mang had long admired Ch'en Tsun's abilities, and there were many people in office who praised and recommended him. Because of this, he selected Ch'en Tsun to become governor of Ho-nan. When Tsun had arrived in his new office and the time came to send a messenger west to the capital, he sent for ten clerks who were good at writing and set them to preparing personal letters of greeting to his old friends in the capital. Leaning on his desk, Tsun would dictate to the clerks, at the same time attending to official business. He sent out several hundred letters, and whether addressed to close or casual friends, each one expressed just the proper sentiment. All Ho-nan was greatly startled by Tsun. After several months, however, he was removed from his post for the following reasons. When Tsun first became governor of Ho-nan, his younger brother Ch'en Chi was made provincial administrator of Ching-chou. When the two were about to set out for their posts, they went together to visit a wealthy household of Ch'ang-an, the Tso family, who were related by marriage to the late king of Huai-yang, where they joined in drinking, eating, and making merry. Sometime later, the director of rectitude Ch'en Ch'ung heard of this and submitted a memorial to the throne accusing the brothers as follows:

"The two Ch'en brothers have received great blessing from Your Majesty, being raised from rank to rank through a succession of offices. Tsun has been ennobled as a feudal lord and appointed governor of a province, while Chi has been made administrator of Ching-chou. Both have been entrusted with the duty of upholding right and exposing wrong, of proclaiming and spreading abroad the teachings of the sages. Yet they have failed to rectify themselves and to exercise caution in their behavior. When Tsun first took office, he and his brother went by closed carriage into the side lanes, visiting the widow Tso A-chün. There wine was served to them and they sang songs. Tsun rose and danced about in the wildest fashion, collapsing in a heap on his mat. When it grew late, he stayed for the night, being helped into bed by the serving girls. Tsun is aware that there is a proper restraint to be exercised in drinking wine and taking part in a feast; he knows it is forbidden by propriety to enter the gate of a widow's house. Yet he guzzles wine until he becomes disgustingly drunk. He brings chaos to the restraints that ought to be observed between men and women. He holds his title and position in contempt and defiles his seal and cord of office. Such evilness one can hardly bear to speak about! I request that he and his brother be dismissed from office."

After Ch'en Tsun had been removed from office, he returned to Ch'ang-an. Guests flocked about him in even greater numbers and he drank and feasted as before. When some time had passed, he again took office, acting as chief commandant of Chiu-chiang and Ho-nei. Three times in all he became an official of the two thousand picul rank. His old friend Chang Sung also rose in rank until he became governor of Tan-yang and was enfeoffed as marquis of Shu-te. Later they both retired from office and returned to live as feudal lords in Ch'ang-an. Chang Sung lived in very modest circumstances, without guests or retainers; only from time to time people who cared about such things would come to him to ask his opinion on some doubtful matter or to discuss the Classics and other literary works. Ch'en Tsun, on the other hand, went about day and night bellowing and shouting; carriages and horsemen filled his gates and there was a never-ending flow of wine and meat.

Sometime earlier, the attendant of the Yellow Gate Yang Hsiung had written a "Remonstrance on Wine" which he hoped would exercise an influence on Emperor Ch'eng. In this piece, a guest who is fond of wine criticizes a strait-laced gentleman and makes the following comparisons:

> You, sir, may be compared to a pitcher.
> Look for a pitcher and one finds it
> Sitting on the brow of the well.

Perched up high, overlooking the depths,
When it moves it is constantly on the brink of danger.
Wine and spirits do not pass its mouth;
Instead it is loaded with a bellyful of water.
It cannot move to left or right,
But is dragged up and down by the well rope.
Then one morning it is lowered too fast
And smashes to bits on a brick in the well wall.
Its body hurtles down to the yellow springs,
Its bones and flesh turn into mud.
This is the way it looks out for itself,
No match, indeed, for the leather wine sack!
The wine sack is a carefree wag,
With a belly like a great big pot.
All day long he is full of wine;
You can always draw another draught.
He is used to being treated like an elder statesman,
Riding with the ruler in the royal carriage.
He goes in and out of the Two Palaces,[9]
And completely runs the affairs of the nation.
Surely when one can say this much,
There cannot be anything wrong with wine!

Ch'en Tsun was extremely fond of this piece and always used to say to Chang Sung, "You and I are like the pitcher and the wine sack. You sit mumbling over your Classics and other texts, spending your life in hardship and self-discipline, not daring to commit the tiniest misstep. But I let my mind roam free, indulging my desires, bobbing and sinking with the common run of men. In position, title, accomplishment, and fame, I am in no way inferior to you. We differ only in the matter of enjoyment, and there I think I have the edge on you, have I not?"

Chang Sung would reply, "Each person has his own nature—he has to decide the long and short of things for himself. Even if you wanted to, you could never become like me, and if I tried to imitate you, I would certainly fail. Nevertheless, anyone who learns from me will find it easy to get along, but anyone who imitates you will have a hard time! Mine is the accepted way."

When Wang Mang was defeated the two men were both living temporarily in Ch'ih-yang. Chang Sung was killed by rebel sol-

---

[9] The palace of the emperor, and that in which the empress dowager and heir apparent reside.

diers. When the Keng-shih Emperor [10] came to Ch'ang-an, the high ministers recommended Ch'en Tsun for the post of grand marshal of the supporting army. With Liu Sa, the marquis of Kuei-te, he was sent as an envoy to the Hsiung-nu. The *Shan-yü* tried to threaten and browbeat him, but Tsun lectured him on what was to his advantage and was not, setting forth the rights and wrongs of the situation. The *Shan-yü* was much impressed and allowed him to return home. When the Keng-shih Emperor was overthrown, Ch'en Tsun remained in the north and was finally killed by rebels. He was drunk at the time he was murdered.

YÜAN SHE

Yüan She's polite name was Chü-hsien. His grandfather in the time of Emperor Wu was among the group of families who, because of their activities as "strong men" and heroes, were ordered to move from Yang-ti to the tomb town of Mou-ling near Ch'ang-an. His father in the reign of Emperor Ai became governor of Nan-yang. At this time the empire was rich and prosperous, and when an official of the two thousand picul class such as the governor of a large province died in office, the collection taken up to provide for his funeral expenses usually amounted to over ten million cash. This sum would be turned over to the wife and family so that they could set themselves up in some kind of business. Also in those days there were few people who observed the old three-year mourning period. But when Yüan She's father died, he returned the funeral donation to the people of Nan-yang and for three years lived in a hut by the graveside, performing the duties proper to a bereaved son. Because of this, his name became known in the capital, and when his period of mourning was ended, the Fu-feng officials visited him and invited him to become an advisory clerk. Men of position admired him and gathered about him like spokes about a hub. He became a clerk under the minister of education and, being recommended for his abilities in governing troublesome areas, he was appointed magistrate of Ku-k'ou. At this time he was only a little over twenty, but because the people of Ku-k'ou were already familiar with his reputation, he did not have to say a word and the district was well ordered.

Some time previously, Yüan She's uncle had been killed by a

[10] A member of the Liu clan who ruled briefly from the time of Wang Mang's overthrow in A.D. 23 until his own death at the hands of rebels in A.D. 25.

member of the Ch'in family of Mou-ling. After Yüan She had been
in Ku-k'ou for half a year or more, he had himself impeached and
dismissed from office, intending to avenge his uncle's death. But
the "strong men" and heroes of Ku-k'ou took it upon themselves to
murder the Ch'in man for him, and as a result he went into hiding.
A year or so later, a general amnesty was proclaimed and he was
able to come out of hiding. The various "strong men" of the provinces and kingdoms, as well as the men of Ch'ang-an and the five
tomb towns around it who prided themselves on their spirit and
sense of honor, all flocked around him in admiration.

Yüan She did all he could to treat others with consideration, and
many kinds of people, both good and bad, crowded his gates.
Wherever he happened to be, the lanes and alleys turned out in
full force to welcome him. One of his visitors criticized him, saying, "You started out as the heir of an official of the two thousand
picul class. From the time when, as a young man, you bound up
your hair, you were careful to act correctly, fulfilling your mourning duties, spurning wealth, and making a name for yourself by observing proper ritual and deferring to others. Even when avenging
a wrong or seizing an enemy, you never violated the principles of
benevolence and righteousness. Why is it that now you behave in
such an unlicensed manner and allow yourself to become identified
with this class of worthless knights?"

Yüan She replied, "Haven't you ever noticed how it is with a
maidservant or a widow? At first, while she is intent on conducting
herself with strict decorum, her heart thrills with admiration for
Princess Po of Sung and the Filial Wife of Ch'en.[11] But then one
day, alas, she is robbed of her virtue by some thieving scoundrel,
and in the end she sinks into a life of wantonness and shame. She
knows it isn't proper, but it is beyond her power to return to the
old life. That's the way it is with me."

Yüan She began to feel that his rejection of the funeral donation
from the people of Nan-yang, which had gained him such fame,
and his overly frugal ordering of his father's grave, had been at

---

[11] In the 6th century B.C. Princess Po, widow of Duke Kung of Sung, chose
to die in a fire in the palace rather than venture abroad at night without her
chaperon. The "Filial Wife," a widow of a man named Ch'en, remained in her
husband's home in order to take care of her mother-in-law. When her parents
tried to persuade her to remarry, she threatened suicide. Emperor Wen of the
Han, hearing of her conduct, rewarded her and gave her the title of "Filial
Wife."

variance with proper filial conduct. So he set about building a mausoleum in the grand manner, with encircling walls and double gates. Earlier, in the time of Emperor Wu, a man named Ts'ao who had held the post of prefect of the capital had been buried at Mou-ling, and the people all referred to the road which led to his tomb as "The Prefect's Road." Yüan She was much impressed with this, so he bought some land, built a road leading to his father's tomb, and set up a sign reading, "Governor of Nan-yang's Road." But people would not go along with this, and referred to it simply as "Mr. Yüan's Road." The funds for these various expenditures were provided by wealthy men and families of prominence. Yüan She's own needs in clothing, horse, and carriage he placed after everything else, and his wife and family often had difficulty making ends meet. His only concern was to relieve the poor and troubled, for he regarded it as his duty to aid those who were in distress.

Once some people prepared wine and invited him to their house. He had no sooner entered the gate of the neighborhood than one of his followers told him that the mother of someone he knew had been taken ill and, in hopes of escaping the sickness, had been moved to a house in the neighborhood where he was visiting. He went immediately to knock on the gate, and when he heard the family wailing, he entered and offered his condolences. Then he asked about the funeral arrangements and, learning that the family was without means, he said, "Just sweep and wash things up, bathe the body, and wait for me."

Then he returned to the house where he was being entertained and said to his followers with a sigh, "That man's mother is lying on the ground without a proper burial. What heart have I to face these things—please take the food and wine away!" His followers rushed forward to ask what they could do to help. Yüan She then moved off his mat in a gesture of mourning, seated himself on the floor, cut up a number of writing slips and wrote out orders for the necessary items, from clothing, bedding, and coffin down to such things as food and the piece of jade for the mouth.[12] He distributed these among his retainers, who hurried off to the market to make the purchases. By the time the sun was beginning to set, they had all reassembled and, after Yüan She had personally inspected the articles, he told the host that he would appreciate some refresh-

[12] A small piece of jade or some other valuable object was customarily placed in the mouth of the dead person.

ment. He and his followers then joined in eating and drinking, but Yüan She alone was careful not to gorge himself. Then he took the coffin and other articles and, accompanied by his followers, went to the bereaved family and prepared the body for burial, comforting and encouraging the others until the funeral was completed. This is an example of how he helped others and treated people. Later, when someone spoke ill of him, calling him "the worst of the evildoers," the sons of the bereaved family immediately killed the man who had made the remark.

Yüan She's followers often violated the law and their crimes frequently came to the attention of the authorities. Wang Mang several times arrested him with the intention of putting him to death, but each time pardoned him and let him go. Yüan She began to grow afraid and attempted to secure a post as a clerk in one of the high ministries, hoping in this way to escape from his followers. When Empress Dowager Wang, the Mother of Culture, passed away (A.D. 13), he was temporarily appointed as a colonel in charge of the construction of the grave mound. After this, he became a palace attendant, but later retired from office.

Yüan She wished to visit the grave mound of his father but wanted to avoid a meeting with his followers, so he decided to go alone and in secret, arranging to meet some old friends there. He drove hurriedly to Mou-ling in a single cart and, when dusk had fallen, entered a friend's house in a certain quarter of the town, hiding there and seeing no one. He sent one of his slaves to the market to buy meat, but the slave, certain that he could do anything he pleased as long as he was on an errand for Yüan She, began to quarrel with the butcher. Eventually he stabbed and wounded the butcher and then ran away.

At this time the acting magistrate of Mou-ling Lord Yin had newly assumed office and Yüan She had not yet paid a call on him. When he learned of the incident, he became very angry. He had heard of Yüan She's reputation as a "strong man" and wished to make an example of him in order to impress people and persuade them to give up such ways. He sent two officers to seize Yüan She and hold him under guard. By the middle of the day, the slave had not been found and the officers wanted to put Yüan She to death on the spot and be done with the affair. Yüan She was in a very difficult position and did not know what to do, when just at that moment twenty or thirty carriages arrived full of people who had arranged to meet Yüan She at the appointed time to visit his father's grave mound, all of them "strong men" of the region. Together they tried to reason with Lord Yin, but he refused to listen. The men then said, "Yüan Chü-hsien's slave broke the law and has not been apprehended. If we make Mr. Yüan bare his back, tie himself up with cords, pierce his ear with an arrow,[13] and proceed to the gate of your office to beg pardon for his crime, this should be sufficient proof of your authority." Lord Yin promised that this would suffice. Yüan She then apologized according to the agreement and was told to put on his clothes and go on his way.

In earlier days Yüan She had become friends with a rich man of Hsin-feng named Ch'i T'ai-po. T'ai-po's younger half brother by the same mother was a certain Wang Yu-kung, who had always hated Yüan She. At this time Wang Yu-kung was a minor official in the district office and he spoke to Lord Yin, saying, "In your capacity as acting magistrate you have subjected Yüan She to humiliation in this fashion. But one day the permanent magistrate will come to take over and you will get in your single cart and go back to being a clerk in the office. Yüan She has assassins flocking around him like clouds—when it comes to killing people, I don't know which of them is the worst offender. It's enough to make your heart turn to ice! When Yüan She built the grave mound for his father, he was very lavish and overstepped the regulations for such things. His crimes and evil deeds are well known and the ruler is aware of them. Now if I were to suggest a plan for you, I'd say the best thing would be to tear down and destroy this grave mound of Yüan She's and submit a memorial enumerating all his old crimes. That way you can surely get the appointment as permanent magistrate for yourself. Then Yüan She would never dare do anything to get back at you."

Lord Yin followed this advice and, as he had hoped, Wang Mang gave him a permanent appointment as magistrate. Yüan She for this reason came to hate Wang Yu-kung. He called his followers together and dispatched his eldest son Yüan Ch'u with twenty carriages accompanying him to force his way into Wang Yu-kung's house. Wang Yu-kung's mother, as has been said, was also the mother of Ch'i T'ai-po, and when Yüan She's followers saw her, they all bowed respectfully and passed word to each other, saying, "Don't frighten Mrs. Ch'i!" Then they killed Wang Yu-kung and his father, cut off their heads, and departed.

[13] A form of punishment used in the military.

In nature Yüan She generally took after Kuo Hsieh. On the out-side he was gentle, kind, humble, and modest, concealing his true feelings within himself. He delighted in killing people, and there were more than a few men who, having given him an angry look, ended up dead in the dust.[14] Towards the end of Wang Mang's reign there were uprisings of soldiers in the eastern regions. Wang Mang's sons and relatives strongly recommended Yüan She for his ability to attract followers who were willing to die for him, urging that he could be of service. Wang Mang therefore summoned him and, after berating him for his various crimes, pardoned him and made him governor of Chen-jung, formerly called T'ien-shui.

Yüan She had not been in office long before Ch'ang-an fell to the rebels. In all the prefectures and provinces there were pretenders to the throne who raised troops in support of the Han dynasty and killed the officials of the two thousand picul class and senior offi-cers. All these pretenders had heard of Yüan She from of old, and they vied with each other in inquiring the whereabouts of "Gover-nor Yüan" and courteously paying their respects to him. At this time the provincial governors and envoys appointed by Wang Mang who attached themselves to Yüan She all managed to stay alive, and they took turns in escorting him on his way to Ch'ang-an.

In the *keng-shih* period (A.D. 23–24) the general of western de-fense Shen-t'u Chien invited Yüan She to visit him and showed him the greatest respect. The former magistrate of Mou-ling Lord Yin, who had desecrated and destroyed the grave mound which Yüan She had built for his father, was at this time secretary to Shen-t'u Chien. Yüan She had originally harbored no great resentment against him, but when Yüan She accompanied Shen-t'u Chien on an outing, Lord Yin made a point of stopping him and, bowing re-spectfully, said, "The world has all changed, hasn't it. I hope you won't continue to think ill of me." Yüan She replied, "Mr. Yin, what do you take me for—some kind of animal?" As a result of this incident Yüan She became enraged and sent an assassin to mur-der the secretary. He intended to run away and hide, but Shen-t'u Chien, though inwardly greatly angered and ashamed of what Yüan She had done, hid his true feelings and said, "I had thought that Yüan Chü-hsien and I together could guard the three areas adja-cent to the capital. Why would I change my plans because of this

[14] Reading *ch'u ssu* instead of *tu ssu*.

affair of one minor official?" Yüan She's followers reported this to She, urging him to tie himself up and beg for pardon before the prison officials; Shen-t'u Chien promised that this would be sufficient. Yüan She's retainers turned out in twenty or thirty carriages, escorting She to the prison, but Shen-t'u Chien sent soldiers out on the road to arrest Yüan She in his carriage. The carriages escorting him all scattered and galloped off and Yüan She was in the end executed and his head hung in the market place of Ch'ang-an.

During the time of emperors Ai and P'ing there were "strong men" and heroes living here and there in the provinces and kingdoms, but none of them are worth listing. Of those whose names were known in the provinces and prefectures, there was Tu Chün-ao of Pa-ling, Han Yu-ju of Ch'ih-yang, Hsiu Chün-pin of Ma-ling, and Ts'ao Chung-shu of Hsi-ho, but all of these behaved in a modest and retiring manner. When Wang Mang was acting as regent, he attempted to wipe out the "strong men" and knights and sent an order naming Ts'ao Chung-shu for arrest, but he was unable to capture him. Ts'ao had originally been friendly with the general of strong bowmen Sun Chien. Wang Mang suspected that Sun Chien was concealing him, and in an offhand manner asked Sun Chien about it. Sun Chien replied, "I know the name very well. If you punish me instead, I trust that that will be sufficient to make amends." Wang Mang was by nature stubborn and vicious and seldom forgave anyone, but since he respected Sun Chien so highly, he did not question him further and thus never captured Ts'ao Chung-shu. Chung-shu's son when young also roamed about and is said to have made a name for himself as a knight.

the Families Related to the Emperors by Marriage (Excerpts) [1]

MADAM LI, CONCUBINE OF EMPEROR WU

MADAM LI, A CONCUBINE OF EMPEROR WU THE FILIAL, originally entered service in the palace as an entertainer. Her elder brother Li Yen-nien, who had an innate understanding of music, was skilled at singing and dancing and Emperor Wu took a great liking to him. Whenever he presented some new song or musical composition, there were none among his listeners who were not moved to admiration. Once when he was attending the emperor, he rose from his place to dance and sing this song:

> Beautiful lady in a northern land,
> standing alone, none in the world like her,
> a single glance and she upsets a city,
> a second glance, she upsets the state!
> Not that I don't know she upsets states and cities,
> but one so lovely you'll never find again!

The emperor sighed and said, "Splendid!—but I doubt there's anyone that beautiful in the world." The emperor's elder sister Prin-

[1] Pan Ku has taken the first part of this chapter almost verbatim from *Shih chi* 49 (translated in *Records of the Grand Historian of China*, vol. 1, pp. 379–92). I have begun at the point where his narrative begins to diverge sharply from that of Ssu-ma Ch'ien and have selected from among the numerous biographies of empresses and concubines those that seem of greatest interest.

cess P'ing-yang then informed him that Li Yen-nien had a little sister, and he forthwith had her summoned and brought before him. She was in fact strikingly beautiful and skilled at dancing as well, and because of this she won his favor.

She bore him a son, known posthumously as King Ai of Ch'ang-i, but died shortly afterwards at a very young age. The emperor, filled with grief and longing, had a portrait of her painted at the Palace of Sweet Springs. Later, Empress Wei was removed from the position of empress, and four years afterwards, when Emperor Wu passed away, the general in chief Ho Kuang, following what he knew to have been the emperor's wishes, had sacrifices performed to Madam Li in the emperor's mortuary temple as though she had been his official consort, posthumously honoring her with the title "Empress of Emperor Wu the Filial."

Earlier, when Madam Li lay critically ill, the emperor came in person to inquire how she was, but she pulled the covers over her face and, apologizing, said, "I have been sick in bed for a long time and my face is thin and wasted. I cannot let Your Majesty see me, though I hope you will be good enough to look after my son the king and my brothers."

"I know you've been very sick, and the time may come when you never rise again," said the emperor. "Wouldn't you feel better if you saw me once more and asked me face to face to take care of the king and your brothers?"

"A woman should not appear before her lord or her father when her face is not properly made up," she said. "I would not dare let Your Majesty see me in this state of disarray."

"Just let me have one glimpse of you!" said the emperor. "I'll reward you with a thousand pieces of gold and assign your brothers to high office!"

But Madam Li replied, "It is up to Your Majesty to assign offices as you please—it does not depend on one glimpse of me."

When the emperor continued to insist on one last look at her, Madam Li, sobbing, turned her face toward the wall and would not speak again. The emperor rose from his seat in displeasure and left.

Madam Li's sisters berated her, saying, "Why couldn't you let him have one look at you and entreat him face to face to take care of your brothers! Why should you anger him like this!"

"The reason I didn't want the emperor to see me," she said, "was so I could make certain he would look after my brothers! It was because he liked my looks that I was able to rise from a lowly position and enjoy the love and favor of the ruler. But if one has been taken into service because of one's beauty, then when beauty fades, love will wane, and when love wanes, kindness will be forgotten. The emperor thinks fondly and tenderly of me because he remembers the way I used to look. Now if he were to see me thin and wasted, with all the old beauty gone from my face, he would be filled with loathing and disgust and would do his best to put me out of his mind. Then what hope would there be that he would ever think kindly of me again and remember to take pity on my brothers?"

When Madam Li died, the emperor had her buried with the honors appropriate to an empress. After that, he enfeoffed her eldest brother Li Kuang-li, the Sutrishna general, as marquis of Hai-hsi, and appointed her brother Li Yen-nien as a chief commandant with the title "Harmonizer of the Tones."

The emperor continued to think longingly of Madam Li and could not forget her. A magician from Ch'i named Shao-weng, announcing that he had the power to summon spirits, one night lit torches, placed curtains around them, and laid out offerings of wine and meat. He then had the emperor take his place behind another curtain and observe the proceedings from a distance. The emperor could see a beautiful lady who resembled Madam Li circling within the curtains, sitting down and then rising to walk again. But he could not move closer to get a good look and, stirred more than ever to thoughts of sadness, he composed this poem:

> Is it she?
> is it not?
> I stand gazing from afar:
> timid steps, soft and slow,
> how long she is in coming!

He then ordered the experts of the Music Bureau to devise a string accompaniment and make it into a song.

He also composed a work in *fu* or rhyme-prose form to express his grief at the loss of Madam Li; it read as follows:

> Beauty soft and yielding, matchless grace,
> A life cut off forever, to thrive no more—

We decked the new temple, waited to greet you,[2]
But firmly you declined to return to your old home.
Grieving in the thicket, rank and weed grown,
Hiding in a dark place, harboring your pain,
You left your horse and carriage at the crest of the hill,
To tarry in that long night that knows no dawn.
Autumn's breath is sad and sharp with chill,
The limbs of the cassia fall and fade away.
Your spirit, lonely, pines for those far off,
Your soul wanders restless to the borders and beyond.
Consigned to sunken darkness for long ages to come,
I pity these lush flowers cut off half way;
Reflecting that for all time you'll return no more,
I recall how you came and went in beauty's prime,
Petals clustered about a center, unfurled to wait the wind,
Blossoms heaped and jumbled in increasing radiance,
Shining serenely, elegantly fair,
Pleasing in gentleness, yet more grave than before.
At leisure, unconstrained, you leaned against a column,
Lifted moth eyebrows, cast your glance around the room.
But when you'd roused my heart to follow after,
You hid your rosy face and shone no more.
Forced to part after intimate joys,
At night I start from dreams, dazed and lost.
So sudden that change from which you'll never return,
Your soul set free to fly far off;
In such perplexity your sacred spirit,
Roaming in grief and consternation;
But the days are many since you took to that road,
And in the end, hesitant, you said goodby,
Traveling ever westward, quickly out of sight.
I am sunk in longing, silent and dumb,
With thoughts that surge like waves, and pain in my heart.
   Reprise:
Beauty wreathed in splendor,
A crimson flower fell.
(Those other jealous wretches,
How could they compare?)
In days of greatest glory,
Cut off before your time!

---

[2] According to commentators, the "new temple" is the curtained area rigged by the magician to summon the dead woman's spirit. As will be seen, the poem shifts restlessly back and forth between descriptions of Madam Li herself and metaphors of blooming or fallen flowers.

Your son and brothers sobbing,
Bathed in tears of woe,
Wailing, lamenting,
Unable to cease their cries,
But such cries must go unanswered—
Let there be an end!
Thin and worn with sighing,
You grieved for the future of your little boy,
And though sorrow left you speechless,
You trusted to the favor you had once known.
No vows are needed among good men,
Much less between those who love!
Though you're gone and will never return,
I repeat once more my pledge to be true!
You left the sunny brightness,
Went to realms of dark,
And though you descended to our new temple,
You come no more to the gardens of old.
Ah, alas,
I dream of your soul!

Later, Li Yen-nien and his younger brother Li Chi were tried on charges of immoral behavior with the women of the palace, and Li Kuang-li, the eldest brother, surrendered to the Hsiung-nu. As a result, all the members of the Li family were put to death.

THE BEAUTIFUL COMPANION LADY CHAO

The Beautiful Companion Lady Chao of the Hook and Dart Palace, a concubine of Emperor Wu the Filial, was the mother of Emperor Chao. She was a native of Ho-chien. When Emperor Wu passed by her home on a tour of inspection, a man who was expert in reading the signs in the sky announced that there were indications of the presence of an unusual woman. The emperor hastily sent a messenger to discover who it could be and bring her to him; the messenger returned with a woman whose hands were doubled up in fists. The emperor tried to see if he could unclench her fists, and immediately the fingers unfolded. As a result of this encounter she won his favor, and was known as the Lady of the Fists.

Sometime earlier, her father had been tried for an offense and condemned to suffer castration; he became an attendant of the Yellow Gate in the inner palace and died in Ch'ang-an, being buried by the Gate of Yung.

The Lady of the Fists advanced to the rank of Beautiful Companion and took up residence in the Hook and Dart Palace, enjoying great favor with the emperor. In the third year of *t'ai-shih* (94 B.C.) she gave birth to the future Emperor Chao, who was accordingly called the son of the Hook and Dart Palace. She was pregnant for fourteen months before finally giving birth. The emperor said, "I have heard that in ancient times the sage Yao was born after fourteen months in the womb, and now the same has happened with my son of the Hook and Dart Palace!" He thereupon ordered that the gate to the quarters where the boy was born be named the Gate of the Mother of Yao.

Later the heir apparent, the emperor's son by Empress Wei, met with downfall, and the king of Yen Liu Tan, as well as the king of Kuang-ling Liu Hsü, other sons of Emperor Wu, were guilty of too many faults and errors to be considered for the position of heir apparent. Madam Wang's son King Huai of Ch'i, and Madam Li's son King Ai of Ch'ang-i, whose mothers had enjoyed favor with the emperor, had both passed away at an early age. The son of the Hook and Dart Palace was by this time five or six years old, a large, husky boy of great intelligence whom the emperor frequently declared took after himself. The emperor also recalled that the boy's manner of birth had been quite different from that of ordinary persons and, being very fond of him and entertaining great hopes for his future, he wished to appoint him as heir. But in view of the fact that the boy was so young and his mother still in the prime of life, he was afraid that she might try to dominate him and exercise power in such a way as to bring ruin to the state. So for a long time he hesitated to make the move.

At this time the boy's mother the Beautiful Companion Chao accompanied the emperor on a visit to the Palace of Sweet Springs, but she committed a fault and, being severely scolded, died of grief. She was accordingly buried at Yün-yang close by.[3]

Later, when the emperor fell gravely ill, he appointed the son of

---

[3] Ch'u Shao-sun, a scholar of the 1st century B.C. who made additions to the *Shih chi*, has appended the following account of this incident to *Shih chi* 49: "A few days later the emperor scolded and berated the lady of the Hook and Dart Palace. She removed her hairpins and earrings and struck her head on the ground, but the emperor said, 'Take her away to the prison of the women's quarters!' As she left, she turned to look at him, but he said, 'Hurry on your way! You cannot be saved!' She died in the Yün-yang Palace; at that time a violent wind blew up clouds of dust and the common people were moved to pity. . . . Later, when the emperor was at his leisure, he asked those about him, 'What are people saying?' They replied, 'People are saying

the Hook and Dart Palace as heir apparent to the throne, and promoted the chief commandant in charge of the imperial carriage Ho Kuang to the post of grand marshal general in chief, instructing him to assist the young ruler. The following day he passed away and Emperor Chao came to the throne. He honored his mother the Beautiful Companion of the Hook and Dart Palace with the posthumous title of empress dowager and dispatched a party of twenty thousand soldiers to construct a grave mound for her at Yün-ling, establishing a town of three thousand households to tend it. He honored his maternal grandfather of the Chao family with the posthumous title of marquis of Shun-ch'eng, and commanded the Fu-feng district of the capital area, in which his grave was situated, to set up a funerary park and village of two hundred households, with officials appointed to guard and maintain it according to the law. The marquis of Shun-ch'eng had an elder sister named Chao Chün-hsü who was presented with a gift of two million cash, as well as male and female slaves and houses in abundance. All the other male relatives of the family were given gifts and rewards depending on how closely they were related to the emperor. None of the Chao family held any office or title except Lady Chao's father, who was enfeoffed posthumously.

LADY WANG, CONSORT OF THE IMPERIAL GRANDSON SHIH [4]

Lady Wang, the consort of the imperial grandson Shih, was the mother of Emperor Hsüan. Her name was Weng-hsü. During the *t'ai-*

---

that if one is about to set up the son, why does one do away with the mother?' 'Ah, yes,' said the emperor, 'but then this is not the kind of thing that children and fools would understand anyway! In past times the state was brought to ruin because the ruler was young and his mother still in her prime. If a woman ruler is allowed to exercise power alone, she will behave in a willful, unlicensed, and wanton way, and nothing can check her. Have you never heard of the case of Empress Lü?' " Pan Ku seldom borrowed material from Ch'u Shao-sun, whom he apparently regarded as unreliable, and he characteristically rejects this passage, with its sinister implication that the emperor deliberately did away with the Beautiful Companion Chao for political reasons.

[4] The imperial grandson Shih was the son of Prince Li, the son of Emperor Wu and Empress Wei who was for a time heir apparent but, because of the suspicion cast upon him by the black magic affair, finally revolted and was wiped out along with all the members of his family. Only his grandson, the son of the imperial grandson Shih and Lady Wang, survived to become Emperor Hsüan.

shih period (96–93 B.C.) she gained favor with the imperial grandson Shih. The imperial grandson's wife and concubines did not have any titles; all are referred to simply as "daughters of commoners."

In the second year of *cheng-ho* (91 B.C.), Lady Wang gave birth to the future Emperor Hsüan, and a few months later the heir apparent, Emperor Wu's son by Empress Wei, and the imperial grandson Shih met their downfall. The imperial grandson's wife and concubines were all arrested and put to death—there was not even anyone left to gather up the bodies and bury them. Only the future Emperor Hsüan was allowed to live. After he came to the throne, he posthumously honored his mother Lady Wang with the title Consort of Tao and his father's mother the Good Companion Shih with the title Consort of Li. Both were moved to new graves, with funerary parks and villages set up and officials appointed to guard and maintain them. (A discussion will be found in the Biography of the Heir Apparent Li.)

In the third year of *ti-chieh* (67 B.C.), Emperor Hsüan finally succeeded in locating his mother's mother, known as Dame Wang. Dame Wang, along with her sons Wu-ku and Wu, accompanied the imperial envoy who had located them and together journeyed to the capital to appear before the ruler. Dame Wang and her sons made the trip in a cart pulled by a yellow ox, and the common people therefore referred to her as "the old lady of the yellow ox."

Earlier, when Emperor Hsüan first came to the throne, he several times sent out envoys to search for the members of his mother's family, but since so many years had gone by, although the officials were often able to locate persons who seemed at first to fit the description, they were never the real ones. When at last Dame Wang was found, the emperor ordered the palace counselor Jen Hsüan, along with various officials attached to the offices of the chancellor and the imperial secretary, to conduct a careful cross-examination of the villagers who were acquainted with her. The villagers all testified that she was in fact Dame Wang.

Dame Wang herself reported that her name was Wang-jen and that her home was originally in P'ing Village of Li-wu in Cho Province. When she was fourteen she married a man named Wang Keng-te of the same village; after his death, she married again, this time a man named Wang Nai-shih of the district of Kuang-wang, bearing him two sons named Wu-ku and Wu and a daughter named Weng-hsü.

When Weng-hsü was eight or nine, she went to stay for a time in the house of Liu Chung-ch'ing, a younger son of Marquis Chieh of Kuang-wang. Liu Chung-ch'ing said to Weng-hsü's father, "Give me Weng-hsü and I will raise her myself." Weng-hsü's mother accordingly made an unlined silk robe for the girl and sent her off to the home of Liu Chung-ch'ing. Liu Chung-ch'ing taught her to sing and dance, and she was allowed to visit her parents and to return home to fetch winter and summer clothes.

After she had lived at Liu Chung-ch'ing's house for four or five years, she came home one time and said to her mother, "There is a merchant from Han-tan named Chang-erh who is looking for singers and dancers and I think Chung-ch'ing wants to give me to him!" Dame Wang immediately took her daughter and fled with her to P'ing Village. Liu Chung-ch'ing came looking for them in a carriage, bringing the girl's father with him. Dame Wang, flustered and at a loss to know what to do, brought her daughter back home, but she said to Liu Chung-ch'ing, "Though the child has been living in your house, my lord, we have never been given so much as a single cash for her! What right have you now to give her to someone else?" Liu Chung-ch'ing, however, hypocritically protested, "I would never do such a thing!"

A few days later, Weng-hsü passed the gate of her mother's house in a horse-drawn carriage belonging to the merchant Chang-erh. As she passed the gate, she called out, "They are taking me away after all! We are headed for Liu-su!" Dame Wang and her husband followed her to Liu-su and managed to get to see her, both parents and daughter bursting into tears when they met. Dame Wang said, "I'll bring a law suit against them for this!" but Weng-hsü replied, "Never mind, mother. Whatever house I go to I'll manage to get along. It wouldn't do any good to try to sue."

Dame Wang and her husband returned home to get more money and provisions and then resumed their journey, following Weng-hsü as far as Lu-nu in the state of Chung-shan. There they located her in a group of five singers and dancers who were all staying at the same place. Dame Wang spent the night with her daughter and the following day, leaving her husband there to keep watch on Weng-hsü, she went home once more to get together more money, intending to follow Weng-hsü all the way to Han-tan. But before she had finished selling grain to raise money and buying what she needed for the trip, her husband Nai-shih returned home, announcing, "Weng-hsü has already gone—I didn't have any money to follow her." According to Dame Wang, they completely lost track of

Weng-hsü and had never heard anything more of her till the present day.

The merchant Chang-erh's wife Cheng and his assistant Shih Sui reported that twenty years earlier a retainer of the heir apparent named Hou Ming had come from Ch'ang-an looking for singers and dancers and had asked for Weng-hsü and others, five persons in all. Chang-erh had accordingly ordered Shih Sui to escort them to Ch'ang-an, and all of them had become members of the heir apparent's household. The elder of Kuang-wang Keng Shih, Liu Chung-ch'ing's wife Ch'i, and others, forty-five persons in all, testified to the truth of these reports. The emperor's envoy Jen Hsüan accordingly submitted a memorial stating that it was absolutely certain that Dame Wang was the mother of Lady Wang, the consort of the imperial grandson Shih.

The emperor, as has been stated, summoned Dame Wang and the others to an audience in the capital and enfeoffed Dame Wang's sons Wu-ku and Wu as marquises within the Pass. Within the space of a month he handed out gifts and rewards to them worth countless sums of money.

The emperor then commanded the imperial secretary to bestow on his grandmother the title of Lady Po-p'ing, assigning to her the two districts of Po-p'ing and Li-wu with their eleven thousand households to be her bath-town. He also enfeoffed his uncle Wu-ku as marquis of P'ing-ch'ang and his uncle Wang Wu as marquis of Lo-ch'ang, each to enjoy the revenue from a town of six thousand households.

The emperor's grandfather Wang Nai-shih had died of illness earlier in the fourth year of *pen-shih* (70 B.C.), three years before Dame Wang was discovered and the family became rich and eminent. He was given the posthumous title of Ssu-ch'eng Marquis and orders were issued to Cho Province to repair his grave and set up a funerary park and village of four hundred households with officials to guard and maintain it according to the law. A year or so later, the emperor's grandmother passed away and was given the posthumous title Lady of the Ssu-ch'eng Marquis. Orders were given to have the body of the Ssu-ch'eng Marquis exhumed and buried along with that of his wife just south of the funerary temple of Feng-ming Ku-ch'eng, where their daughter was interred; a funerary park and village was set up with officials to tend it. The funerary park that had earlier been established for the Ssu-ch'eng Marquis in Cho Province was accordingly done away with.

Two members of the Wang family were enfeoffed as marquises, Wang Wu-ku and Wang Wu. Wang Wu-ku's son Wang Chieh became grand marshal and carriage and cavalry general. Wang Wu's son Wang Shang rose to the post of chancellor and has his own biography.

EMPRESS HSÜ, CONSORT OF EMPEROR HSÜAN

Empress Hsü, the consort of Emperor Hsüan the Filial, was the mother of Emperor Yüan. Her father Hsü Kuang-han was a native of Ch'ang-i and at an early age became an attendant in the palace of the king of Ch'ang-i. He had occasion to be among those accompanying Emperor Wu on an outing to the Palace of Sweet Springs and mistakenly took the saddle belonging to another attendant and put it on his own horse. He was charged with the crime of stealing while in attendance upon the emperor, for which the penalty was death, but Emperor Wu ordered that he be allowed to undergo castration instead. After punishment, he was made a clerk in the office of eunuchs.

At the time when Shang-kuan Chieh was plotting revolt, Hsü Kuang-han was alloted the task of searching for evidence of misdoing. In the quarters where Shang-kuan Chieh stayed when he was at the palace, pieces of rope several feet in length were found; there were several thousand of them, suitable for tying people up, and they were packed away in a sealed box. Hsü Kuang-han, however, failed to find them when he made his search; they were discovered by another official who went to the room afterward. Hsü Kuang-han was accused of negligence and was condemned to become a provider of "firewood for the spirits." [5] He was assigned to the women's quarters of the palace and was later made an orderly in charge of the women's sickroom.

At this time the future Emperor Hsüan, known as the imperial great-grandson, was being brought up in the women's quarters of the palace and lived in the same lodging as Hsü Kuang-han. The supervisor of the women's quarters at this time was Chang Ho. He had originally been a clerk in the household of the heir apparent, Emperor Wu's son by Empress Wei, and when the heir apparent met with his downfall, Chang Ho was arrested and condemned to suffer castration. Because of the kindness he had formerly received

[5] A form of convict labor; persons condemned to it had the task of cutting firewood for the ancestral temples.

from the heir apparent, he was careful to look after the imperial great-grandson, the heir apparent's grandson, and treat him very generously.

When the imperial great-grandson grew to manhood, Chang Ho wanted to give him his granddaughter as a wife. At this time Emperor Chao had just undergone the capping ceremony, having grown to a height of eight feet two inches.[6] Chang Ho's younger brother Chang An-shih was general of the right and, being on very good terms with the general in chief Ho Kuang, assisted in affairs of government. When he heard Chang Ho praising the imperial great-grandson and saying that he wanted to give him his granddaughter for a wife, he became very angry and said, "The imperial great-grandson is, after all, a descendant of the heir apparent! He has been lucky enough to be made a commoner and to receive an allotment of food and clothing from the government, but that's all he deserves. I don't want to hear you say anything more about giving him your granddaughter for a wife!" Because of this, Chang Ho abandoned his plan.

At this time Hsü Kuang-han had a daughter named P'ing-chün who was fourteen or fifteen and had been promised as a bride to the son of Ou-hou, the supervisor of the inner palace. When the time came for the wedding, however, Ou-hou's son died. The girl's mother than took her to be examined by a diviner; he predicted by the signs in her face that she was destined to become highly honored, which secretly pleased the mother greatly.

Meanwhile, Chang Ho, hearing that the orderly of the sickroom Hsü Kuang-han had a daughter, laid out wine and invited Hsü to his quarters. When the wine had begun to take effect, Chang Ho said, "The imperial great-grandson is closely related to the ruler. Even if he should turn out to be a person of limited ability, he is certain to be made at least a marquis within the Pass. It would be well to give him your daughter as a wife." Hsü Kuang-han gave his consent to the proposal. The next day when the girl's mother heard what he had done, she was furious, but Hsü Kuang-han repeated his request that Chang Ho act as go-between, and eventually the girl was married to the imperial great-grandson. A year later she gave birth to the future Emperor Yüan, and a few months afterwards, the imperial great-grandson was made emperor. His wife Hsü P'ing-chün was advanced to the rank of Beautiful Companion.

[6] On the capping ceremony, see n. 1, p. 47; the Han foot, it will be recalled, was about two thirds of the English foot.

At this time the youngest daughter of the general in chief Ho Kuang was still unmarried and Ho Kuang was on very close terms with the empress dowager.[7] When the ministers and high officials were instructed to discuss who should be made empress, they all tended to favor Ho Kuang's daughter, though none of them actually spoke out on the matter. The emperor meanwhile ordered that a search be made for the "old sword" that had been by his side in his humble days, and the high ministers, perceiving his meaning, recommended that the Beautiful Companion Hsü be made empress. The recommendation was adopted.

The question of the enfeoffment of her father then arose, but Ho Kuang argued that, since Hsü Kuang-han had in the past been condemned to corporal punishment, he was not qualified to become the lord of a fief. Only after a year or so was he finally enfeoffed as lord of Ch'ang-ch'eng. Ho Kuang's wife Hsien continued to have hopes of raising her youngest daughter to a position of eminence, but she could think of no way to accomplish this.

The following year Empress Hsü became pregnant. She was taken ill, and a woman doctor named Ch'un-yü Yen, who was a great favorite with the Ho family and who had been summoned to the palace to treat the empress in the past, was sent for. Ch'un-yü Yen's husband Shang was a guard of the gate of the women's quarters and he said, "Before you enter the palace, you should go pay a call on the lady of the Ho household. Ask her if I may have the post of overseer of the salt ponds of An-i!"

Ch'un-yü Yen went and reported what her husband had said to Ho Kuang's wife Hsien. Hsien looked as though she had suddenly thought of something and, sending the servants out of the room and addressing Ch'un-yü Yen by her polite name, she said, "Shao-fu, you have been kind enough to speak to me about this matter, and now I have a little matter I would like to speak to you about —I wonder if you will listen?"

"What could madam possibly ask that I would be unwilling to do!" protested the woman, whereupon Hsien said, "My husband the general in chief has always been extremely fond of our youngest daughter Ch'eng-chün and would like to see her given some position of special honor. We would like you to help us, Shao-fu."

"What do you mean?" asked Ch'un-yü Yen.

"It is a very serious thing for a woman to give birth," said Ho

---

[7] The consort of Emperor Chao and granddaughter of Ho Kuang on her mother's side.

Hsien. "Hardly one woman out of ten survives. Now the empress is about to bear a child. It would be quite possible to put poison in her medicine and do away with her, and then Ch'eng-chün could be made empress in her place. If you agree to help and the affair is successful, you may be sure that we will share the wealth and honor with you, Shao-fu!"

"But the medicine is prepared by a number of people, and someone always tastes it first!" said Ch'un-yü Yen. "I don't see how it could be done!"

"All it takes is a little arranging on your part," said Ho Hsien. "The general in chief is master of the whole empire—who would dare say anything! If there should be any trouble, he will protect you. I'm only afraid that you may not be interested in the proposal."

Ch'un-yü Yen was silent for a long time and then said, "I will do my best." Then she ground up some aconite plants and took the mixture to the Ch'ang-ting Palace, where the empress was in residence. After the empress had given birth, Ch'un-yü Yen combined the mixture of aconite with the big pill prepared by the chief doctor and gave it to the empress to drink. When some time had passed, the empress said, "My head is splitting with pain!—are you sure there wasn't poison in the medicine you gave me?"

"Of course not," said Ch'un-yü Yen. The empress continued in greater and greater discomfort and agony until she passed away. Ch'un-yü Yen left the palace and went to call on Ho Hsien, who thanked her for her trouble but did not dare to make any elaborate show of gratitude.

Later someone submitted a letter to the throne accusing the doctors and others who had attended the empress in her illness of negligence of duty. All those involved were arrested and taken to the prison for persons under imperial indictment, being charged with unprincipled behavior of the most serious kind. Ho Hsien, fearful that the situation would get out of hand, confessed to her husband exactly what she had done, adding, "Since the plot has failed and things have come to this pass, you mustn't let the law officials press Ch'un-yü Yen too severely!"

Ho Kuang, horrified, listened in silence and made no reply, but later, when a memorial was submitted to the emperor concerning the case, he managed to add a notation, as though by the emperor, ordering that Ch'un-yü Yen was not to be prosecuted further.

Empress Hsü held the position of empress for three years before passing away. She was given the posthumous title Kung-ai, the "Reverent and Pitiful Empress." She was buried at Tu-nan, the funerary park south of Emperor Hsüan's grave at Tu-ling.

Five years later, when Empress Hsü's son was made heir apparent, her father Hsü Kuang-han, the lord of Ch'ang-ch'eng, was enfeoffed as marquis of P'ing-en, and was granted a special advancement in rank. Four years later, Hsü Kuang-han's younger brothers were enfeoffed, Hsü Shun as marquis of Po-wang and Hsü Yen-shou as marquis of Lo-ch'eng. Thus three members of the Hsü family became marquises.

When Hsü Kuang-han passed away, he was given the posthumous title of Tai, the "Sustaining Marquis"; since he left no sons, his fief was abolished. He was buried beside his daughter's funerary park at Tu-nan, with a village of three hundred households set up and officials appointed to guard and maintain the grave in accordance with the law. Emperor Hsüan appointed Hsü Yen-shou as grand marshall and general of carriage and cavalry, making use of his services in the government.

When Emperor Yüan came to the throne, he enfeoffed Hsü Yen-shou's second son as marquis of P'ing-en so that he could carry on the line of his uncle, the Sustaining Marquis. Hsü Chia was also appointed grand marshal and general of carriage and cavalry.

THE BEAUTIFUL COMPANION PAN, CONCUBINE OF EMPEROR CH'ENG

The Beautiful Companion Pan was a concubine of Emperor Ch'eng the Filial. When the emperor first came to the throne (32 B.C.), she was selected to enter the women's quarters. At first she held the rank of Young Attendant, but she very quickly won great favor with the ruler and was advanced to the rank of Beautiful Companion, taking up residence in the Tseng-ch'eng Lodge. She twice moved to other quarters because of pregnancy, but though she bore a son in each case, both died a few months after birth.

Once Emperor Ch'eng was amusing himself in the women's quarters and invited Lady Pan to ride with him in his hand-drawn cart, but she declined, saying, "In the paintings of ancient times one always sees the sage rulers with eminent ministers by their side; only the last rulers of the Three Dynasties, the men who brought destruction to their lines, have their women favorites beside them.

Now if you invite me to share your cart, will you not appear to resemble the latter?"

The emperor, impressed with her words, abandoned the idea. When his mother the empress dowager heard of the incident, she was pleased and said, "In ancient times it was Lady Fan, nowadays it's the Beautiful Companion Pan!" [8]

Lady Pan was thoroughly versed in the *Odes* and other works such as "The Modest Maiden," "Emblems of Virtue," and "The Instructress." [9] Whenever she was summoned to an interview or communicated with anyone by letter, she always followed the dictates of old-time ritual.

From the *hung-chia* period on (20–17 B.C.), the emperor took an increasing interest in his ladies in waiting. Lady Pan recommended to him an attendant of hers named Li P'ing, who won favor with the emperor and was promoted to the rank of Beautiful Companion. The emperor said, "In earlier times Empress Wei also rose from humble origin to a place of honor," and he accordingly bestowed upon Li P'ing the surname Wei, so that she became known as the Beautiful Companion Wei. [10] Later Chao Fei-yen and her younger sister likewise rose to prominence from humble beginnings, but they overstepped all the bounds of ritual and regulation and in time came to outshine all their predecessors. Lady Pan and Empress Hsü both lost favor with the emperor and were seldom summoned into his presence.

In the third year of *hung-chia* (18 B.C.) Chao Fei-yen slanderously accused Empress Hsü and Lady Pan of resorting to sorcery to win favor, attempting to put a curse on the other women of the palace, and extending their imprecations even to the person of the ruler. As a result of the charges, Empress Hsü was removed from her position. When Lady Pan was cross-examined by the law officials, she replied, "I have heard that life and death are decreed by Fate, and wealth and eminence are decided by Heaven. [11] Even when one follows correct behavior he cannot be certain of good

---

[8] Because the king of Ch'u in ancient times was excessively fond of hunting, his concubine Lady Fan refused to eat meat as a form of protest. Lady Pan has shown herself to be a similar model of behavior in correcting the faults of her lord.

[9] Commentators identify these as works on correct behavior; the translations of the titles are tentative.

[10] Empress Wei, the consort of Emperor Wu, began her career as a dancing girl.

[11] Lady Pan is quoting from *Analects* XII, 5.

fortune, so what could he hope for by committing evil? If the gods have understanding, then they will not listen to the pleas of a disloyal subject; and if they have no understanding, what good would it do to offer pleas to them? Therefore I would never resort to such actions!"

The emperor, impressed with her answer, took pity on her and awarded her a gift of a hundred catties of gold. But the Chao sisters continued in their arrogant and jealous ways and Lady Pan, fearful that before long she would meet with disaster, asked to be allowed to wait upon the empress dowager in the Palace of Lasting Trust. The emperor gave his permission and she accordingly retired from court and took up residence in the eastern palace, the Palace of Lasting Trust. There she composed a poem in *fu* or rhyme-prose form giving vent to her sadness; it read:

> Virtue of ancestors handed down
> Bestowed on me precious life as a human being,
> Allowed me, humble creature, to ascend to the palace,
> To fill a lower rank in the women's quarters.
> I enjoyed the holy sovereign's most generous grace,
> Basked in the radiance of sun and moon.
> Burning rays of redness shone on me,
> I was granted highest favor in the Tseng-ch'eng Lodge.
> Already receiving blessings beyond what I deserved,
> I yet ventured to hope for more happy times,
> Sighing repeatedly, waking or asleep,
> Undoing my girdle strings with thoughts of the past.[12]
> I spread out paintings of women, made them my mirror,
> Looked to my instructress, queried her on the *Odes;*
> I was moved by the warning of the woman who crows,
> pained at the sins of the lovely Pao-ssu;
> I praised Huang and Ying, wives to the lord of Yü,
> Admired Jen and Ssu, mothers of Chou.[13]

[12] When a girl was about to be married, her father fastened the strings of her girdle and gave her words of instruction and warning; Lady Pan is recalling that time.

[13] A hen that crows at dawn in place of the rooster is an ancient symbol for a domineering woman; the specific reference here is to Ta-chi, concubine of the evil last ruler of the Shang dynasty. The beautiful but treacherous Pao-ssu brought about the downfall of King Yu of the Chou. O-huang and Nü-ying were daughters of the sage ruler Yao; he gave them in marriage to his successor to the throne Shun, the lord of Yü. T'ai-jen and T'ai-ssu were the mothers of kings Wen and Wu respectively, the founders of the Chou dynasty. Most of these women are mentioned in the *Book of Odes* and were no doubt depicted in the paintings that Lady Pan was perusing for her instruction.

Though I'm foolish and uncouth, no match for these,
Would I dare turn my thoughts away, let them be forgotten?
The years pass in sorrow and apprehension;
I grieve for lush flowers that no longer flourish,[14]
Weep for the Yang-lu Hall, Hall of the Wild Mulberry,[15]
Babes in swaddling clothes who met with woe.
Surely it was due to no error of mine!
Heaven's decrees—can they never be changed?
Before I knew it, the bright sun had veiled its light,
Leaving me in the dusk of evening,
But still the ruler's kindness sustains and shelters me;
In spite of faults, I have not been cast off.
I serve the empress dowager in her eastern palace,
Take my place among lesser maids in the Palace of Lasting Trust;
I help to sprinkle and sweep among the curtains,
And shall do so till death brings my term to a close.
Then may my bones find rest at the foot of the hill,
A little shade of pine and cypress left over for my grave.
  Recapitulation:
Hidden in the black palace, gloomy and chill,
Main gates bolted, gates to inner quarters barred,
Dust in the painted hall, moss on marble stairs,
Courtyards rank with green grass growing,
Spacious rooms shadowy, curtains dark,
Chamber windows gaping, wind sharp and cold,
Blowing my skirts, stirring their crimson gauze,
Flapping, rustling them, making the silk sound.
My spirit roams far off to places secret and still;
Since my lord departed, who finds joy in me?
I look down at red flagstones, remembering how he trod them,
Look up at cloudy rafters, two streams of tears flowing;
Then I turn to left and right, my expression softening,
Dip the winged wine cup to banish care.
I reflect that man, born into this world,
Passes as swiftly as though floating on a stream.
Already I've known fame and eminence,
The finest gifts the living can enjoy.
I will strive to please my spirit, taste every delight,
Since true happiness cannot be counted on.
"Green Robe"—"White Flower"—in ancient times as now.[16]

[14] The flowers are her own fading youth and beauty.
[15] The halls are the places where she bore her two sons.
[16] The song in the *Book of Odes* entitled "Green Robe," Mao #27, is said to describe a wife whose place has been usurped by concubines; "White

When Emperor Ch'eng passed away (7 B.C.), Lady Pan was assigned to tend his grave and funerary park, and when she herself passed away, she was buried there in the funerary park.

EMPRESS CHAO, CONSORT OF EMPEROR CH'ENG

Empress Chao, the consort of Emperor Ch'eng, was originally a government slave of Ch'ang-an. When she was born, her father and mother declined to pick her up, but when three days had passed and she was still alive, they finally decided to raise her.[17] When she grew up, she was attached to the household of Emperor Ch'eng's elder sister Princess Yang-a, where she learned singing and dancing and came to be called Fei-yen or Flying Swallow.

Once when Emperor Ch'eng had left the palace on one of his incognito outings, he stopped at the home of Princess Yang-a, where he was entertained with music and dancing. There he saw Fei-yen and took a liking to her. She was summoned to the palace and won great favor with the emperor. She had a younger sister who was also summoned to service in the palace. Both were assigned the rank of Beautiful Companion and soon outshone in eminence all the other ladies of the palace.

When Empress Hsü, Emperor Ch'eng's earlier consort, was removed from her position,[18] the emperor wanted to set up the Beautiful Companion Chao as empress in her place, but his mother the empress dowager, considering Lady Chao to be of much too humble origin for such a position, strongly objected. Ch'un-yü Ch'ang, who was the son of the empress dowager's elder sister and an attendant in the inner palace, went back and forth a number of times carrying messages between the emperor and the empress dowager, until the latter was finally persuaded to give her consent. The em-

---

Flower," Mao #229, is traditionally interpreted as censuring King Yu of the Chou for putting aside his consort Queen Shen in favor of the evil Pao-ssu. Lady Pan compares herself to these unfortunate women of antiquity. Though Pan Ku does not mention it here, in ch. 100, the chapter devoted to the history of his own family, he reveals that Lady Pan was his father's aunt.

[17] When a child was born, it was laid on the ground before its parents. If they lifted it up, it meant they recognized it as their own and intended to raise it; if not, the child was left to die.

[18] Empress Hsü (a distant relative of the Empress Hsü, consort of Emperor Hsüan, whose death by poisoning has been described above), was removed from the position of empress in 18 B.C. because of jealousy and suspicion of black magic, as already mentioned in the biography of Lady Pan.

peror then enfeoffed Lady Chao's father Chao Lin as marquis of Ch'eng-yang, and a few months later finally promoted Lady Chao from the rank of Beautiful Companion to that of empress. He also enfeoffed Ch'un-yü Ch'ang as Ting-ling Marquis, ostensibly because of the merit he had acquired earlier by advising the emperor to abandon plans for a new mausoleum at Ch'ang-ling.[19]

After Lady Chao had become empress she declined somewhat in favor; all the emperor's attentions now became fixed upon her younger sister, who was promoted to the rank of Bright Companion and assigned to quarters in the Bright Sun Lodge. Its courtyards were painted vermilion and its halls lacquered, with sills of bronze coated with a layer of gilt. It had steps of white jade, and where the laths of the walls were exposed to view they were studded at intervals with golden rings inlaid with decorations of Lant'ien jadeite, shining pearls, or pieces of kingfisher feather. Since the time when women's quarters first began to be built, there had never been anything to match it.

The two Chao sisters monopolized the emperor's affections for over ten years, but in the end neither of them bore any children. In the latter years of their period of favor, Emperor Yüan's grandson the king of Ting-t'ao was brought to court, and his maternal grandmother Empress Dowager Fu sent bribes in secret to Empress Chao and her sister the Bright Companion. As a result, the king of Ting-t'ao was designated heir apparent to Emperor Ch'eng.

In the spring of the following year (7 B.C.), Emperor Ch'eng passed away. He had always been strong in constitution and was not afflicted by any illness. At the time of his passing, King Ssu of Ch'u Liu Yen and the king of Liang Liu Li had come to court and were due to return to their territories the following day; the emperor accordingly entertained them in the evening at a banquet in the White Tiger Hall. In addition, he made preparations to bestow upon the general of the left K'ung Kuang the position of chancellor, and had already had the seals of the marquisite that would accompany the advancement carved and had prepared the text of the pronouncement he would make at the time of the presentation. In the evening he was in perfectly normal health, but towards morning, when he put on his leggings and socks and tried to get out of

[19] Emperor Ch'eng had already built a mausoleum for himself at Yen-ling but was proposing to abandon this site and build a new one at Ch'ang-ling. Ch'un-yü Ch'ang spoke out against the extravagance of such a move, and his opinion was seconded by all the ministers and high officials.

bed, he found he could not dress himself any further and that he had lost the power of speech. By the time the water clock pointed to the tenth notch [8:30 A.M.], he had passed away. A rumor spread among the common people placing the blame for his demise on the Bright Companion Chao.

The empress dowager issued an edict to the grand marshal Wang Mang and the chancellor and minister of works,[20] saying, "His Imperial Majesty has passed away with great suddenness and among the populace there is a buzz of suspicion and speculation. The supervisor of the women's quarters and his assistants shall cooperate with the clerks of the censorate, the chancellor, and the commandant of justice in questioning all those persons in the women's quarters who served the emperor and were in personal attendance upon him in order to determine what his movements were and the exact circumstances attending his illness."

At this point the Bright Companion Chao committed suicide.

When Emperor Ai ascended the throne, he bestowed the title of empress dowager upon Empress Chao and enfeoffed her younger brother, the attendant of the inner palace and commandant of the imperial horses Chao Ch'in, as marquis of Hsin-ch'eng. Thus two members of the Chao family were enfeoffed as marquises.

A few months later the commander of convicts Chieh Kuang submitted a report describing the results of the investigation which read as follows:

"I was told that the Comely Person Lady Hsü and the former female scribe of the empress's palace Ts'ao Kung both enjoyed the attentions of Emperor Ch'eng the Filial and bore him sons, but that the sons had disappeared. I accordingly dispatched my attendant clerk Yeh and my secretary Wang to question all those who might have knowledge of the matter. The keeper of the jail in the women's quarters Chi Wu; the former eunuch attendants of the Yellow Gate Wang Shun, Wu Kung, and Chin Yen; the government slave women Ts'ao Hsiao, Tao Fang, and Chang Ch'i; and the former coachmen of the Bright Companion Chao, Yü K'o-tzu, Wang P'ien, and Tsang Chien, all joined in giving the following testimony:

" 'The woman named Ts'ao Kung was the daughter of the government slave woman Ts'ao Hsiao. She was formerly attached to

[20] The empress dowager was Emperor Ch'eng's mother, the consort of Emperor Yüan; Wang Mang was her nephew. The post earlier called imperial secretary was renamed minister of works in the time of Emperor Ch'eng.

the empress's palace, where she learned to read and became a scribe. After mastering the *Book of Odes,* she gave the empress instruction in it. She was on very intimate terms with the slave woman Tao Fang, and in the first year of the *yüan-yen* period (12 B.C.) she said to Tao Fang, "His Majesty has favored me!" Several months later her mother Ts'ao Hsiao came to the apartments where the girl was living and noticed that her belly had grown large; when she questioned her about it, Ts'ao Kung replied, "I have received the imperial favor and I am pregnant." In the tenth month of that year, she was taken to the lodge of the supervisor of cattle for the women's quarters and there bore her child, with six slave women in attendance.

" 'At that time the eunuch attendant of the Yellow Gate T'ien K'o arrived with a written message from the emperor contained in a message pouch tied with a heavy green cord and sealed with the seal of the middle aide to the imperial secretary.[21] The message was handed to the keeper of the jail of the women's quarters Chi Wu and it said, 'Take the woman, the newborn child, and the six slave women who are in the lodge of the supervisor of cattle and confine them all to the sick room jail. Do not ask whether the child is a boy or a girl, or whose child it is.' Chi Wu accordingly went and fetched the women and child and took them to the jail. Ts'ao Kung said to him, 'Be sure to dispose properly of my baby's afterbirth. I wonder if you are aware whose child it is?'

"Three days later, T'ien K'o came again with a message from the emperor and gave it to Chi Wu. It inquired whether the child was still alive or not and instructed Chi Wu to write the answer on the back of the message board in his own hand. Chi Wu accordingly wrote a reply saying that at the present time the child was still alive.

"After a little while had passed, T'ien K'o appeared once more and said, 'The emperor and the Bright Companion Chao are very angry and want to know why you haven't killed the child!'

"Chi Wu struck his head on the ground and said weeping, 'I know I deserve to die for not killing the child, but if I kill it, I will also be doing something for which I deserve to die!' Then he asked T'ien K'o to deliver a sealed memorial to the emperor from him; it said, 'Your Majesty does not yet have an heir to succeed you.

---

[21] The official whose duty it was to investigate irregularities of behavior within the palace.

When it comes to sons, there is no such thing as wellborn or humble—perhaps you will think it over a little longer.'

"After the memorial had been submitted, T'ien K'o came back with a message for Chi Wu saying, 'Tonight at the fifth notch of the water clock [around 7 P.M.] bring the child and the eunuch Wang Shun and wait at the eastern inner gate of the women's quarters.' Chi Wu asked T'ien K'o, 'When His Majesty received my letter, how did he react?' 'He stared straight ahead,' replied T'ien K'o.

"Chi Wu handed the child over to Wang Shun, who received an imperial command saying, 'Bring the child into the palace and select a wet nurse for it. Instruct her to take good care of it, as she may soon expect some reward. She is not to let word of what has happened leak out.' Wang Shun accordingly selected the slave woman Chang Ch'i to be the baby's wet nurse. The baby at that time was eight or nine days old.

"Three days later, T'ien K'o again came with a message from the emperor, sealed as before, and gave it to Chi Wu. Inside the message pouch was a small green box, also sealed, with a note attached to it that read, 'Instructions to Chi Wu: take the letter and the other things in the box and give them to the woman in the jail. Stand by personally while she drinks the contents.' When Chi Wu opened the box, he found two packets of medicine and a small piece of red paper [22] which said, 'Instructions to Wei-neng: be brave and drink this medicine—you can never come to the palace again, as you yourself must know.' Wei-neng was Ts'ao Kung's other name.

"After Ts'ao Kung had finished reading the note, she said, 'Just as I thought—he's going to let those two sisters run the whole empire for him! My baby was a boy and had beautiful hair on his forehead—he looked just like Emperor Yüan the Filial. And now where is he? They've probably killed him! If only I could get word to the Palace of Lasting Trust!' [23] Then she drank the medicine and died.

"Later, the six slave women were summoned to the palace, and when they had returned from the interview, they said, 'The Bright

[22] Though paper was not supposed to have been invented until the 1st century A.D., all commentators insist that the word *t'i* here refers to a kind of paper.
[23] Where Emperor Ch'eng's mother Empress Dowager Wang was in residence.

Companion said she knows that we have not done anything wrong, but she gave us a choice of committing suicide or of being taken somewhere else to be killed. We asked to be allowed to commit suicide.' They then proceeded to hang themselves, after which Chi Wu submitted a report to the throne describing these various events.

"The slave woman Chang Ch'i took care of the child entrusted to her for eleven days, whereupon the chief of palace women Li Nan received an imperial command to take the child away. No one knows what became of it.

"The Comely Person Lady Hsü formerly resided in the Cho-mu Hall of the Shang-lin Park. She was often summoned to the Decorated Chamber or to such-and-such a lodge of the palace, sometimes remaining there for several months, sometimes for half a year. She enjoyed the imperial favor and in the second year of *yuan-yen* (11 B.C.) became pregnant. She bore a child in the eleventh month of that year. The eunuch Chin Yen received an imperial command to escort the doctor in charge of childbirth to Lady Hsü's rooms, at the same time taking along three pills made of a blend of five kinds of medicine.

"Later Yü K'o-tzu, Wang P'ien, and Tsang Chien, coachmen of the Bright Companion, overheard their mistress say to Emperor Ch'eng, 'You lied to me all those times you said you had just come back from the empress's palace! If you were always returning from the empress's palace, then how does it happen that Lady Hsü has given birth to a child? I suppose in the end you are going to set up another Empress Hsü!' In her fury she beat herself with her own hands, struck her head against the walls, doors, and columns, and flung herself off the bed to the floor, where she wept and wailed and refused to eat, saying, 'Now what are you going to do with me? Just send me home, I suppose!'

"The emperor said, 'I made a point of telling you about the baby and instead of being grateful you fly into a rage over it. You never understand anything I say!' The emperor likewise refused to eat.

"The Bright Companion said, 'If you are so certain you are in the right, why don't you eat? You always used to promise that you would never be unfaithful, but now if Lady Hsü has a baby, it means you broke your promise, doesn't it?'

" 'For the sake of the Chao family, I promise never to make Lady Hsü an empress,' said the emperor. 'No one in the empire will ever be allowed to stand higher than the Chaos—you don't have to worry about that!'

"Later, the eunuch Chin Yen received orders to deliver to Lady Hsü a green letter pouch and was instructed as follows: 'Lady Hsü will have something to give you. Bring it here and place it on the south side of the blinds of the Decorated Chamber.' When he had done so, Lady Hsü put her newborn baby in a reed hamper, tied and sealed it, and gave it to Chin Yen along with the green letter pouch in which she had deposited her reply. Chin Yen took the hamper and the letter pouch and placed them on the south side of the blinds of the Decorated Chamber, after which he withdrew. The emperor, who was sitting in the room with the Bright Companion, instructed the coachman Yü K'o-tzu to untie the cord around the hamper, but before he had finished untying it, the emperor ordered Yü K'o-tzu, Wang P'ien, and Tsang Chien all to leave the room, personally shutting the door after them. He remained alone in the room with the Bright Companion for some time, after which he opened the door and called to Yü K'o-tzu, Wang P'ien, and Tsang Chien, ordering them to tie up the hamper and seal it, push it around to the east side of the screen, and leave it there, along with a message pouch tied with a green cord.

"The eunuch Wu Kung then received an order to take the hamper and the message pouch and give them to the jailor Chi Wu; both were sealed with the seal of the middle aide to the imperial secretary. The message read, 'Instructions to Chi Wu: there is a dead baby in the hamper—bury it in a secluded spot and let no one know about it.' Chi Wu thereupon dug a hole at the foot of the wall surrounding the jail tower and buried it.

"Sometime earlier, the government slave women Wang Yeh, Jen Li, and Kung-sun Hsi, who had originally been attached to the Ch'ang-ting Palace where the former Empress Hsü resided, the household of the late marquis of Ch'eng-tu Wang Shang, and the household of the marquis of P'ing-a Wang T'an respectively, had been manumitted and given the status of commoners. Later they had been summoned to the palace and assigned to the Bright Companion as her private maids. When Emperor Ch'eng passed away and his body was lying in state waiting to be placed in the coffin and the wailing and lamentation were at their height, the Bright Companion, aware of the enormity of her sins and misdeeds and knowing that the three maids had previously been attached to the Hsü and Wang families, began to fear that they might let word leak out as to what had happened. She therefore presented a certain Yang-tzu and other elderly slave women to them as a gift, assigning ten slaves to each of them in order to put them in a kindly mood, enjoining them at the same time not to say anything about any faults or errors she might have committed.

"In the fifth month of the second year of *yüan-yen* (11 B.C.), the former supervisor of the women's quarters Wu-ch'iu Tsun said to the jailor Chi Wu, 'The clerks and officials under me are all in league with the Bright Companion and I don't dare say anything to them; you are the only one I can talk to. I have no children, but you have, and the party we are dealing with would think nothing of wiping out a whole family—I expect therefore you would prefer not to become involved. But the fact is that all the women here in the women's quarters who are favored by the emperor and bear him a child die immediately afterwards, and there are countless others who have been forced to drink medicine and abort. I would like for the two of us to report the situation to one of the high ministers, but the general of swift cavalry Wang Ken is only interested in squeezing money out of people and it would not do to try to work through him. If only there were some way to get word to the Palace of Lasting Trust!'

"Later, when Wu-ch'iu Tsun fell gravely ill, he said to Chi Wu, 'It looks as though I'm going to die. That matter we talked about earlier—you had better not try to carry it our alone. Keep it to yourself!'

"All of the events described above took place before the general amnesty which was issued on the day *ping-ch'en* of the fourth month of the present year (May 17, 7 B.C.) and hence have technically been pardoned. I would like respectfully to point out, however, that in the third year of the *yung-kuang* era (41 B.C.), a man named Chung and others looted the grave of Lady Fu at the mausoleum of Emperor Kao-tsu at Ch'ang-ling. Later there was a general amnesty, but when the matter came to light, Emperor Yüan the Filial handed down an edict saying, 'This is something which I find it impossible to forgive!' and accordingly the offenders were all prosecuted and brought to punishment. Moreover, the people of the empire regarded it as only proper that they should be.

"When the consort of Duke Chuang of Lu brought about the murder of the legitimate heir, Duke Huan of Ch'i summoned her and had her put to death, and the *Spring and Autumn Annals,* which records the events, indicates its approval of his action.[24]

---

[24] The events are recorded in the *Spring and Autumn Annals* and its commentaries, Duke Chuang 27th and 32d years, and Duke Hsi 1st year. Duke

Now the Bright Companion Chao has brought danger and chaos to
our sacred dynasty and is personally responsible for wiping out the
line of succession—her family and associates deserve to suffer the
punishment of Heaven!

"Earlier, Hsü Yeh, the consort of Marquis Kang of P'ing-an, was
accused of major treason and all the members of her family were
scheduled to be tried along with her, but she was granted pardon
and was allowed to return home to her native province.[25] Now the
crimes which the Bright Companion has committed are of the grav-
est nature and her guilt is far greater than was that of Hsü Yeh,
and yet her brothers and associates are all allowed to occupy positions of eminence and even to approach the imperial curtains of
state. As one of the lesser officials, may I say that it is enough to
make the heart turn cold with fear. This is no way to set an example for the four quarters in censuring evil and displaying respect
for right! I request that the matter be subjected to thorough investigation and that the chancellor and lesser officials deliberate as to
the correct way to apply the law."

Emperor Ai thereupon relieved Chao Chin, the marquis of
Hsin-ch'eng, and his elder brother's son Chao Hsin, the marquis of
Ch'eng-yang, of their titles and reduced them to the rank of commoner. Along with their families and followers they were removed
to the province of Liao-hsi.

At this time the palace attendant in charge of deliberations Keng
Yü submitted a memorial which read:

"I have heard that in matters of succession, to depart from the
legitimate line, setting aside the son of the legal consort in favor of
one born of a concubine, is something which the law of the sages
strictly forbids and which men have warned against in both past
and present. And yet T'ai-po, the eldest son of Ta-wang of the
house of Chou, observing his younger brother Chi-li and knowing
that he was the one who ought to become heir, withdrew and adamantly refused the succession himself, retiring instead to live in the
distant region of Wu. It was a measure taken because of the unusual circumstances, not one based upon ordinary procedure, and
as a result of it Chi-li became heir, carrying on the sacred line of

---

Huan of Ch'i at this time exercised the power of a hegemon or dictator over
the other feudal states.

[25] Hsü Yeh was an elder sister of Emperor Ch'eng's first consort, Empress
Hsü. When Empress Hsü lost favor, Hsü Yeh and others of her group attempted to put a curse on the women who had succeeded her in the emperor's attentions.

his ancestors, and his son and grandson, kings Wen and Wu, in the end gained possession of the empire. Their descendants in turn inherited the throne, ruling for seven or eight hundred years, their achievements placing them at the head of the kings of the Three Dynasties, their virtue and understanding of the Way perfect above all others. As a result of what happened, the ancestors of the Chou kings as far back as Ta-wang came to be honored with posthumous titles. Thus we may say that, when there are extraordinary circumstances attending the matter, then and only then may such extraordinary measures be resorted to.

"Emperor Ch'eng the Filial realized that he had failed to produce an heir when the time was right, and he considered that, even if he should sire a son in his later years, the boy would be incapable of ruling the nation after he himself had passed away, for all the real power and authority would fall into the hands of the boy's mother. When a woman in a position of authority finds she can do as she pleases, then there is no end to her cravings and desires, and when a ruler is still a mere child, the high ministers will not obey him. At such a time, unless there is someone suitable to act as regent, as the Duke of Chou did for his nephew, the infant King Ch'eng, then the altars of the soil and grain will be imperiled and the empire will be in danger of chaos and subversion. Emperor Ch'eng recognized that Your Majesty is endowed with the virtue of a sage and a man of superior understanding, and is rich in works of benevolence and filiality, pity and loving kindness; he possessed a clarity of perception that was all his own, and he made his decision without revealing it to others. Thus he put an end to his visits to the lodges of the palace women and eliminated the source from which a youthful heir might spring, all because he wished to make certain that the throne would pass to Your Majesty and the safety of the ancestral temples would be assured.

"Now these stupid officials with their report are incapable of taking deep thought for the security of the nation and producing any masterly and enduring plan of action, nor do they understand how to spread abroad the holy virtue of the dynasty and honor the wishes of the former emperor; instead they go about turning things upside down, poking and prying, exposing to public view the private affairs of the ruler, slandering and defiling the former emperor with charges of blind infatuation and accusing his favorite concubine of the sin of jealousy, completely failing to understand his sacred and far-sighted wisdom and frustrating all his plans to save the nation from distress.

"When discussing matters of great virtue, one does not stick by mundane standards; when aiming for great accomplishments, one does not follow the way of the masses. Thus, because Emperor Ch'eng's vision was of the highest order, so it surpassed that of the common run of officials by ten thousand times; and because Your Majesty's virtue flourishes with such abundance, so you are able to carry out the will of august Heaven. How could any of the petty officials of the present age with their mere modicum of talent ever be capable of equaling such vision and virtue!

"Moreover, to praise and encourage the good points of one's ruler or father, and to work to correct and eliminate the errors he has made in the past, is the accepted procedure of both ancient times and the present. But these men failed to speak out in stern reprimand at the proper time and to attempt to head off disaster before it had occurred; instead they each followed along with the ruler's will in flattery and assent, hoping thereby to ingratiate themselves with him. Yet now, after he has passed away and the title of empress dowager has already been bestowed upon the former Empress Chao—when in effect the entire matter has been closed—now they try to search out and alter what can no longer be changed, bringing to light faults that should remain dark and hidden. This is something that pains me deeply!

"I beg that this memorial be handed down to the authorities for discussion and, if it is agreed that what I have said is true, then a proclamation to that effect should be made to the empire so that all may know and understand what the sacred intentions of the former emperor actually were. If this is not done, and instead these slanderous charges are left unrefuted, to become known to the departed ancestors above and handed down to later ages, to be transmitted far off to the hundred barbarian tribes and noised abroad in the region within the seas, this will be a grave departure from what the former emperor intended when he passed away.

"A true filial son is one who is careful to abide by his father's wishes and to bring to completion what his father began. I only hope that Your Majesty will give the matter close examination."

Emperor Ai had received considerable assistance from Empress Dowager Chao at the time when he became heir apparent, and therefore in the end he did not investigate further the charges against her.

Emperor Ai's grandmother, Empress Dowager Fu, was grateful to Empress Dowager Chao for the help she had given to her grandson, and Empress Dowager Chao returned her friendship.

Empress Dowager Wang, the mother of the late Emperor Ch'eng, and the other members of the Wang clan, however, all hated Empress Dowager Chao. When Emperor Ai passed away (1 B.C.), Wang Mang spoke to Empress Dowager Wang about the matter of Empress Dowager Chao, and she issued an edict to the authorities saying: [26]

"Empress Dowager Chao and the Bright Companion both attended the emperor within the curtains of his chamber; elder and younger sister, they replaced all the other palace ladies in the ruler's affections. But they turned to schemes of violence and disorder, destroying and wiping out the line of succession and thereby betraying their duty to the ancestral temples. A profaner of Heaven and offender against the former rulers, Empress Dowager Chao is not fit to act as mother of the empire.[27] She shall be deprived of the title of empress dowager and called simply "Empress of Emperor Ch'eng the Filial," and shall move her residence to the Northern Palace."

A month or so later a second edict was handed down which read:

"Empress Chao herself knows the depth and magnitude of her crimes—negligent in paying her respects at court, lacking in the proper ways of a woman, failing to wait on her superiors according to ritual, she possesses the malice of a wolf or a tiger. Hated by the imperial household, loathed by all within the seas, she is yet allowed to occupy the rank of empress—truly this is an offense against the heart of august Heaven! A little misplaced kindness can undo the greatest plans; that which mercy would put up with, justice shall wipe out! The empress shall hereby be deposed from her rank, made a commoner, and sent to her old home!"

The same day, the empress committed suicide. She had held the position for sixteen years in all before being deposed.

In earlier times there had been a children's song going around which said:

> Swallow swallow
> tail sleek and shiny

[26] Empress Dowager Wang, Wang Mang's aunt, was exercising the power of rule on behalf of Emperor Ai's successor Emperor P'ing, who was nine years old at the time.

[27] Because Empress Chao had been the official consort of Emperor Ch'eng, Emperor Ai, who had been adopted as Emperor Ch'eng's heir, had treated her as his mother and bestowed on her the title of empress dowager. The edict now dissolves that relationship.

Young gentleman Chang
   in time comes to call
Wooden gates
   gray-green fixtures
Swallow comes flying
   pecks imperial grandsons
Imperial grandsons die
   swallow pecks turds [28]

When Emperor Ch'eng used to go out on incognito expeditions, he would always be accompanied by Chang Fang, the marquis of Fu-p'ing, and would identify himself as a member of the marquis's household; therefore the song mentions "young gentleman Chang." The "gray-green fixtures" are the bronze rings on the palace gates.

LADY FENG, CONCUBINE OF EMPEROR YÜAN [29]

The Bright Companion Lady Feng, concubine of Emperor Yüan the Filial, was the grandmother of Emperor P'ing. In the second year of Emperor Yüan's reign (47 B.C.), she was selected to enter the women's quarters; at the same time, her father Feng Feng-shih held the post of chief of the capital police. She first held the rank of Superior Attendant, but after a few months advanced to that of Comely One. Five years later she moved to the parturition lodge and bore a son; she was honored with the rank of Beautiful Companion.

At this time her father held the posts of general of the right and keeper of the palace gate, and her elder brother Feng Yeh-wang was serving as left prefect of the capital, so that both father and son were members of the court. It was the opinion of the persons of the time, however, that they had attained these positions because of their talent and ability, and not because of the favoritism enjoyed by Lady Feng. Within the palace, Lady Feng held a place in the affections of the ruler equal to that of the Bright Companion Fu.

[28] Children's ditties of this kind were believed to be prophetic and are therefore carefully recorded by the historian. The interpretation of the song is found in the "Treatise on the Five Elements," *Han shu* 27B1, which says that it appeared shortly before Emperor Ch'eng first met the Chao sisters. The image of the swallow derives of course from Chao Fei-yen's name, "Flying Swallow;" the last line refers to the final downfall of the sisters.

[29] The biography is part of the section devoted to Empress Fu, the consort of Emperor Ai.

During the *chien-chao* era (38–34 B.C.) the emperor, accompanied by the women of the palace, once visited the so-called tiger pens to watch the wild animals fight. The group had taken their seats when a bear broke out of the pen, climbed up the railing, and was on the point of entering the hall where the emperor and his party were sitting. The Bright Companion Fu and the other ladies in attendance all ran away in terror, but Lady Feng walked straight towards the bear and stood in its way. Meanwhile the guards in attendance attacked the bear and killed it.

The emperor said, "It is only human nature to be terrified in such a situation. What made you walk in the direction of the bear?"

Lady Feng replied, "If a wild beast has a human being to seize upon, it will halt its attack. I was afraid that the bear would advance to where Your Majesty was seated, and therefore I put myself in its way."

Emperor Yüan sighed with admiration, and because of the incident his affection for Lady Feng doubled. The Bright Companion Fu and the others were all filled with shame.

In the summer of the following year Lady Feng's son was set up as king of Hsin-tu and she was honored with the rank of Bright Companion. When Emperor Yüan passed away, she received the title of queen dowager of Hsin-tu and resided with her son the king in the Ch'u-yüan Palace. During the *ho-p'ing* era (28–25 B.C.) she accompanied her son to his fief in Hsin-tu. He was later moved to the fief of Chung-shan and is known posthumously as King Hsiao of Chung-shan.

Ai, Emperor, 9; shields Empress Dowager Chao, 275

Analects: quoted, 45, 88, 101, 170, 180, 223, 224, 262; alluded to, 49n, 80n, 119n; studied, 112, 137, 163, 198, 212

"Bath and hair-washing day," 125n
Bath-towns: explained, 71n; assigned to Lady Po-p'ing, 256
Black magic affair, 47, 76-77, 186, 253n
Book of Changes (I Ching): quoted, 77, 94, 182; studied, 81, 112, 174; debate on interpretation of, 114; alluded to, 182-83, 213
Book of Documents: quoted, 65, 88, 213; studied, 79, 97, 118; alluded to, 206
Book of Odes: quoted, 50, 51, 72, 98, 99, 102, 105, 120, 135, 190, 204, 212; studied, 79, 97, 137, 171, 190, 198, 262, 263, 268; alluded to, 264
Burials: lavishness condemned, 108, 119n; simple burial of Chu Yün, 117; lavish burial of Ho Kuang, 139-40; funeral donations, 240; burial of commoner, 242

Capping ceremony for boys, 47n, 89, 128, 258
Chang An-shih, 43, 44, 129, 131, 151, 187, 258
Chang Ch'ang, 203-7
Chang Ho, 257-58
Chang Sheng, 34-36
Ch'ang Hui, 34-42 passim, 207-8
Ch'ang-i, king of, see Liu Ho
Chao, Bright Companion, concubine

of Emperor Ch'eng, biography, 265-77
Chao, Emperor, 8, 251; mausoleum, 112n; birth and childhood, 252
Chao, Empress, consort of Emperor Ch'eng, 8, 262; biography, 265-77
Chao, Lady, consort of Emperor Wu, 122; biography, 251-53
Chao Ch'ung-kuo, 44
Chao Fei-yen (Flying Swallow), see Chao, Empress, consort of Emperor Ch'eng
Ch'en Tsun, biography, 235-40
Ch'en Wan-nien, 168, 193
Cheng P'eng, 215-19
Ch'eng, Emperor, 3, 8; infatuation with Chao sisters, 265-77; sudden death, 266-67; mausoleum, 266n; murder of sons, 267-72
Ch'eng Pu-chih, 14
Chiang Ch'ung, 47-50, 153; see also Black magic affair
Ch'iang tribes, 19, 181, 203-7
Chieh-yü or Beautiful Companion, 125n; see also Pan, Beautiful Companion
Chien-chih, crime of, 205n
Chin An-shang, 142, 149, 156, 202
Chin Mi-ti, 123-24; biography, 151-57
Ch'ing, size of, 22n
Chou K'an, 214-19
Chu Chia, biography, 225-26
Chu Yün, biography, 112-17
Ch'u Shao-sun, 147n, 252n
Ch'u Tz'u, alluded to, 120
Ch'un ch'iu, see Spring and Autumn Annals
Ch'un-yü Yen, woman doctor, 143, 259-60

Chü Chang, biography, 231
Chü Ch'ien-ch'iu, 52, 77, 175
Chü Meng, biography, 226
Ch'üan Pu-i, 59; biography, 158-62
Confucian scholars, 114, 145, 230, 236;
    cap worn by, 159n; gathering in
    Stone Conduit Hall, 171; see also
    Hsiao Wang-chih
Confucianism, 4, 205n, 214, 225

Death, view of, 108
Dubs, Homer H., 10, 123n
Dwarfs, 80-81

"Elders" or san-lao, 49n
Entertainers and actors, 55, 66, 81, 94,
    106
Eunuchs, power of, 214-21; see also
    Shih Hsien

Feather and Forest Guard, 60, 61n,
    126, 131, 143-44
Feng, Lady, concubine of Emperor
    Yüan, biography, 277-78
Filial Piety, Classic of: quoted, 108,
    136; studied, 137, 163
Five Elements: "Treatise on the Five
    Elements," 6, 71n, 277n; theory of,
    54n, 167n, 183n
Five Marquises of Wang family, 232
Former Han, summary of history, 8-9
Fu or rhyme-prose form, poem in, 105,
    249-51, 263-64

Guessing games, 81

Han shu: described, 2-5, 9; style of, 10
Han-shu pu-chu, 10; see also Wang
    Hsien-ch'ien
Han Tseng, 43, 44, 209
Han Yen-nien, 28-29
Hao, "strong men," 222n, 225-46 pas-
    sim; "Four Strong Men," 224
Hightower, J. R., 30n
Ho Ch'ü-ping, 20-23 passim, 121-22,
    139, 151, 225
Ho Hsien, wife of Ho Kuang, 141-49,
    177, 259-60

Ho Kuang, 6, 8, 32, 40, 44, 59-62, 71-
    73, 112, 154-55, 161, 166, 175, 187,
    198-99, 248, 253, 259-60; biog-
    raphy, 121-51
Ho Shan, 138-49, 176-77, 200
Ho Yü, 138-49, 176-77, 200
Ho Yün, 138-49, 177
Honda Wataru, 10
Hsia-hou Sheng, 44, 135, 190, 198
Hsiao Wang-chih, 44, 112, 171; biog-
    raphy, 198-221
Hsin dynasty, 9; see also Wang Mang
Hsiu-t'u king, Hsiung-nu leader, 151-
    52, 157
Hsiung-nu: relations in reign of Em-
    peror Wen, 12; relations in reign
    of Emperor Ching, 13-14; relations
    in reign of Emperor Wu, 14-40 pas-
    sim, 55n, 151; relations in reign of
    Emperor Chao, 40-41; relations in
    reign of Emperor Hsüan, 44, 178,
    213; relations with Wu-sun, 207;
    internal troubles, 209-10; relations
    in time of Keng-shih Emperor, 240
Hsü, Empress, consort of Emperor
    Hsüan, 143, 146; biography, 257-61
Hsü, Empress, consort of Emperor
    Ch'eng, 262, 265
Hsü Kuang-han, 141-42, 163, 176-77,
    257-61
Hsüan, Emperor, 8, 52; selected to
    become emperor, 137-38; infancy
    of, 186-88, 194-95, 258; good order
    in time of, 197; life as a commoner,
    235
Hsüeh Kuang-te, biography, 171-73
Hsün Tzu: quoted, 99; alluded to, 219
Hu Chien, biography, 109-12
Huang Pa, 44, 167, 193, 212
Hulsewé, A. F. P., 10
Hun-yeh king, Hsiung-nu leader, 35,
    151-52
Hung Kung, 214-19

Kai, Princess, 42, 56, 59, 62, 111-12,
    125-28, 198
Kao-tsu, 8, 60, 63, 135, 225
Keng-shih Emperor, 240

Kou king, Hsiung-nu leader, 35
Ku-liang Commentary, studied, 47
Ku Yung, 232
Kung-sun Ao, 31
Kung-sun Ho, 47
Kung-sun Hung, 96, 230
Kung-yang Commentary: studied, 47;
　alluded to, 135n, 177n, 209n
Kung Yü, 113, 168, 171
Kuo Hsieh, biography, 226-31
K'uang Heng, 113

Lao Tzu, 106, 107; *Tao-te-ching*,
　quoted, 163
Legalist philosophy, 96
Li, Madam, concubine of Emperor Wu,
　biography, 247-51
Li, Prince, *see* Liu Chü
Li, length of, 13
Li Ch'iang, 203-7
Li Kan, 18, 22-23
Li Kuang, 5; biography, 12-23
Li Kuang-li, 24, 249, 251
Li Ling, 2, 5; biography, 24-33; meet-
　ings with Su Wu, 38-41
Li Yen-nien, 31, 247-51
Liang Ch'iu-ho, 44
*Liang-Han wen-hsüeh-shih ts'an-k'ao
　tzu-liao*, 10
Liu Chü, the heir apparent Li, 8,
　253n, 257; biography, 46-54; man
　pretending to be, 160-62
Liu Ho, king of Ch'ang-i, 8; biog-
　raphy, 69-76; summoned to throne
　and dismissed, 129-37
Liu Hsiang (Keng-sheng), 105, 214-19
Liu Hsin, 105n
Liu Hsü, King Li of Kuang-ling, 128;
　biography, 65-69
Liu Hung, King Huai of Ch'i, biog-
　raphy, 54
Liu Pang, *see* Kao-tsu
Liu Po, King Ai of Ch'ang-i, 69, 248
Liu Tan, King Tz'u of Yen, 126; bi-
　ography, 54-65
Liu Te, 44, 70, 129, 136, 138
Liu Yü, 3
Lou Hu, biography, 232-34

Lu Po-te, 25
Lü, Empress, 8, 58, 252n

Ma Ho-lo, plot of, 123, 153-54
Marquis within the Pass, title ex-
　plained, 23n, 188n
Mei Fu, 117n, 120
Mei Kao, 46, 96
Miki Katsumi, 10
Ming, Emperor, 3
Ming-t'ang or Bright Hall, 104, 182n
Mou: size of, 22n; price of, 86
Music Bureau, 249

Paintings, 261, 263; portraits in Uni-
　corn Hall, 44; Hall of Paintings,
　127; on hand-drawn cart, 141; por-
　trait of mother of Chin Mi-ti, 153;
　portrait of Madam Li, 248
Pan, Beautiful Companion, concubine
　of Emperor Ch'eng, biography, 261-
　65
Pan Ku, 2, 265n; Confucian outlook,
　4; treatment of wandering knights,
　6; treatment of empresses, 7
Pan Piao, 2
P'eng Hsüan, 172n
Ping Chi, 43, 44, 70, 129, 162, 176,
　185, 198, 207, 208, 210-12; biog-
　raphy, 186-97
P'ing, Emperor, 9, 118
P'ing Tang, 172n
Portents: Han theory of, 6, 85, 145-46,
　169, 179n, 200; before death of
　king of Yen, 62; before death of
　king of Kuang-ling, 67; pertaining
　to king of Ch'ang-i, 71-72; banner
　of Ch'ih Yu, 76; attempt to frighten
　Wang Mang with, 118; before down-
　fall of Ho family, 147-48

Records of the Historian, see *Shih chi*
Rules of the Marshal, 17; quoted, 111

Sang Hung-yang, 42, 59, 123, 126-28,
　174
Shamans, 48-49, 66-67

Shan-yü, title of Hsiung-nu leader, 15*n;* discussion on how to receive at Chinese court, 212-13; *see also* Hsiung-nu

Shang-kuan, Empress, consort of Emperor Chao, 69*n,* 71, 125, 126*n,* 130-38 *passim,* 142*n,* 149, 259*n*

Shang-kuan An, 42, 61, 111-12, 125-28

Shang-kuan Chieh, 32, 42, 59-62, 112, 123-28, 198, 257

Shang-lin Park, 141; creation of, 84, 87; sacrifices at, 133

Shih chi: described, 1-2; a "dangerous" book, 3; treatment of wandering knights, 6; treatment of empresses, 7; contrasted with *Han shu,* 7; additions made by Ch'u Shao-sun, 252*n*

Shih Hsien, 115, 214-21, 231

Shih Kao, 214-18

Shou-ni, crime of, 205*n*

Shu Kuang, biography, 162-65

Shu Shou, 162-65

Spring and Autumn Annals, 1, 3; quoted, 135; studied, 158, 162, 167; alluded to, 161, 176, 200, 209, 272

Ssu-ma Ch'ien, 1, 96; defense of Li Ling, 29-30; see also *Shih chi*

Su Chien, biography, 33-34

Su Wu, 5, 60, 126; biography, 34-45

Sutrishna general, 30; title explained, 24*n*

Swann, Nancy Lee, 10

Tan, crown prince of Yen, 12

Taoism, 107; *see also* Lao Tzu

Tou, Elder Princess, 89-93

"Treatise on the Five Elements," *see* Five Elements

Tso chuan, 1; quoted, 77

Tso Commentary, see *Tso chuan*

Tu Yen-nien, 44, 131, 193

Tung-fang Shuo, 5, 46; biography, 79-106

Tung Yen, 89-93

Tzu or polite name, use explained, 33*n*

Tzu-chih t'ung-chien, 124*n*

Wang, Dame, mother of Lady Wang, 254-57

Wang, Empress Dowager, consort of Emperor Yüan, 9, 267, 269

Wang, Lady, mother of Emperor Hsüan, biography, 253-57

Wang Feng, 117*n*

Wang Hsien-ch'ien, 10, 67*n*

Wang Mang, 2, 3, 9, 65, 233, 246, 267; kills his son Yü, 118-19; uprisings in time of, 234, 236, 245

Wang Shang, 233, 257

Wang Yü, 118, 233

Wei, Empress, consort of Emperor Wu, 8, 46-52 *passim,* 262*n*

Wei Ch'ing, 18-21, 23, 33, 225, 229

Wei Hsiang, 43, 44, 142, 146, 163, 200, 207; biography, 174-86

Wei Lü, 31-33, 35-37

Wen, Emperor, frugal ways, 94; temple name, 135

Western Ch'iang, *see* Ch'iang tribes

Widows: virtuous, 165, 241*n;* forbidden to enter house of, 238

Wu, Emperor, 8; summary of accomplishments, 56, 79-96 *passim;* extravagant ways, 94; dependence on eunuchs, 215; mausoleum, 229, 240

Wu-ch'iu Shou-wang, 84, 85, 87

Wu-sun people, 207-8

Yang Hsiung, 105-6; "Remonstrance on Wine" quoted, 238-39

Yang Wang-sun, biography, 107-9

Yen Shih-ku, 10, 124*n*

Yu-hsia or wandering knights, 6, 112; biographies, 222-46

Yü Ch'ang, 35-36

Yü Ting-kuo, 44, 193, 212; biography, 165-71

Yüan, Emperor, 8; natural disasters in time of, 168-69, 171-72; education, 212; birth of, 258

Yüan She, biography, 240-46

Yün Ch'ang, biography, 118-19

Translations From The Oriental Classics

Major Plays of Chikamatsu, tr. Donald Keene   1961

Records of the Grand Historian of China, translated from the Shih chi of Ssu-ma Ch'ien, tr. Burton Watson, 2 vols.   1961

Instructions for Practical Living and Other Neo-Confucian Writings by Wang Yang-ming, tr. Wing-tsit Chan   1963

Chuang Tzu: Basic Writings, tr. Burton Watson, paperback ed. only   1964

The Mahābhārata, tr. Chakravarthi V. Narasimhan   1965

The Manyōshū, Nippon Gakujutsu Shinkōkai edition   1965

Su Tung-p'o: Selections from a Sung Dynasty Poet, tr. Burton Watson   1965

Bhartrihari: Poems, tr. Barbara Stoler Miller. Also in paperback ed.   1967

Basic Writings of Mo Tzu, Hsün Tzu, and Han Fei Tzu, tr. Burton Watson. Also in separate paperback eds.   1967

The Awakening of Faith, attributed to Aśvaghosha, tr. Yoshito S. Hakeda   1967

Reflections on Things at Hand: The Neo-Confucian Anthology, comp. Chu Hsi and Lü Tsu-ch'ien, tr. Wing-tsit Chan   1967

The Platform Sutra of the Sixth Patriarch, tr. Philip B. Yampolsky   1967

Essays in Idleness: The Tsurezuregusa of Kenkō, tr. Donald Keene   1967

The Pillow Book of Sei Shōnagon, tr. Ivan Morris, 2 vols.   1967

Two Plays of Ancient India: The Little Clay Cart and the Minister's Seal, tr. J. A. B. van Buitenen   1968

The Complete Works of Chuang Tzu, tr. Burton Watson   1968

The Romance of the Western Chamber (Hsi Hsiang chi) tr. S. I. Hsiung   1968

The Manyōshū, Nippon Gakujutsu Shinkōkai edition. Paperback text edition.   1969

Records of the Historian: Chapters from the Shih chi of Ssu-ma Ch'ien. Paperback text edition, tr. Burton Watson   1969

Cold Mountain: 100 Poems by the T'ang Poet Han-shan, tr. Burton Watson. Also in paperback ed.   1970

Twenty Plays of the Nō Theatre, ed. Donald Keene. Also in paperback ed.   1970

Chūshingura: The Treasury of Loyal Retainers, tr. Donald Keene   1971

The Zen Master Hakuin: Selected Writings, tr. Philip B. Yampolsky   1971

Chinese Rhyme-Prose, tr. Burton Watson   1971

Kūkai: Major Works, tr. Yoshito S. Hakeda   1972

The Old Man Who Does as He Pleases: Selections from the Poetry and Prose of Lu Yu, tr. Burton Watson   1973

The Lion's Roar of Queen Śrīmālā, tr. Alex & Hideko Wayman   1974

Courtier and Commoner in Ancient China: Selections from the History of The Former Han by Pan Ku, tr. Burton Watson   1974

Studies In Oriental Culture

1. *The Ōnin War: History of Its Origins and Background, with a Selective Translation of the Chronicle of Ōnin*, by H. Paul Varley ... 1967
2. *Chinese Government in Ming Times: Seven Studies*, ed. Charles O. Hucker ... 1969
3. *The Actors' Analects (Yakusha Rongo)*, ed. and tr. by Charles J. Dunn and Bunzō Torigoe ... 1969
4. *Self and Society in Ming Thought*, by Wm. Theodore de Bary and the Conference on Ming Thought ... 1970
5. *A History of Islamic Philosophy*, by Majid Fakhry ... 1970
6. *Phantasies of a Love Thief: The Caurapañcāśikā Attributed to Bilhana*, by Barbara S. Miller ... 1971
7. *Iqbal: Poet-Philosopher of Pakistan*, ed. Hafeez Malik ... 1971
8. *The Golden Tradition: An Anthology of Urdu Poetry*, by Ahmed Ali ... 1973
9. *Conquerors and Confucians: Aspects of Political Change in Late Yüan China*, by John W. Dardess ... 1973

Companions To Asian Studies

Approaches to the Oriental Classics, ed. Wm. Theodore
   de Bary   1959
Early Chinese Literature, by Burton Watson   1962
Approaches to Asian Civilizations, ed. Wm. Theodore
   de Bary and Ainslie T. Embree   1964
A Guide to Oriental Classics, ed. Wm. Theodore de Bary
   and Ainslie T. Embree   1964
The Classic Chinese Novel: A Critical Introduction, by
   C. T. Hsia   1968
*Chinese Lyricism: Shih Poetry from the Second to the
   Twelfth Century*, tr. Burton Watson   1971
A Syllabus of Indian Civilization, by Leonard A. Gordon
   and Barbara Stoler Miller   1971
Twentieth-Century Chinese Stories, ed. C. T. Hsia and
   Joseph S. M. Lau   1971
A Syllabus of Chinese Civilization, by J. Mason Gentz-
   ler, 2d ed.   1972
A Syllabus of Japanese Civilization, by H. Paul Varley,
   2d ed.   1972
An Introduction to Chinese Civilization, ed. John Mes-
   kill, with the assistance of J. Mason Gentzler   1973

Introduction To Oriental Civilizations

Wm. Theodore de Bary, *Editor*

Sources of Japanese Tradition 1958   Paperback ed., 2 vols. 1964
Sources of Indian Tradition 1958   Paperback ed., 2 vols. 1964
Sources of Chinese Tradition 1960   Paperback ed., 2 vols. 1964

ASIAN STUDIES

COURTIER AND COMMONER IN ANCIENT CHINA

Selections from the *History of the Former Han* **by Pan Ku**

BURTON WATSON, TRANSLATOR

Pan Ku's celebrated and influential *History of the Former Han* has been a model for dynastic history since its appearance in the first century A.D. The narrative is rich in detail and characterized by a purity and economy of style. Covering the period from 206 B.C. to A.D. 23, the work consists of annals, chronological tables, treatises, and biographies, the last of which often include excerpts from writings by the subjects of the biographies.

Burton Watson has translated ten chapters from the biography section, including the lives of imperial princes, generals, officials, and some lesser figures: a court jester, wandering knights, court ladies, and concubines. All the chapters have been selected for their literary interest and their influence on Chinese literature and culture.

"The reader of this admirable translation . . . will be able to appreciate why the *History of the Former Han,* a great work of literature as well as of history, is, for the Chinese, what the work of Thucydides is for the Western world."—*Times Literary Supplement*

Translations from the Oriental Classics

Columbia University Press
New York

ISBN 0-231-08354-8